THE YEAR THE WORLD
WAS MINE

THE YEAR THE WORLD WAS MINE

An Anglophile Hits a Half Century

Rochelle Almeida

Hamilton Books

Lanham • Boulder • New York • Toronto • London

Published by Hamilton Books
An imprint of The Rowman & Littlefield Publishing Group, Inc.
4501 Forbes Boulevard, Suite 200, Lanham, Maryland 20706
Hamilton Books Acquisitions Department (301) 459-3366

6 Tinworth Street, London SE11 5AL

British Library Cataloguing in Publication Information Available

Library of Congress Control Number: 2019914687

ISBN 978-0-7618-7156-9 (pbk)
ISBN 978-0-7618-7157-6 (electronic)

For Cynthia Colclough, Susan Colclough,
Loulou Cooke, Barbara Cookson, Raquel Grossman,
Rosemary Massouras, and Bina Ullal
who offered shelter during storms in Blighty.
With love and gratitude.

CONTENTS

ACKNOWLEDGMENTS

This book started its life as a blog called *Rochelle's Roost in London* expertly set up, ten years ago, by the multi-talented, Tony Award-winning Meredith Lynsey-Slade.

Fred Schwarzbach, former Director of Liberal Studies at New York University, posted me to teach in London for a year. Beth Haymaker smoothed my departure from the US. And Karen Karbeiner, my comrade-in-arms, offered hilarious Thursday dinner conversations and fond memories of Jane Austen in Chawton. The Metropolitan Museum of Art in New York City granted me a year's leave from my weekend volunteer duties as Highlights Tour docent.

Former Director of the NYU site in London, a decade ago, the dynamic David Reuben made my academic year in the city most stimulating by supporting my research and teaching.

Administrative staff-members at NYU-London then and now, David Crout, Nigel Freeman, Yvonne Hunkin, Anna Maguire, Robert Pinkerton, Eric Sneddon and Ruth Tucker provided all the administrative and personal assistance I could possibly need including organizing student field trips and directing me to Accidents and Emergency at Euston Hospital.

My British colleagues at NYU-London were stimulating companions. I remember Clive Bloom for friendship and collegial guidance; Phillip Drummond for introducing me to quality British Cinema through screenings at the British Film Institute; Michael Hattaway for permitting me to tag along to Shakespearean plays at the Globe Theatre; Stephen Inwood for enlightening me about the history of London; Nesta Jones for West End theatre tickets; Dennis Judd for chats about Indo-British History; Julia Pascal and Emma Claire Sweeney for writerly exchanges; Hagai Segal for teaching me about international terrorism; Valerie Wells for an unforgettable weekend in Cornwall; Matt Wolf for sharing his theater reviewer's press passes with me and Phillip Woods for lunch-time discussions over hot soup and cold sandwiches in the basement Faculty Lounge.

Doormen Mark Walters, "Mo" Ali and Ron Malin always made my entries and exits at odd times from the premises of NYU-London cheerful, kept track of my "pigeon-hole" and assisted with postal deliveries around the world.

Arben Hasa and Marta Cybulska were the most caring staff in the best residential building in Holborn, if not in all of London. As for Milan Thacker, Barbara Cookson and Tim Freeman, seriously . . . an expat couldn't have prayed for better neighbors. I will never forget frequent dinners of kedgeree, bacon and onions, Irish stew and *eiswein* on snow-bound evenings.

Bina and Navin Ullal and Michelle Misquita, Bombay transplants in London, were the school and college classmates who saw me through varied phases of physical immobility. My Bombay classmate Charmayne Rodrigues arrived in London from Australia to introduce me to Sushil Velu who pulled me along to Calais for Wine Jaunts and introduced me, in turn, to Owen Berkely-Hill, Cecil Colaco and Michael Anderson, Bombay Cathedralites, whose parties were a blast. Bande Hasan, trusted long-time family friend and confidant, was always ready with a helping hand, fancy wheels and fancier teas.

My UK-based relatives, Cheryl and David Crane on the Isle of Sheppey in Kent and Joel and Sybil Gonzalves in Guilford, Surrey, watched my back telephonically and in reality through a year of unexpected ups and downs.

The Colclough Family (Michael, Aiden and Edward) became (and remain) my surrogate family in London while Cynthia became (and remains) the sister I never had. Among other things, they kept my spirits up through endless pukka cuppas in the domestic warmth of their Renaissance abode. Joining them in the endeavor were Rosemary Massouras whose grilled nectarines, hazelnuts pavlovas and incessant good humor saw me through a sudden change of accommodation; Janie

Yang nurtured friendship at Syon House and while antiquing in Rochester, Kent; Matt, and Rosa Fradley acquainted me with Thaxted, Saffron Walden and Bishop's Stortford in Essex on Mother's Day weekend. Allan and Cathy Low assisted me in royal-spotting in Scotland. Daily blogging led me to the brilliant Murali Menon who shares my love for Gresham College lectures and *flaneuring* and to Hilary Melton-Butcher who kept me cheerfully supplied with suggestions for footloose exploration. The irrepressible Stephanie Provost whose chauffeuring prowess matched Bashir Jooma's and mapped countless British miles with me on their vehicles' odometers. Rahul D'Silva lent brains, brawn and sound foodie advice in London's East End.

William and Caroline Symington in Connecticut connected me with Caroline and Robert Cummings, former Director of Boston University in London, who made Thanksgiving significant in South Kensington. Through that interlude, I was befriended by Belgians Marilyn, Phillipe and Emma-Louise Rixhon, fellow-expats in London, who served me superb home-cooked meals in their Queens Park residence and by Paul, Loulou, and Jack Cooke who unlocked their homes (literally!) and hearts to me with the utmost warmth and generosity. Thanks to their open hands of friendship, we have stayed closely linked through the past decade.

My former NYU students (now buddies) who made their own homes in London were a wonderful resource and a warm comfort to me. Among them are Elise (Trafton) Purchas and husband James as well as Kent Lui (now in Hong Kong).

Among the seventy-five Anglo-Indians through whom I conducted field-interviews in the UK are Dorothy Dady, Gerry and Coreen Gilbert, Henry and Marion Holley, Ashley and Dulcie Jacob, Dennis and Joy Ribeiro, John Thomas, the late Owen Thorpe, Cecil and the late Mary Wilson. They treated me to meals of hot samosas and hotter curry and rice in their suburban homes and their insights led to my book *Britain's Anglo-Indians: The Invisibility of Assimilation* (published in 2017).

David Washbrook, now at Trinity College, Cambridge, facilitated my election to the positon of Senior Associate Member at St. Antony's College, Oxford, while Julie Irving's hard administrative labor facilitated my rewarding research at the Bodleian Library. Liza Denny and Sandie Bryne made lecturing at Oxford my dream-come-true. David and Elizabeth Longrigg run an extraordinary academic home-away-from-home in the city of dreaming spires and have gifted me enduring camaraderie.

Through umpteen trips to Europe, I shared accommodation with friends old and new who offered local hospitality, tourist advice and national delicacies. Among them I count Jack and Julia Anderson, Anja Brug, Genevieve, husband Frederic and sons Louis and Amaury Ducote, Annalisa Oboe, husband Giorgio Giuliari and sons Giovanni and Giacomo, Jacques and Florence Lerouxel and children Jean, Marius and Julia and the late Madame Lisette Tougne. Through a decade of frequent stays in the UK, Susan Colclough and Tony Cox in Oxford and American expats in London Raquel Grossman, Chris Costanza and son Jonas also frequently offered a sheltering roof over my head. My cousin-in-law Sr. Rosie Veigas, organized tickets to the Papal Mass in Rome. The staff that run youth hostels all over the Continent were knowledgeable, polite and helpful towards the most frugal of penny-pinching globe-trotters. In Bombay, Firdaus Gandavia readily lent his studio apartment at short notice.

Writers are endlessly influenced by those who have published before them. In the process of putting this fictional memoir on paper, I read dozens of travelogues and narratives from best-selling authors such as Bill Bryson (*Notes From a Small Island*), Elizabeth Gilbert (*Eat Pray Love*), Frances Mayes (*Under The Tuscan Sun*), Peter Mayle (*A Year in Provence*) and Cheryl Strayed (*Wild*) and to lesser-known ones such as Elizabeth Bard (*Picnic in Provence*), David Elliot Cohen (*One Year Off*), Chris England (*From Balham to Bollywood*), Suzy Gershman (*C'est La Vie*) and Mary-Lou Weisman (*Traveling While Married*). While their accounts eventually blurred in my mind, each author inspired and encouraged me, subliminally, in the challenging quest of attempting to tell my own story by speaking in my own voice.

The first draft of this manuscript was read, reviewed, edited and revised by members of the New York Writers Workshop in Manhattan that was recommended to me by my NYU-colleague Tim Tomlinson and held under the sterling direction of best-selling novelist Charles Salzberg.

Close friends Alison Barry, Agnes Branigan, Bonnie Britz-Thurnauer, Margaret Deefholts, Susan De Souza, Susan Hood, Leslie Mathani, Amy Tobin, and KK Streator read early and late drafts of the manuscript and offered many invaluable recommendations for revision following close textual attention to detail.

Fellow-writers Emma Claire Sweeny in the UK, Naresh Fernandes and Jerry Pinto in Bombay and Shashi Tharoor in New Delhi championed my efforts and endorsed them heartily.

This manuscript was awarded a publications grant from the Center for the Humanities at New York University which was facilitated by Gwyneth Malin and Billy Helton.

The editorial staff at Hamilton Books, especially Mikayla Mislak, Katherine Mullineaux, and Brooke Bures were wonderfully supportive through the production process. Their caring hand-holding was invaluable as the manuscript went into print.

Family members in India and the United States rah-rahed me. My loving mother Edith who was still with us when I lived in London provided intellectual input through lengthy telephonic chats that I profoundly miss. My father Robert, also in Bombay, has been my biggest fan through every book I've published. My daughter Chriselle in California read extracts from the manuscript and provided pertinent editorial advice.

As for my husband, nomadic partner and best friend Llewellyn, well . . . his love, loyalty, devotion, support and encouragement cannot be described or acknowledged in words. One could find no better companion on the road of life.

Hitting a chronological half-century during a spectacular innings in England was possible only because you made it so. To every one of you, this Anglophile says, in the best British way she knows, Cheers!

I

BLUNDERING IN BARCELONA

"When I journeyed to Venice, my dreams became my address."

—Marcel Proust

"If you're a professor, why are you staying in a Youth Hostel?" asked my macho German suite mate Artie. It was a question I'd ask myself repeatedly over the next four days in mid-October 2008 on a demented whirlwind walking tour of Barcelona that aggravated the foot soreness with which I had been plagued for weeks.

What had possessed me to make an online booking in a hostel on a bustling avenue called *Las Ramblas* which did not even have separate male and female dorm rooms? Briefly put, I was coursing through a mid-life crisis having reached the glorious age of fifty. I recalled an enjoyable backpacking tour around Europe in my roaring twenties when youth hostels had been the mainstay of a slender budget. Granted, I was no longer an impoverished grad student counting pennies but it seemed urgent to live again through some of my happiest memories of almost a quarter century previously.

I was eager to give such possibilities another shot as a pre-menopausal matron. Plus, it was rumored that youth hostels had come a long way since my youth. They offered mod cons such as 24-hour running hot water, even private rooms with *en suite* bathrooms—if you could dig deeper in your pockets—and three magical words: unlimited free Wi-Fi! Yessss! But although I was often told that I appeared far younger than my age, I wasn't fooling anyone that I was still a gawky youth. So, Artie's question was valid.

Truth to tell, there was the issue of price. Given the large number of European cities I intended to traverse during my year of adventure, youth hostels were the only form of accommodation to which my limited euros would stretch. I convinced myself that when traveling solo, I could resist indulgence. Being alone, I would rough it out with the best of the young 'uns. I would make one last ditch effort to regress into days of bunk bed crawling, tepid showers in unisex bathrooms and breakfasts *en masse* with inmates upon whose energy I could feed. So, with a huge sense of bravado in the face of trepidation, I made a booking online. The least I could expect was that the hostels be gender segregated, right?

Wrong. The one on lively *Las Ramblas* was "Mixed." When I protested on arrival at Reception after a far-from-flush flight from London on Ryanair—Europe's premier budget airline—to Barcelona, the teen-aged staff eyed me wearily. What's wrong with men and women sharing the same dorm room, they demanded, like *I* was mental. We do have separate showers, you know. *Gracias a Dios* for little mercies. Cursing impulses that had led me to make the booking without checking out this crucial detail, I listlessly climbed the stairs to my third floor dorm room. All around me teeny-boppers behaved the way teeny-boppers do—raucous, loud and oblivious to anyone else but themselves. I retreated quietly to my room wondering how I would endure the next few nights in sunny Espana. Serves me right for indulging a frantic desire to drink deeply, one last time, from the Fountain of Youth.

By the time I climbed the ladder to crawl into my upper-level bunk, I was tired, famished, glum and too annoyed to make friends with anyone. Exulting in the silence of my six-bedded dorm room and praying that no one else would join me, I stared agog at five German hunks who burst in suddenly, bristling with testosterone. They looked up and gazed at me, dumb-founded, and, in barely comprehensible English, asked if I would consider switching dorm rooms. I assured them that I had tried and failed. They burst into rapid-fire German all at the same time. I understood nothing. Nada. Not a word. When they paused for breath, they looked again at each other, then shrugged as if accepting the inevitable and deciding to give in with good grace.

From then on, they sportingly tried to include me in their activities. Would I like a beer? Would I like to join them on a late-night outing? They were going "clubbing." They knew the best one in town and, they assured me, with their influence, I could get in for free as their guest.

I have to admit the offer was tempting. Five virile Aryan youth fitting Hitler's ideal of the Super Race to the tee with boyish blonde hair, bulging biceps, and six-pack abs asking me out! This was every woman's Fiftieth Year Fantasy. But there was the issue of my aching back from a flight during which I had been squeezed in my seat tighter than canned sardines and a stressful interaction with the Reception staff that had left me feeling far from sociable. Were I twenty-five years younger, I might have insinuated myself into their habitual nightlife. As it was, I politely declined.

Not that they let me off the hook. My twenty-something suitemates, tanned golden and exuding fitness with every move, students of engineering, took me under their wing, as if I were their aged auntie. With all hopes of an early night and precious privacy wiped from my mind, I had no choice but to postpone bedtime. That evening, they shared their beer and nibbles with me as they sat in an expanded ring on the floor with their I-Pods blaring, their necks nodding in time to some earphoned beat.

I had assumed from their enthusiasm for 'clubbing', that the city meant just one thing—Party Central—which would pretty much leave my room empty all night. When their beers ran out, the Jerries left me to my own devices. I prepared for sleep in my bunk bed for my hunky companions had disappeared leaving few signs of their occupancy. Not intending to be awoken by their midnight return, I turned to the two devices that youthful experience had taught me to carry for nights in Youth Hostels. Stuffed up with ear-plugs and donning an eye-mask, I intended to remain undisturbed through the night.

But I need not have worried for my dorm mates had far more consideration than most youth hostel-dwelling *habitués*. In deference to my mature years, they had tip-toed back into the room at daybreak. Vaguely aware of their entry somewhere in the small hours of the morning, I turned over and pulled my blanket closer around me as they hurled themselves on their bunks face down and passed out.

But when I awoke in time for breakfast at 8:00 am, I took one look around and recoiled in horror. Our room resembled a war zone in a cabaret-studded nightclub. Stilettos were strewn in unmatched pairs. Glittery T-shirts, tiny tube tops, the tightest trousers. Padded bras and itsy-bitsy panties, feather boas and chandelier ear-rings littered the floor. I stared in bewilderment. What had gone on whilst I was asleep? Had they brought girls in? Well, I would have heard female voices and conspiratorial whispers, had that been the case. Besides, judging by the number of skimpy garments lying around, an army of women had barged in. I could hardly imagine them having communal hi-jinks on hostel bunk beds. Besides, would they feel comfortable bringing hotties in whilst I, old enough to be their *mutter*, was comatose in a neighboring bunk? Hardly likely. And then if these garments belonged to a bunch of women, where were they now? Were they still in bed with my club-crawling suitemates, unrecognizable in the darkened room beneath their blankets? Or had they left already after their quickies? Well, they could hardly have left naked, could they? They'd need to take their seductive clothing with them, one way or the other. None of it made any sense.

Grabbing my toiletries, I crept out of the room and headed to the Ladies bathroom for a shower before breakfast. The place buzzed—literally, as a dozen hair-dryers whirred simultaneously. I dived into my bag for a toothbrush when I heard someone say, "Well, well, well . . . if it isn't the manager of our darling Drag Queens!"

Silence descended suddenly on the premises as all eyes focused on me. I could only stare. Whatever did she mean? Drag Queens? Manager? Who? Not *moi*, surely? "So, what's it like?" continued the catty brunette whose tone I could not read. "What percentage of their pay do they pass on to you?" Was she being funny? Or accusatory? I continued to stare at her, struck dumb. "Speak English, don't ya?" When I eventually found my tongue, I said, "Look, there must be some mistake. I have absolutely no idea what you mean or whom you have mistaken me for. But it isn't me you want!" "Your roommates. You manage those drag queens, don't you?" What?? I stared and stared some more until, finally, the coin dropped. And then each piece started to fit into place like one colossal, three-dimensional jigsaw puzzle. That's what they were. Transvestites! The confusing attire did not belong to any women at all, but to the very guys fast asleep in their bunks below and around me. They'd had to have stripped off their party threads *sans* lights so as not to disturb me, had dived under their own covers and were, very possibly, at that very moment, clad in their birthday suits as I stood flabbergasted in my PJs in the Ladies' loo. In fact, all the time that I had been downing their beer and suggesting tourist itineraries for what I had thought were merely party-hearty grad engineering students on a crazy weekend binge from Munchen, I was sharing space with a pack of cross-dressers who Jekyll and Hyde-d their way through blurry days and naughty nights hugging a secret.

If I was indignant at being forced to share a mixed dorm with them, just imagine how perturbed they might have been at my presence. And yes, being the consummate thespians they were, they had taken my company in their stride, dealt with what must have been a harrowingly difficult situation for them and run (or danced!) with it. There was something—a lot—to be said for their determination to get on with the show. And all the time they kept inviting me to join them at their Club, they were probably looking to show off their transgender skills—their ability to see-saw between masculinity—all that beer-guzzling straight from cans with heavy metal music for company—and femininity—manifested through the most girly of clothing. Seeking validation for the salacious life they led at night, my roomies had invited me into their clandestine world only to be turned down. Had they been disappointed at my rejection? Or simply relieved?

"How do you know? About the . . . er . . . drag queens in my room?" I asked, as the accusing young slip of a thing turned away.

"We were in the lounge when they got back from the club last night," she laughed. "Togged out in far wilder clothing than anything from *Moulin Rouge*."

What were the odds that I would be allocated a bunk in a room with a troupe of male disco performers who preferred to be females? If it were not so disconcerting, it would have been hilarious.

Even as my situation grew more awkward, my attitude towards my newest German cronies became weirdly protective. Almost maternal. I would keep my roomies' secret. I would protect them against the censure of my fellow-hostelites. I would shield them against all of Barcelona, if I had to.

"Ah . . . and because I happen to be sharing their dorm room, you assumed I was . . . what? Their manager?"

"Well, we thought . . ."

"Well, you were mistaken," I heard myself interrupt. "And although it really isn't any of your business, you might like to know that they are the nicest, sweetest guys in the world."

Back in my room surrounded by five strip-teasers still fast asleep, I assessed my position afresh. I had walked into the youth hostel with my eyes open never expecting to be confronted with so odd a position. Although raised as a conservative female in India, I had lived a life far from sheltered. I was not unfamiliar with homosexuals. Growing up in Bombay, I had a few gay classmates in college and had closely be-friended at least a couple. But finding myself in close quarters—literal-ly!—with transvestites . . . well, that was a first time for me. How would this new knowledge of my roomies' talents as cross-dressing performers affect my attitude towards them going forward?

I left them asleep, quiet as dormice, innocent as angels, after I washed, dressed and made my way downstairs. The dining room at breakfast was Carb Central. Cornflakes. Muffins. Toast. More toast. Violently-colored preserves in plastic bowls. Adios Dr. Atkins! Funny but in a past life, when I'd been on intimate terms with youth hostels throughout Europe, consuming carbs by the shovelful had never been an issue. Age and a thickening waistline were clearly catching up with me; but left with no choice, I filled up as of old, tied shoe laces firmly on my sneakers and was off in search of Gaudi. And I honestly did not stop walking for the next four days, foot soreness notwithstanding!

As a lone explorer striding across the globe, the *Lonely Planet* series of travel books had become my Bible. In London, the neighbors I had started to refer to as Next Door Tom and Brenda had introduced me to *Stanford's*, a book store in Covent Garden devoted entirely to travel literature. In this virtual Aladdin's cave for intrepid sojourners, I had spent long hours studying maps and had purchased a copy of *Lonely Planet Barcelona*. As was my wont, I had photocopied pages relevant to my visit and carried them in my backpack to devour on the flight into Spain. Acquainted thus with Not-To-Be-Missed Venues for the first-time visitor, I armed myself with information in English and set out to meet Antoni Gaudi.

Born in the mid-nineteenth century, Gaudi represented the spirit of the Catalan people who had searched long and hard for an identity that would become distinctly their own—that is to say, different from that of the rest of Spain dominated by the colonial capital of Madrid. In incorporating into his designs a vast variety of material that included ceramics, mosaics, stained glass, wrought iron, terracotta, plaster of Paris and poured concrete, he created structures in which every aspect, from exterior chimney pots to interior mantelpieces, were entirely born in his imagination. From such holistic conceptualization was created buildings that are a burst of color, shape and form. It was perhaps fated that he would be killed by a passing tram while in his seventies within sight of the slowly-developing cathedral dedicated to the Holy Family (La Sagrada Familia) to which he had devoted a lifetime.

Parc Guell (say "Goy") was where I would begin my attempts to enter Gaudi's mind and grapple with the uniqueness of his perception of our world. At the bus-stop outside the youth hostel, I found myself waiting with a person I'd spied in the dining hall. She smiled shyly, I smiled back equally tentatively and a new acquaintanceship was born. It did not take much persuasion to team up with the middle-aged German solo sojourner like myself who was named Gisela. Wasn't that what solo travel was all about? Reaching out to fellow-travelers on the journey of life and forming new friendships?

Gisela was a blonde, bespectacled titan from Frankfurt equipped with bulging backpack and multi-lensed camera. And she had a voice that boomed. We communicated in halting English and took pictures for each other in Parc Guell where I discovered that she made a living as a freelance photographer. The purpose of her visit to Barcelona was to capture the essence of Catalunya through its architecture. I could not have found a more fitting companion. And, as her presence in the youth hostel made clear, I was not the only mature resident in the house for she had seen fifty long years before I did.

After becoming introduced to Gaudi's whacky aesthetic in the park, we decided to take another bus to La Sagrada Familia—still a work a progress more than a half century after Gaudi's demise. Ironically enough, I'd arrived in Barcelona prepared to be unimpressed. Modernist architecture is not really my cup of *sangria*. Or so I had thought. But when I viewed a special exhibit in the cathedral—Gothic in the most Modernist kind of way—explaining the influence of nature-derived images—wheat stalks, lavender, sunflowers, pine cones—on Gaudi's architectural motifs, I had my Ah-Ha Moment. The Master had converted iconography from the natural world—from earth to ocean—to decorate the most ecclesiastical of spaces. For in fashioning the complexity of a nautilus and in devising the facets of a snowflake, God had manifested His Divinity. What Gaudi was suggesting to the unbeliever was that Man had only to look to Nature to find God Himself enwrapped therein.

Reeling under the impact of this Renaissance Man who was artist, painter, ceramist, watercolorist, architect, landscape designer and gardener rolled into one, I became dazzled and simply could not get enough of him.

When I suggested we move on to Casa Battlo (say "Baatyo"), Gisela acquiesced and soon we were roaming its corridors. I remained so transfixed for the next couple of hours—audio guide wand plastered to my ear as I surveyed the rooms—that I wandered off. Lost in thought, I realized that I had fallen head over heels in love with Antoni Gaudi. Though physically fatigued and deeply conscious of aching soles, I trudged through his buildings enwrapped in wonder.

When I finally surfaced from my chaotic rumination, I looked around for Gisela. She was nowhere to be seen. Had she actually just evaporated into thin air? Where was she? How could I possibly find her? I had no Spanish vocabulary to help me approach someone who might have assisted me. No, I didn't have a posse to send out for her. Plus, five-floored *Casa Battlo* was enormous. It'd be like searching for a needle in the proverbial haystack. I'd intended to cover much ground that day and, fully conscious of fleeting time and my protesting feet, resisted the temptation to seek and find her. Back on my ownsome, I drifted along *Rambla de Catalunya* saying "Hola" to the Modernistas.

When I returned to my room at about 6:00 that evening, it was like entering a convent after spending a year in a war zone. Every last square foot of my room was meticulous. Had I not known better how cleverly gender-benders conceal evidence of their double lives, I might have thought I had hallucinated. The floors shone, each bed was immaculately made up, every item of clothing impeccably folded away. Any sign of occupancy by a crop of kinky cross-dressers had been wiped clean away.

And then at around 7:30 p.m. as I relaxed in my bunk deciding where my explorations ought to take me the next day, my roomies returned. On seeing me again, Artie said, "Ah, hello, hello. We thought you had went home. When we waked up, your bed . . . it was so neat."

His buddy Wolfgang piped in, "*Ja*! We thought we must clean also. The room, it is looking good, no?"

If they believed that I had made informed guesses about the goings-on in their lives, they gave no indication at all. For my part, I pretended I had noticed nothing amiss that morning. They drew me once again into their social circle and for the second evening I joined my German suitemates on the floor to swallow more Lowenbrau.

Half an hour later, my companions wanted to know if I would join them at the discotheque that evening. They searched my face closely as I responded. I searched their expressions with equal scrutiny. We were like teams of diplomats negotiating with guarded cordiality around a delicate matter with neither party wishing to give anything away. I ended the *détente* when I thanked them for trying to include me in their nocturnal plans and, feigning fatigue, declined.

But by 8:00 pm, I became aware of insistent hunger pangs. It was time to seek out a delicatessen for a sandwich or a pizzeria for a slice. Excusing myself, I left my room to find *La Boqueria*, a covered market-place conveniently located on the vibrant Las Ramblas. Some Serrano ham for which Iberia was famed and equally well-renowned Manchego cheese would make a mean sandwich.

Armed with my meal and a Coke, I hurried back to the hostel in order to follow my own golden rule of solo travel survival—getting back to my room before it turned dark. With remnant daylight still faintly evident on that evening in early autumn, I took the stairs to my third floor dorm room.

And then, lo and behold, whom should I see descending towards me but the Germanic Titan, Gisela.

"Ah!" I exclaimed. "Found you!"

Gisela sized me up and scowled. If I expected her to embrace the situation with a sense of humor, I could not have been more mistaken. Her expression became menacing as she approached me. She stuck her finger in my face and said, "You. You go away without me. I look everywhere for you."

"I'm so sorry. I really am. I became so absorbed in Gaudi . . ."

"I look for you one hour. No, I look for you two hour. Everyone I ask for you . . ."

She advanced closer as her echoing voice grew in power with every syllable she uttered in the stairwell's narrow confines. I looked around desperately for someone to come to my aid only to find that there was no one else in that isolated space but the two of us.

"You try to get lost," she continued. "You don't want be my friend, you just say. Why you leave me behind?"

"I didn't really mean to. We just drifted apart. Honestly, I was sorry to have lost you."

By this point in our exchange, she had me up against the wall as every inch of her nearly six feet of beefy Germanness towered threateningly above me. Any minute I expected her to strike me. Seriously. If she had raised her hand and clouted me on the head, I would not have been surprised and there would have been no one around to witness the assault.

Then, quite as suddenly, just when I thought I'd be wiping bits of my face off the floor, she switched to German and loosened her grip on my elbow. A tirade that remained unintelligible followed me as I raced up the stairs and fled to my room. Casting one last glance at her on the landing below, I found her watching me disappear with a venomous look in her eyes.

Heart racing, I entered my empty room and sank down on a bunk. What was my best plan of action? My roomies had apparently left for yet another night on the town. Ought I to go downstairs to Reception to report the near-assault? My mangled sandwich, clutched in my trembling hands, all at once seemed like the most unappetizing thing in the world. I had five roommates built like Greek gods who got their kicks from wearing women's underwear. And I'd had a near-death confrontation with a European photog who had appeared shy and docile as a doe in the morning and had metamorphosed before my very eyes into a neo-Nazi with the strength of an ox by the time night struck! Well, I'd asked for it. He who sups with the devil must have a long spoon.

I returned to London, two days later, seriously debating the sagacity of continuing to haunt youth hostels. Barcelona had been an architectural revelation but I'd had the most curious encounters and had seriously abused my poor feet. Estimated mileage logged over four days was nothing less than thirty!

Back in my Holborn flat—which suddenly seemed like the sanest, safest place on earth, I sank into my bathtub for a relaxing soak and contemplated my proposed interview, the next day, with the first of the many Anglo-Indians I would meet as part of my field-research. With any luck, they would be more normal than the oddballs I had left behind in Barcelona.

2

GETTING THERE . . . AND OVER THERE

So how did I find myself holed up in a flat in Holborn?

A month previously, I'd awoken in my favorite city—London! Aka T'Smoke. It was the perfect mid-life birthday present to assuage a perfectly plausible mid-life crisis. Was it possible that following umpteen good years as a dutiful wife and mother, university professor and museum docent in America, this Bombay-born Anglophile had been granted the opportunity of a lifetime? A fantasy I'd shelved for decades suddenly became real when I was offered the opportunity to spend one academic year teaching in London. Strictly speaking, it was not a Sabbatical—merely a chance to continue to do the work I'd done for years but in my dream venue.

Long years before I boarded the trans-Atlantic flight that made my dreams come true, I'd nursed a recurrent one that involved escape to England. Mind you, it wasn't as if I was dissatisfied or unfulfilled. I wasn't stuck in the proverbial rut. I wasn't recovering from a bitter divorce. I wasn't fed up with my family or burned out by my job. I had neither lost my livelihood nor my mojo. Far from it. In fact, my favorite reverie was often accompanied by guilt. I simply did not think I had the right to expect a new and improved life. I already had a perfectly happy one for which a lot of people would trade both arms.

No, my fantasies were not the brainchild of discontent. They were born out of a challenge I wished to set myself. An urge, if you prefer, to spend a year *sans* spouse and grown-up daughter in a city I adored, doing exactly as I pleased. I cherished a desire to awake each morning asking myself, "So what shall I do today?" and know that there were no needs to cater to other than my own. Supremely selfish, I'll grant you that, but honestly, what woman, pushing fifty, aware that youth has been left behind and that menopause is lurking around the corner, has not asked herself the questions: What would I do if I had a year, just one year, to call my own? How would I spend a sabbatical of sorts? A Fauxbattical? Convinced that there is no life, however perfect, that cannot be enriched by the opportunity for fantastical escape, I'd contemplated the answers. Before I knew it, ideas that I unimaginatively christened "My London To-Do List," emerged beneath my fingertips.

Ever since I'd fallen in love with Great Britain as a backpacker who'd arrived to undertake grad study at Oxford nearly a quarter century previously, the notion of a year-long stay in the UK had simmered on the back burner of my brain. It bubbled and squeaked when I commenced spadework for an academic study on the UK's elderly Anglo-Indians—a community of mixed racial descent, part-European, part-Indian, created on the Indian sub-continent as a result of three centuries of Western colonialization. To truly become enmeshed in the immigrant fabric of these hyphenated lives, I'd need to enter their milieu, not as an outsider but as one who lived and breathed their Anglicized air.

Enter the Dean of Liberal Studies at New York University, where I'd spent fourteen years teaching South Asian Studies. During a chance encounter with him, I'd mentioned my London-based research initiative. My objective was to obtain information about the immigrant lives of Anglo-Indians as an ethnic, diasporic minority in Britain's multicultural mosaic. Following India's independence, soon after World War II, in 1947, they'd uprooted themselves from the sub-continent, to sink new ones in Great Britain. That first generation, having arrived in England in its twenties, was limping towards its seventies and beyond. Large numbers had passed away and a larger number were no longer physically or mentally able to recount their stories.

I was curious to meet them and listen to their tales before it was too late. Conscious of the Publish Or Perish conventions of the American academe, I was keen to record their oral histories in the hope of publishing them in a scholarly volume. Knowing that my proposal required me to spend prolonged periods in London, the Dean made a suggestion: Would I like to take on a posting to teach at NYU's campus in Bloomsbury for a year?

Would I just?

So, long before birthday cards poured in, my milestone year took substantial mental shape. This would be it, I decided. My Gap Year at Fifty. There would be no stopping me as I savored the year ahead fully, zestfully, passionately. But then, after my initial excitement subsided, doubt jostled for space in my imagined scenario. Could I really pull it off? Leave home and family far behind for a year of self-fulfillment? Hypothetical arguments commenced. Was it fair to leave my husband alone for a year? Would this self-imposed separation have a negative impact on our marriage? I could not bear the thought. But my excitement at grasping the opportunity outweighed my fears about possible marital disharmony. My husband was a terrific homemaker in great physical shape, fully absorbed in his international banking career. He could take good care of himself. My twenty-something daughter had flown the nest years previously. The patter of little feet that would weld me more firmly to my domestic pivot was probably years away in the distant future. If I wished to flee my nest, spread my wings and fly to T'Smoke, there wouldn't be a better year. England, I thought, here I come!

When I put the Dean's proposal before Hubs, he only said, "One whole year? In London? My God, your favorite city! How you will love it!" And in those few words lay the consent I needed to bolt. If he was sorry to see me go, he didn't say so. But then, I'm married to a man of few words. As for Dot . . . well, her face fell, but she took it stoically, seeking consolation, I suppose, in having found what she then thought was her own soul mate. By February, I announced to envious friends that I'd be spending an academic year in Ole' Blighty, as the British Isles were known among Indian natives during the Raj. "Bi-la-ya-ti," they'd called it in Hindi. Abroad. Overseas. When the syllables rolled off English tongues, they'd boiled down to "Blighty."

For the next six months, I floated on Cloud Nine. Anglophilia is built into my DNA. Despite three decades as a first-generation immigrant in America, I exhibit symptoms of a British colonial hangover, culled from my birth and upbringing in the colonial city of Bombay in India where I'd lived for the first thirty years of my life and graduated with university degrees in English literature. What could be more natural for someone weaned on Waterbury's Compound Gripe Water? Though I was firmly rooted in coastal Connecticut physically, cerebrally I dwelled way across the Atlantic.

While photographed ("snapped") and finger printed for a UK work permit, I conjured up parts of Great Britain I had yet to explore—like Cornwall and Northern Ireland. With London as a base, I'd hotfoot it to the B hives: Berlin. Belfast. Barcelona. Oh, and Belgium (Brussels and Bruges)—bits I'd skipped on previous European jaunts. Budget airlines let me envisage long weekends coursing through cobbled Continental alleys and a stint in Oxford where I'd recently been elected to the position of Senior Associate Member at St. Antony's College. As each piece fit into an expansive jigsaw puzzle, I foresaw a year of teaching followed by a summer of pure research in Matthew Arnold's "city of dreaming spires." I ceased to dream in abstract and began to plan in concrete. When UPS delivered my passport with a stamped year-long British work permit, it felt like "Take Out Service." Like *Dominoes* on my doorstep. Cloud Nine grew fluffier.

There was one more thing to clear before I skittered across the Atlantic: the green light for leave of absence as a docent in the Metropolitan Museum of Art where I'd given tours for ten years. My co-docents co-operated and ate their hearts out. Phew! London for a year? All those museums . . . and free of charge to boot. They wished they could heave their bags over their backs and join me pronto. I attached a blog to my website to mull over each day's doings and enable loved ones I'd leave behind to arm-chair trot with me. I signed up for Aetna's Global Insurance coverage, courtesy of NYU. I hadn't a clue that, three months later, I'd be a pro at navigating the Kafkaesque corridors of the UK's National Health Service as I became afflicted with a condition I had never heard of previously and could barely pronounce! Plantar Fasciitis! Suggested cures, it turned out, were every bit more fanciful that the causes. But I get ahead of myself when I say that afflicted I was and cope I did.

Solitary I would stay for most of the year, but accompanied I would be at the outset, for Hubs offered to see me settled in my new digs. Because his own measly weeks of summer holiday would be chomped by the chore of dropping me off across the pond, I planned us a motoring trip in Scotland—his choice of venue. He was the only guy I knew who felt at ease driving a stick-shift car on the wrong side of the UK's murderously narrow roads where the risk of decimating stray sheep was always a real possibility. So, it was resolved that he was coming with me for what would be two weeks together in bonnie Scotland before he scooted back home leaving me to muse on my ownsome.

But, surrounded by unzipped baggage, I still remained clueless about their ultimate destination as I hadn't yet received my London address. So, I did a mini Morris dance when my new domicile was disclosed just three days before our departure. My flat would be in High Holborn ("Ho-bin") in the heart of legal London. My virtual dance became physical when UPS delivered a packet, two days later, and not a moment too soon. In fact, less than twenty-four hours before we boarded an American Airlines aircraft, my feverish fingers closed around the keys to my new London pad.

Life-changing, I knew, Holborn wouldn't be. After all, it wasn't as if I was shipping off through the Peace Corps to sub-Saharan Africa. Would I return home transformed? Not likely. What then did I expect from my year away from home? Well, primarily, the chance to reflect on the strange turns my life had taken through the years. My immigration from India to the USA, for instance, twenty years previously had occurred when I least expected or desired it. A simple offer to undertake post-doctoral research on a full fellowship at St. John's University, New York, had changed my life completely. It had led to a job offer at New York University even as I met and married Hubs and settled down to an immigrant life in The Big Apple. My stab at life in London was a chance to find out if I could conquer an irrational fear, inherited from my mother, that had dogged me from childhood—of living alone for an extended period. I wished to conquer latent internal demons—such as my solitude-induced anxieties. Finally, it would be an opportunity for discovery—nothing on a Columbian scale, of course. Minor ones would be just fine by me.

Persistent doubts surfaced and my attempts to quell them commenced: Can I face the emotional challenge of life *sans* spouse and daughter for twelve whole months? Having left money matters to my banker husband for most of my life, will I balance books successfully, given dismal dollar-pound exchange rates? There was my health to consider. Am I buff enough? I wondered. Although I've been a regular gym-goer for two decades and thrive on endless walking, will my physical and psychological energy hold up? And then there was the issue of company. How will I bond with the traditionally reserved English? And the folks I meet on my travels? Will they make overtures and accept my complex background as a brown-skinned, Indian-born, naturalized American? Or will I be victimized by Europe's notorious racism? What troubled me most was the prodigious scope of my plans.

"I'm afraid," I told Hubs, "I'll have too much fun and not get any work done."

"Not if I know you," said my loyal spouse. "Want to bet?"

"Well . . . I don't know," I replied, riddled with doubt. "Just take a look at my To-Do List."

His jaw dropped as his eye ran over my plans determinedly spelled out in black and white. After reading each objective more frivolous than the next such as Learn to Bake Bread and Visit Every Wren Church. Hubs said, "This is not an itinerary. It's a syllabus!"

A few days later, in August 2008, dawn had broken over American *terra firma* when Hubs and I were hoisted from Kennedy airport into wide open skies. I called my new haven Rochelle's Roost in London—a nest in which to do my brooding.

I awoke in Economy on a flight path less traveled—not southwards from Scotland through the backbone of England, but eastwards over Cornwall and Devon. A sharp left turn north exposed the green patch-work blanket of Surrey and the M25 motorway encircling Greater London. And then, there it was—the Thames, and as my eyes followed bends in the river, I saw it, glorious from above, reduced to Lilliputian dimensions, on that rarest of weather possibilities in England—London on a cloudless day.

The Reception Hall at Heathrow was bedlam. Our taxi driver was AWOL. We sat amidst Himalayan baggage mounds and waited. Things had already begun to fall apart. Suddenly, Sri Lankan Mahen material-ized out of thin air to usher us into his waiting vehicle. He barked into his mobile in barely discernible Tamil, then turned to us and smiled. "Mistake happened So sorry. Your driver . . . .he pick up another pas-senger. But come-come with me. I take you to High Holborn No wear-ries."

At 10: 45 pm, long after London's barristers and solicitors had ad-journed for the weekend, we drew up outside my new building, *Bishop House*. Chancery Lane Tube stop, reminiscent of Dickens' *Bleak*

House, was only twenty steps away, the answer to a prayer. Any closer and I'd be living underground!

Pound sterling changed hands. Mahen grinned, pleased with our generous tip, exposed his sparkling white Chiclets, and gave me his card. "Call me anytime," he urged. Fat Chance. His fare, when converted to dollars, had cost just a fraction less than our trans-Atlantic tariff.

The magnetic fob on my key ring opened street-level glass security doors into the spiffy vestibule usually occupied by the doorman ("concierge"). I almost uttered a giddy "Open Sesame," fancying myself at the entrance to Ali Baba's cave, as I inserted the key that had initiated an impromptu Morris Dance in my Southport kitchen. Pausing at the threshold, I wondered if we ought, in Hindu fashion, to break a coconut and utter a few choice Sanskrit *mantras* for luck before we crossed it? But then we're not Hindus. We're practicing Catholics. We were neither carrying coconuts nor knew any *mantras* and Hubs was already feeling around the walls for light switches, as if playing Blind Man's Bluff. Deeper inside, lights from the very modern office building across the street bounced comfortably off into our new home—the answer to another prayer ("Please, God, do not let my flat be located in some dark alley").

One tiny room after the other lay virginal and waiting to be discovered as we explored them gingerly. It was one of those trendy new "boutique one-bed" apartments (flats) with a bathroom so disproportionate you felt you could do the Viennese waltz in it. Still. I was far from disappointed.

Hubs surveyed the room. "Ikea," he pronounced. "Very contemporary." Standard issue furniture: warm maple pieces, black leather sofa bed, well-equipped kitchen drawers, black granite countertops, winking stainless steel backsplash, and appliances. Paradise had taken Modernist shape. Traditionalist Me wanted to rebel; but I reined in my aversion. You are here to embrace difference, I scolded myself sternly. Surely you can deal with stark white walls and Scandinavian cellular furniture. I noted that though we were located in the heart of Central London, not a squeak reached our ears from the streets below. Boy, what effective double glazing! I thought as I dropped off that first night.

Discovery commenced at daylight. Awaking at six on our first day in London, I took stock of my new surroundings. My entire flat would fit into our bedroom suite in Southport! I reviewed the inventory of furniture. In the clear light of day, a desk remained conspicuous by its absence. How could a writer function without a desk? Some things could simply not be compromised. It was my cue to start another list: Things To Buy. But it would take me months, many months, before I would finally find the perfect desk to suit my writerly ambitions.

Holborn slumbered that Saturday morning. Thirteenth century Staple Inn sat catty corner to my building, all weathered black beams and multiple brick chimneys, a miraculous lone survivor of London's Great Fire of 1666. Antiquity would stare me in the face each morning as I drew up window blinds. This history buff had lucked out big time. We walked towards Bloomsbury to discover my new place of work—New York University's campus. Prayers were answered with every stride. My flat was surrounded by trendy shops in a 'happening' neighborhood. Its location had none of the isolation I'd dreaded. Minutes later, I surveyed my new campus that carried an impressive pedigree: a white Georgian townhouse on Bedford Square that, as the blue disc on the wall proclaimed, had once housed Lord Eldon, Chancellor of London. As we sauntered past the Neo-Classical edifice of the British Museum, my heart said hello to my new stomping ground.

My first week in London with Hubs started tamely enough. We devoured the city as tourists, revisiting favorite haunts from previous vacations ("holidays") and discovering new ones. We walked everywhere, covering a minimum of five miles that very first day. It was the beginning of the manic walking that would finally do me in. But again, I am racing too fast forward.

London during that first week was nothing if not lively. My spirits soared. Afloat on an optimistic high, I hadn't the slightest premonition of the pitfalls lying ahead that would turn my proposed More Perfect Year into a Nearly Perfect One.

3

STALKING ROYALTY IN THE HIGHLANDS

"The Queen! It's the Queen! There she comes! Oh my stars!"

I had transplanted myself into British soil in the fervent hope of living through a whole year of discovery. Little did I dream that, in the manner of the pussy-cat in the nursery rhyme, I'd be going to London to see the Queen. Well, to be exact, Scotland. In the second week of Hubs' summer vacation with me, we scooted off to Scotland in a rented Vauxhall Astra at the start of our Highland Fling.

Britain's royal family makes an annual pilgrimage in August to stalk deer around Scotland's Balmoral Castle. Remember that unforgettable scene in *The Queen* when Helen Mirren playing Elizabeth II stares transfixed at a magnificent stag? Well, we'd arrived Dee-side and, unwittingly, attempted to stalk the Royal Family in their favorite summer hidey-hole. And like Mirren in the movie, we were rewarded for our pains by the perfect sighting—the Windors in their Sunday best at Crathie Kirk—which is 'church' in Gaelic—or Crrrathie Kirrrrk—if you pronounce it like the locals.

Scotland contributed immensely to my year of discovery. Not only did I find out just how beautifully eighty plus years can sit upon a reigning face, but I mustered the courage to taste haggis, Scotland's gastronomic contribution to the world. In fact, the Royal Deeside village of Ballater makes a major part of its living from visitors who come with no more complicated plans than to linger amidst the lakes ("lochs"). And right in the midst of this idyll sits Balmoral, a castle that contributes to the area's economy by attracting gawking tourists who fork out cold hard cash to traipse through its opulent interiors while hoping, on the castle lawns, to spot Holly, Willow, Candy and Vulcan. For those not acquainted with preferred pets, these are the royal corgis. For when Queenie moves house Northside, pampered pooches follow in her wake. Hubs and I planned to join the gawkers. Sewn into Plan A was a guided tour of the Windsors' summer retreat.

Early on Sunday morning, we arrived at the regal venue. Balmoral lay bathed in late-summer sunshine surrounded by vibrant green meadows and low-slung hills. But at the gates, we were sorely disappointed.

"Sorry, Madam, but we cannot let you in." The guard was as frosty as the air on the estate.

What? Were we too early? Was the castle closed on Sundays? Did we need to book tickets in advance? None of the above. Well, it turned out that when the Royal Family was in residence, tourists were prohibited. Hadn't we spotted the flag flying from its ramparts? Duh.

I was shattered. But swift consolation was offered by said guard. If we crossed the street and walked to Crrrrathie Kirrrrk, he helpfully suggested, we could attend Sunday service with the royal family.

Blimey! (Note that after only a week in Britain, my lexicon had already started to reflect decidedly British affectations). A Royal Sighting! And so quickly into my year of discovery! Needless to say, at this point in my travels, I had no way of knowing that as the year went by, I would have occasion to stalk members of the British royal family at several other venues.

Plan B went into motion.

Crathie Kirk resembles a nondescript stone cottage with an unpretentious spire. Each August, its Sunday services are glammed up by the presence of assorted royal family members. Sighting and waving at them proves ample compensation for frustration garnered by not being able to enter their home. A long sloping driveway leads from the parking lot to the church door.

"Let's join the onlookers on the driveway," I said, excitedly to Hubs. If the stars were in alignment, perhaps we would glimpse some regal ones.

Behind velvet roping strung along the slope, we watched as security personnel equipped with walkie-talkies did politely quiet rounds, eyed cameras and said, "No snaps please." Bummer! Even if our patience was rewarded by the practiced wave of a royal wrist, there would be no pictorial proof of our encounter.

As the hour for Sunday service approached, my animation mounted. The Highlands' sun shone golden upon conifer-covered mountains. The air was as crisp as a lettuce leaf, as cool as a cucumber and deliciously fresh. In the nippy mountain air of a perfect day in Scotland, I stood as if in a salad.

Just when I started to feel a bit foolish amidst the eager but very well-behaved audience, a Bentley pulled up.

"They're here!" said someone quite unnecessarily near my right ear.

The car passed within four yards of our waiting feet. I recognized Camilla, Duchess of Cornwall, immediately. She smiled warmly in the passenger seat where she wore one of her signature wide-brimmed beige hats and coat looking not nearly as horsey as cartoonists suggest. Besides her sat the Heir Apparent, the dapper Prince of Wales. I made another discovery in that instant: Prince Charles does not see the need for a chauffeur and is quite happy to drive his car himself! Two royals down. How many more to go? My eyes darted to the back seat where I spied the elegant Sophie Rhys-Jones, Countess of Wessex and wife of Charles' youngest sibling, Prince Edward. Oooh, three royals in the bag! Result!

The audience was satisfied; but an unspoken question hovered on every lip. Where was Her Nibs? We were elated at what we had seen whizz by, but we clearly expected more. Several minutes went sluggishly by. No more cars appeared on the horizon. Public mood deflated quickly for, as Hubs convincingly said, "The show is over".

Then, a few breathless seconds later, it sailed along: a burgundy Rolls Royce began its slow climb uphill.

"It's her!"

"There she comes!"

"Wow . . . wow . . . wow—Oh my God!"

The car stopped a nose-length from us. I spotted Prince Edward smiling away for all he was worth in the front passenger seat. I was beside myself. Public adulation was infectious and like the unabashed Anglophile I am, I waved frantically too. Then, just when it seemed as if my elation was complete, I made eye contact with Her Maj in the back seat and at the window right by where we stood. Resplendent in a bright pink silk hat and coat, she sported pearls at neckline and earlobes. We saw the famous royal wave as she smiled brightly and appeared, if such an oxymoron is possible, seriously happy. Seated alongside, her husband Prince Phillip, Duke of Edinburgh, waved, his head stooped slightly to catch better sight of fans.

"Those eyes!" said someone near me. "Who would know hers were so blue?"

Can she be nearly eighty? I wondered. "What gorgeous skin!" I heard myself think.

What a highlight for an Anglophile! Viewing the Queen with her kids in tow not four feet away from where we were standing was the least anticipated part of our travels. Had I been searching for something to write home about, I had just earned bonafide bragging rights.

Our morning ended after church service, with an unexpected souvenir. Inside Crathie Kirk—tiny, almost cozy, rather dark and heavily beamed—a satin coverlet in royal purple lay draped over the pew that the royal family had occupied at the very front. I strolled over to it nonchalantly, picked up for preservation in my scrapbook a printed copy of the day's liturgy that the Queen had left behind after using it at the service. I left the church wondering how much it would fetch on E-bay! Not that I intended to sell. No Siree Bob! I proposed to hang on for dear life to a church pamphlet that had been handled by the fingers of a ruler whom I found to be in the pink of health and likely to live long enough to become the longest reigning monarch in the country's history.

Ballater produced one more incident to cause prolonged excitement, thanks to Cora and Simon Love, all wide smiles and blazing warmth, proprietors at our *School House Bed & Breakfast*.

"Cuppa Tea?" they asked as we unloaded our cases.

We soon discovered that Cuppa Tea means Hello. It can also mean Dreadful Weather, Bloody Headache, Fecking Traffic and Four 'o Clock.

After we downed the first of many cuppa teas, the Loves informed us about a little-known gem in the neighborhood.

"Make sure you don't miss the old Victorian graveyard," they'd advised. "Across the street from the church, you can see the tombstone of John Brown, Queen Victoria's dedicated groomsman."

"The same one that's immortalized in the movie?" I asked.

"That's the one," said Cora. Billy Connolly played him opposite Judi Dench who was Queen Victoria. Have you seen it?"

You bet your last farthing I had! The iconic Judi Dench was my favorite British actress. Victoria's close platonic friendship with John Brown had been unknown to me until I'd seen her play the bereft monarch in the film. Nothing, I decided, would keep me from paying tribute to the unconventional man who had nursed her through inconsolable grief following the death of her beloved husband, Prince Albert.

Stumbling through a deserted field, we reached the burial ground filled with scratchy undergrowth, bedraggled thistles and blackened Gothic tombstones so worse for wear that their engravings had all but eroded. Amidst the recording of lives snatched a hundred or more years ago by consumption, malnutrition and ague, Hubs spied it—the aged marble tombstone describing Brown as Victoria's "good and faithful servant." Weedy, neglected, forgotten though poor John Brown's grave may be, I was glad not to miss this concealed jewel of Scottish history well documented in the film *Mrs. Brown.* It is true, as the old British ditty goes that "John Brown's body lies a-moldering in his grave." Standing there, in that desolate, sadly melancholic graveyard, I felt haunted by history. How briefly Time credits those whose humblest gestures of kindness most comfort celebrity lives.

Our exploration of Scotland had begun in Edinburgh (say "Ed-in-bruh") at Kristen's Farmhouse B&B in Carnoch, across the Forth River from the capital city that was overtaken by the summer's annual Dramatics Festival and Fringe.

"Cuppa tea?" asked Kristen, as she welcomed us in.

Under her guidance, we took a crash course in Scottish gastronomy for our good proprietress plied us with Balls and Crappin—don't ask! They translated to Shetland meatballs and stuffing! For breakfast, she inquired if we'd like to have Crowdie with Car-cakes or if we'd prefer Brochan with Brose.

Much later, we found out that she had offered Highland cream cheese with pancakes or porridge made with chicken stock-softened oatmeal. And just when I felt the urgent need to fumble around for a dictionary, she offered Haggis. Lest you wonder, Scotland's greatest poet, Robert Burns, described it as "great chieftain of the sausage race!"

As Kristen disappeared for a few minutes, the American guest also sharing our B&B and who introduced himself as Hank told us in a conspiratorial whisper, "Don't go for the haggis. It's all sorts of garbage stuffed in a boiled animal bladder."

No way! What would she offer next? Testicles?

I was about to request a more familiar repast: toast and Dundee's famed orange marmalade with heather honey perhaps. But then I decided quite suddenly, in keeping with my new resolve, to take a walk on the wild side.

"Haggis, please," I heard myself say.

"Oh, I'm glad you want to trri some," said Kristen, beaming. "Do you know what it is? You're not vegetarrrian, are you? Because it's the belly, you see."

Hank the Yank listened, horrified at the choice I'd made. "Now, look 'ere," he began, "It's just tripe."

Ignoring him, Kristen continued, "I mean the gut. The stomach bag of the sheep."

"So not the bladder then?"

"The bladderrr?" She threw her head back. "Who's been feeding you such rrrubbish?"

I glanced at my helpful compatriot.

"We stuff the gut with sheep's pluck."

"Sheep's what?"

"Pluck. You know. Innarrds. Liverr, hearrt, lights."

"Lights?"

"Those arrre the intestines."

"Tripe!" said Hank, triumphantly. "That's what I just said."

"It's offal," said Kristen.

"There. Ya see? I told her so," said Hank. "It's awful."

"Not awful. Offal."

"That's what I said, 'Mam. Just awful."

The much-misunderstood haggis finally arrived on warmed plates looking like the most appealing piece of finest French pate. Good job I hadn't seen a printed recipe that made mention of paunch, windpipe and gristle or I'd have converted instantly to vegetarianism. Kathleen provided a basket of crisp oatcakes and instructed us to spread haggis on them with a butter-knife. Then, thankfully, she disappeared to bring us coffee.

I took a first small bite, gingerly. The sausage was rendered palatable by the heavy-handed use of a pepper mill. It is unlikely that haggis had existed before the colonial conquest of Kerala's peppercorns. Thankfully, onions, oatmeal and cayenne masked the flavor of boiled internal organs. Frankly, you'd have to twist my arm to get me seconds. Then, just when I turned, out of sheer politeness, to finish my oatcake, I saw Hubs reach for the nearest potted plant. Hank the Yank stared with an expression that most eloquently proclaimed, I Told Ya So.

Glasgow was a washout but we ought not to have been disappointed. Tourists do not go to Scotland for its weather. Enough said. It poured rain so torrential we could have betted we were in Bombay during the monsoon. Furthermore, some Council strike closed down every museum in the city. We readjusted our agenda and sought refuge in Charles Rennie Mackintosh's famous *Willow Tea Rooms* where we discovered how to pronounce scone (say "skon") and relished the fleeciest ones that melted like clouds in my mouth when slathered with clotted cream and strawberry jam. As rain drummed on outside, we remained closeted in restaurants where we found out that Cock-A-Leekie is an obscenely scrumptious soup and Cullen Skink, made with mashed haddock, has absolutely nothing to do with a kitchen sink or a smelly skunk. Had we more time to linger in the Land of the Rolled R, doubtless we'd have found occasion to relish Hotch-Potch (Harvest Broth), Powsowdie (Sheep's Head Broth), and Bawd Bree (Hare Broth). Glasgow reinstated our faith in Scottish cuisine.

For the rest of our days in Scotland, we moseyed along scenic miles of countryside never very far away from low mountain ranges whose peaks seemed close enough to touch. Closer to Fort William en route to Loch Ness, we stared blankly out through a weeping windshield to find the location of our next B&B opposite the tallest peak in the land, Ben Nevis, shrouded beneath ominous storm clouds.

"Cuppa Tea?" asked Hamish and Maira McDonald as they ushered us into their abode.

Nothing could have been more welcome to our frozen ears. Later, in their drawing room, overlooking cloud-obscured peaks, they bad-mouthed the English making us fully aware that Anglo-Scots rivalry is alive and kicking this side of the border.

"Hffmmph," Hamish fumed. "Good thing we have our own Parliament now. And they finally returned our Stone. What a kerfuffle they made about that! And after nicking it too. I mean they could have asked nicely." He meant the Stone of Scone (say "skoon", not "skon"). The symbolic Coronation Rock had been snatched from Scotland by the English as one of the spoils of warfare, fitted into the coronation chair of England's King Edward I in 1296 and only recently returned to its rightful owners. Old grudges die hard, it would seem, north of the border.

Our rooms were furnished in tartan plaids and Old McDonald served locally-sourced venison sausages at sunrise in Scottish breakfasts that resembled full blown heart attacks on a plate.

"Would you like some more meat with your meat?" whispered Hubs, as he eyed rashers of bacon, bursting sausages ("bangers") and an un-recognizable fried disk ("black pudding") on his plate.

Thoroughly spoiled by the Anglo-bashing McDonalds, we left their fine hostelry and proceeded towards Loch Ness. But, alas, though Nessie the Monster remained elusive, we did spy a hobo who thumbed our vehicle down just past the Lake.

"Stop right there," I said to Hubs at the sight of the lone hitchhiker.

"Is that wise?" he muttered.

"Let's do our good deed for the day." I was living on the edge, remember?

Egged on by me and the benevolence of the scenery, Hubs stopped our Astra to pick up Brendan, who up close and personal looked far more menacing than he did when we were several yards away. An Irishman, he wore hardware all over his face. Rings and studs winked from assorted extremities. I noted strong combat boots and a leather jacket and my heart plummeted.

"Thank you verrrrie much," he said, heaving his duffel bag as he scrambled into the backseat bringing a most unpleasant whiff in with him. "I missed the last bus to Holyhead, y'see," he continued in his heavy brogue, exposing more silver in his teeth than on Wimbledon trophies. As I eyed him warily in our rear-view mirror, I wondered what had induced me to pick up so odiferous a passenger. God alone could guess what dangers lay ahead on the road with our scary companion.

Each second that we cruised along, I sat on tenterhooks expecting a revolver held to the back of our heads any second. There go our credit cards. There goes our Scottish money. There go our peace of mind and highway-induced complacency.

Somewhat anti-climactically, Brendan was a pussycat in cougar clothing. He told us about his eight-year old son Liam waiting for him at home in Dublin. How disappointed he'd be if Daddy didn't arrive home on schedule. Thanks to our ride, Daddy'd probably make it back before his anxious son fretted.

Brendan alighted just after we crossed Skye Bridge en route to the Isle of Skye. As we saw the last of him, I thought: we have never done this before. What made me suggest, so spontaneously, that Hubs slow down for our malodorous hitchhiker? It would have to be my new state of mind, liberated from the shackles of convention. Wasn't Total Living a matter of daring to undertake what I'd never done before? Stretching beyond my comfort zone? I had made a successful beginning, albeit with Hubs by my side. The true test would come, I knew, when I did something way beyond the pale, entirely on my own.

Our drive to St. Andrews along the banks of the River Spey in the flourishing midst of malt whisky distilleries remains unforgettable for the landscape. Fortunately, better sense prevented us from taking the whisky tasting trail—there was no way we were driving in a straight line after imbibing innumerable pegs of single malt samples available for the asking.

We made two other detours before we crossed the border into England—at Glamis ("Glahms") to tour the Castle of *Macbeth* fame ("Thou hast it now, King, Cawdor, Glamis, all"). In Walter Scott's heart of Midlothian, we found Roslyn Chapel that Dan Brown's *Da Vinci Code* had introduced to the world. Alas, although we descended into its depths, we did not find the Holy Grail buried in its crypt!

We'd entered Scotland, ten days previously, in driving rain. We left the country under the same soggy skies having treated ourselves to a holiday that had opened up stunning natural vistas and led to Close Encounters of the Royal Kind. As we crossed the border and drove into England, Hubs turned towards me and said, "Now, me lassie, let's find ourselves a wee dram."

One week in Scotland and he was speaking like Braveheart.

In Northern England's border town of Carlisle, clouds parted to reveal weak sunlight. Hubs and I greeted its anemic rays like an old friend at Hadrian's Wall. Near the small town of Birdoswald, we tried to imagine how the spreading fields might have appeared in 122 AD. Hundreds of laborers had hauled tons of locally-quarried stone to enable Roman conquerors demarcate their southern territory from marauding Highland clansmen. When I clambered up the wall and had Hubs take my picture, I ticked off one more item on my To-Do List for my year of heightened living. Ta-Da!

Roman mission accomplished, we commenced our literary forays into The North and Midlands. Decades of devotion to Britain's diverse literary offerings had made enthusiasts of us both. On earlier travels in the UK with Dot, we had scoured Shakespearean Country and the Cotswolds. Never, however, had we dallied among the aged ghosts of fictional giants in Yorkshire for the county had produced The Brontes, Sylvia Plath and James Herriot and remains a region much frequented by bibliophiles obsessed with Evelyn Waugh. Their masterpieces would map out our route, I resolved, as we hit country roads lined with snaking stone walls.

Along a remote road off the Pennines' moors whose barrenness and howling winds gave me goosebumps, we found *Haworth*, the Brontes' realm, steeped in Victoriana. Magically transported to another era—one of high necked blouses, floor-length dresses, lace trimmed collars and bonnets—I climbed narrow stairs gingerly as if expecting to trip any minute on my taffeta petticoat. Gazing across miles of sterile moorland from an upstairs window, the impact of that emptiness on a set of three sibling imaginations became clear. The minds of Charlotte, Emily and Anne sought escape from relentless monotony through their creation of haunted householders and mad women in the attic. On visiting *Haworth*, the stream-of-consciousness novelist Virginia Woolf had written: "Haworth expresses the Brontes; the Brontes express Haworth. They fit like a snail to its shell."

And then, at the bottom on a low-growing hill, at Heptonstall, we swung back to the modern era again as the haunting poetry of Sylvia Plath rang in our ears. Among the town's serpentine stone walls, we were surrounded by the tragic spirit of the American poet that lingers in the churchyard where she lies buried as her husband Ted Hughes, once England's Poet Laureate, had hailed from these parts. There, in that dramatically remote landscape that had provided the Brontes with the inspiration to pen their bizarrely plotted novels, Plath found her own muse. Being there, gazing at those vast, tanned plains and shuddering against the wind that whipped around us, I could see for myself how the creative spirit would be moved toward productivity.

It was a slow drive eastwards to Newcastle where a bonus was a glimpsing on the motorway of a stupendous sculpture that stretched its arms out as if embracing all earth and heaven too.

"Just turn your head around for one quick glance," I urged Hubs. "You simply mustn't miss this."

It was Antony Gormley's *Angel of the North* that saw us into the North York Moors and James Herriot Country. Of course, Hubs wisely ignored my advice and we arrived safely in Thirsk to look for our next B&B, *Golden Sheaves Farm*, where I'd secured a booking on the internet weeks in advance. But futile driving for miles in Thirsk led us nowhere close to our destination.

Annoyed and fatigued, we discovered that not all B&Bs have honest owners. *Golden Sheaves* had been falsely advertised as located in Thirsk where the real James Herriot had lived for decades. It was, as a matter of fact, situated in Sindersby, a village about twelve miles away as the crow flies but a good half hour by road along winding cornfields.

When we did eventually find the proprietor who'd fibbed about his location on the Net to attract tourists in search of the Herriot lifestyle, there was not a sound of Cuppa Tea to be heard. He was surly, cold even.

"You're not in Thirsk," I began, accusingly, when he cut me short and mumbled about being in the same general area.

I remained disgruntled.

"Let it go," whispered Hubs.

"But I'd prefer to stay in Thirsk," I insisted. "It's what I believed we'd paid for." Sub-consciously, I wanted to live the Herriot life—if only for a fraction of a second.

Getting to know Giles Gower was to alter the favorable impression we'd received of your friendly British inn-keeper. *Golden Sheaves* hadn't been revamped in at least thirty years. It was dark, dinghy, dusty. Our lackluster, barely-furnished room had two threadbare brown towels tossed across its bed. *En suite* showers? Forget about them. A quest for the bathroom found it tucked half a mile away along pitch dark corridors lit by faint night-lamps—even in broad daylight! Lacking an exhaust fan, the bathroom steamed up cloudily.

Not one to dwell too long or hard over unforeseen travel nightmares, my misgivings about our location were quelled when we discovered that our horrid host stabled two beautiful chocolate farm horses and owned a friendly black lab that answered to Sam. They almost made me believe I was back in the 1950s when James Herriot had paid house calls to ailing animals and their gruff peasant owners. For the next two days, we resolved to toss His Surliness from our minds and enjoy isolated drives along one-lane roads punctuated by waving Breughel sheaves of sun-toasted grain. In Thirsk, we asked a group of friendly pensioners for James Herriot's home.

Born James Alfred Wight (Alf for short), the Glaswegian vet who took the pseudonym James Herriot, became an author well past the age of fifty after writing stories based on professional experiences in the Yorkshire dales where he had first arrived to work in the 1930s. My excitement was palpable as we entered Herriot's ivy-draped home, *Skeldale House* at 23 Kirkdale. Outside the lipstick red door, a blue plaque, found all over the British Isles, proclaimed to passers-by that it had once housed a noteworthy vet-author.

In the garage, I slid into the vet's vintage Austin Severn for a photograph. *Skeldale House* is time warped by the 1950s which allowed me to regress into the decade of my birth. For Herriot fans, a visit to his home is a terrific opportunity to slink away into the past to a place of stringent work ethics and a time before tractors or mechanized farming when farm owners, horses and oxen were truly salt of the earth. No wonder it is such a compelling stop on a tour of Yorkshire.

From the humble to the opulent, we pressed on.

"Waugh. Castle Howard is all about Waugh," I declared.

"You mean Wow?" asked a puzzled Hubs. "Or woe?"

"Waugh. As in Evelyn Waugh. Yet another literary goliath."

Castle Howard, near Malton, could not have been further from the modesty of a 1950s vet's home. The extravagant country estate had stolen my heart away, decades previously, when I had watched Jeremy Irons playing Charles Ryder and Anthony Andrews playing Lord Sebastian Flyte stride through its echoing corridors in the Granada TV version of one of my favorite novels of all time, *Brideshead Revisited* by Evelyn Waugh.

"Whoa!" exclaimed Hubs, as we entered the house for a guided tour. "And I don't mean Evelyn! How OTT is this place?"

Truly Over The Top, Castle Howard was designed in the Italian Baroque vein by John Vanbrugh who took a break from his day job during the Restoration—writing satiric plays associated with the genre known as the Comedy of Manners—to conceive a home for the Eighth Earl of Carlisle in 1699. Vanbrugh is credited as the brains behind two of England's most spectacular homes—Castle Howard in Yorkshire and Blenheim Palace in Oxfordshire. But I'd have to wait until almost the end of my solo year before I romped through his rooms at Blenheim.

At Castle Howard, the Wow Factor is seriously off the charts. It's most stunning feature is its entrance hall where marble flooring, profuse sculpture and lavish gilding coalesce to produce jaw-dropping effect. Ceiling paintings by the Italian artist Antonio Pellegrini on the inside of the dome are the foyer's focal point. I risked slipping a few discs in my spinal column each time I tilted my head back towards the soaring ceiling to admire his genius or swiveled my body around to size up the wall-paneling.

As the tour wound towards the top floor, we entered the bedroom that still housed remnants of movie-making paraphernalia from the previous week's shooting. In the center sat an outsized bed draped luxuriantly in coriander-mint chutney green, an important prop in the new film version for Lord Marchmain's religious conversion became complete as he lay within its roomy dimensions surrounded by his children during climatic breath-holding moments. All of a sudden, I broke every rule in the touring book. Focusing my camera on the scene, I slid it into Hubs' hands, and after looking around stealthily for censorious guards who might have curbed my impulsive juvenility, I raced to stand between the bed to hold on to the drapery for a picture. I am not ashamed to say that it takes pride of place in my scrapbook—a matter that vastly increased my street cred when the movie starring Michael Gambon and Emma Thompson was released, and I found out how intrinsic that bed remains to the plot's *denouement*.

On our return homewards, Hubs logged seriously swift mileage on our pedometer while I made pained efforts to navigate through rush hour traffic. By dexterous zigzagging behind double decker buses and black cabbies slippery as eels, we arrived a whisker short of 5:00 pm, at our car rental company in Victoria. High Fives were exchanged as we made our vehicle-return deadline with neither dent nor ding. But only just.

After returning from our literary exploration of The North, Hubs and I spent one last day together awaking as dawn cracked over London to attend 8:00 a.m. service at St. Paul's Cathedral, only a short saunter from my flat. In its Baroque interior, I became vaguely conscious of an Indian woman flanked on each side by a strapping young man. As service concluded, the friendly prelate—tall, regal and sporting a wide pink sash—said, "Hello. I'm Bishop Carrington. Are you visiting London?"

"Well, I am," began Hubs, "but my wife here will be staying for the year."

"Ah. And where are you from?" asked the good priest.

"From the States, but originally from India."

"Would you happen to be from Goa?" he asked. When he saw our startled expressions, he continued, "Well, my wife is a Goan, you see. Where is she?" He looked around searchingly. "She was here a minute ago. Celia was a D'Silva . . . no, wait a minute . . . she was a D'Souza."

"So was my wife!" laughed Hubs.

"Well then . . . you're practically family! You *must* find Celia. She just left with our boys. Hurry. Hurry after her. Go on. Chop-chop."

Weird as it appeared, it was not a suggestion to sneeze at. A chance to make a new friend already! And a Goan one at that! My chance encounter with the Carringtons, in a cathedral of all places, held the promise of warm forthcoming friendships.

Without a second to lose, we hurried out Wren's splendid portals to find the lady and her handsome escorts halfway across Paternoster Square.

"Celia," I called loudly, cupping hands to mouth. "Ceeeeelia."

She turned and smiled in bewilderment. "Hello," I said, panting shyly forward. "Your husband suggested we find you. I've just arrived from the States to live here for a year."

"How lovely! Welcome to London!" As she shook our hands, she introduced her "boys", young lawyers ("barristers") in the making.

Then extending spontaneous Goan hospitality that did not surprise us one bit, she said, "You *must* come home with us for breakfast. Just around the corner."

We smiled, thanked her and declined. We were off to Lords for the cricket, we said.

"Well then, a cup of coffee at least. I insist. I *must* give you my phone number. Call me."

The 'Boys' looked on bemused as we walked companionably to *Amen Court* where the Carringtons lived in a seventeenth century Christopher Wren confection of red brick walls, tall chimney pots and bold brass door knockers. Celia led us to squishy sofas, put the kettle on and jotted down contact numbers. The Bishop joined us as we sipped coffee while I surveyed their grandly imposing home—marble fireplace and mantle, broad sweeping staircase, built-in bookcases—an antique home after my own heart. Being Catholic, it would take me a while to get accustomed to a priest with a complete household that included a wife and children.

As we hurried off to Lord's for a one-day international match, Hubs said, "You just made your first friends in London! And without even trying!"

Who could have guessed it would be that easy? It was the start of many unlikely associations that embraced me through an unforgettable year when the most fledgling of friendships ended up being far from mere passing encounters.

Not long afterwards, Hubs' departed for the States and I sashayed into my new life as a Singleton in swinging London. That's when the fun really began.

4

A SOLITARY SEPTEMBER

Hubs would not be around when I had my first sinister brush with British bobbies. Fast-forward to eight months. It had been the perfect English summer's day in London, in June of 2009, as I stood behind the solid human wall blocking my view of Pall Mall on a red-letter day in the city's social calendar when I heard someone bellow: "If you do not get off this terrace immediately, I will arrest the lot of you. Start climbing down. NOW."

It had promised cavalry on horseback ("squaddies"), fancy-schmancy Cinderella carriages and, if one was really lucky, the swivel of a royal head or two. It seemed a worthy sight to witness and if I, Samuel Pepys-like, intended to provide a comprehensive account of an unusual year, I figured it had to include some legit Union Jack-waving!

And then, it happened. Within half an hour, I had a run-in with the law—read your usual garden-variety English bobby. As I'd searched for a gap in the human wall to squeeze through, steps leading to a terrace had presented themselves almost magically. If I marched to the pedestal that hoisted the carved Duke of York on high, I'd catch a glimpse of the pageantry. Then, quite handily, a terrace appeared upon which two pre-teenaged boys had parked themselves. Losing little time, I flung my backpack over and scaled a ladder to join them, pleased to have found an elevated, if solitary, perch. But then, to my horror, I saw, within seconds, that like the Pied Piper of Hamlyn, I'd attracted a steady spate of fellow-adventurers who also climbed the rusty ladder to swarm the terrace.

In two ticks, my ambitious plan for an uninhibited view of the spectacle shot the dust.

"You are trespassing on private property," the policewoman boomed. "Get off this terrace straight away."

Most of my companions were foreign tourists who understood little English; but there was no mistaking her menacing tone. Although I tried, I could not ignore her as the possibility of being arrested appeared imminent.

Imagining the worse, I visualized *The Mail's* headlines: "Indian-American Professor Arrested at Trooping of the Color." It was the last thing I needed—prosecution in London—when all I'd been hoping for was a better view of Britain's legendary pomp and splendor.

And the embarrassment of it all! Although, truth be told, were I still at home in the USA, the cop would have bellowed, "Yo Dude! Get your frickin' ass down here now!" Thankfully, I was in a country where a modicum of politeness still prevailed.

Needless to add, I wimped out. Before you could say "God Save the Queen," I, the ringleader, who'd led the crowd up the ladder, scrambled down and scrammed. But not before I caught a passing glimpse of the Princess Royal, Anne Herself, on horseback. Seconds later, the equestrian who'd represented her country at the Montreal Olympics in 1976, had ridden on leaving me stunned that I'd courted arrest for a paltry moment's participation in a ceremony that made little sense to me. Frankly, I took the risks I did merely for the cheap thrills of royal-spotting.

The Trooping of the Color has been arranged since the seventeenth century to mark the Monarch's birthday. Having celebrated her diamond jubilee, the Queen has gone through the routine of inspecting the 'colors' of her troops more than sixty times—and on each occasion, she looks so unfailingly enthusiastic you could be forgiven for believing she was doing it for the very first time. After regiments on foot and horseback sport their colors to rousing cheers of fawning crowds, ten-thick, lining the Union Jack-strewn Mall, horse-drawn carriages bearing royalty follow and head to the Horse Guards Parade where lucky ticket-holders are treated to the sounds of fife, drum and accompanying spectacle. Her Anointed Majesty and assorted minions are then whisked off to Buck House, aka Buckingham Palace, for the Royal Air Force fly past.

No, I had not scored a fortunate spot that would have permitted me to wave to the First Family appearing on the balcony, a couple of hours later. Nor did I spy streaks of beribboned color, left behind by half a dozen aircraft to dissolve into the cloudless sky. But I'd had yet another royal sighting and a pretty hairy escapade to boot. And with it, I added another notch to my belt of blighted adventures in Blighty.

For nine months—the entire time it takes for human gestation—I'd been collecting them like stamps: close encounters with blue bloods and all the capers my heart had desired. You would not be blamed for believing, by my juvenile antics, that I was some backpacking undergrad rather than someone who had just celebrated a Golden birthday and was determined to mark the year in the most singular way imaginable. If having my own extraordinary year of adventure and discovery meant taking a few calculated risks, hey, who was I to refrain?

But let me begin at the beginning . . .

Rendered sudden single, after Hubs' return Stateside way back in September, I had resolved to take refuge in the practical. I would trawl through London's supermarkets. I would cook. I would find solace in nourishment. I was sizing up my options at home in Holborn when I heard an unusual sound in the hall outside. It was the unmistakable jingling of keys. In a trice, I raced to open my door to find a tall, blond woman with an enviably thick waist-length braid, laden with shopping bags, fumbling at her keyhole.

"Hi. I'm your new neighbor," I blurted. "I just moved in from the States to teach university students here." She dropped her bags in a rush, turned to me in surprised delight, grinned and extended her hand.

"Brenda Sutton. Welcome!" Her tone assured me she meant it fervently. "It's so nice to have you next door."

Much later, I would learn that among former occupants of my flat had been a mafia boss from Moscow who'd stomped around periodically like the demented Bolshevik he was. A party-crazy Brazilian collegian who grew marijuana in window-sill pots had followed. Why, then, would Brenda not be relieved to find a university professor next door?

Pleased to have met my new neighbor and liking what I had seen, I reached for a writing pad to make a grocery shopping list. I'd have loved to have sampled such improbable items as only the British will eat— such as kippers and ox-tongue or lemon curd and Marmite. But pragmatism surfaced. Discovering a giant *Sainsbury* supermarket, a block away from my building, I had difficulty stopping myself from running like Archimedes all the way down High Holborn screaming "Eureka."

The capital was bursting with ethnic eateries to suit every pocket and much as I'd have loved to embrace the Food Revolution that had presumably swept across Britain, I was averse to eating alone in public. While I had no qualms about traversing the world as a Singleton, I drew the line when it came to entering a restaurant, taking a seat and going through the motions of ordering and enjoying a professionally-cooked meal without becoming sick with embarrassment. I had simply no choice but to put pot and pan to work and rustle up my own sustenance.

And then just as I walked into my bathroom for a shower, I heard a slight unfamiliar sound in the hallway outside. I jumped and my wild heart began to thump. Was someone lurking outside? I was surrounded by neighbors in a building with no less than twenty units on each floor—yet I did not really know any of them. I cocked my fearful ears and listened for reassuring sounds of occupancy in any of the flats around me, but not a sound reached me. As I held my breath and waited motionless for a few minutes, images of blood-draped corpses rushed through my mind. Clearly I had watched more than my fair share of British crime drama and simply too many detective TV series. I listened closely willing the imagined intruder to leave. Nothing. No one. I exhaled in relief. Because I had resolved never to open my door after 9:00 pm, I was loath to investigate. Better secure than sorry. As I prepared for my first night alone, I struggled hard to quell my inherited anxiety. And then, inevitably, night fell. I moved to my front door, bolted it, turned up the safety lock and clasped on the security chain. Despite being trebly protected, I was deeply uneasy.

So I almost succumbed to cardiac arrest when my doorbell shrilled quite close to 10.00 pm. Who on earth could it be? My flat was equipped with a peephole and I could peer out into the hallway, of course. But my long-time timidity and imagined fear of prowlers led me to pretend I wasn't inside as I crept into bed and, as if I were four years old, pulled my comforter closely around me. As I tussled with the thought of what I would do if my night visitor rang the bell a second time, I hear the door adjoining my flat close gently. It had to have been Brenda, I convinced myself, as I stilled my beating heart and switched off the light.

Hubs' departure made far bigger a dent in my sanity that I'd hoped it would. Through long years of marriage, we had been rarely separated as he never traveled professionally. His position in international banking had kept him firmly rooted in the world's financial capital—New York. My time in the UK, apart from Hubs, was virtually a first after decades for me—and therein lay the challenge. It seemed I could barely get through one night. How would I manage to pull off a whole year successfully? If I were going to put myself through the kind of petrified response I had each time I heard a movement in the corridor outside my flat after dark, I was in for a most nerve-wracking time—and I certainly did not welcome the prospect. I fell asleep that first night in my flat feeling profoundly troubled and when I awoke at 5.00 am, in time to hear the jangling of the metal accordion gate as Chancery Lane Tube station right below my window opened to traffic, I continued to wrestle with my demons.

At about 9:00 am, after comforting daylight had flooded my flat—on yet another grey and dreary morning—my doorbell rang. This time, I peered through the peephole to see a bald head shining like a beacon as a man outside inspected his feet while waiting. When my door swung open, I discovered that the gleaming pate belonged to a tall, lean, white man who said, in a clipped private school accent, "Hello. We wondered if you'd be free to come over for lunch on Sunday."

We? Who was we? Out of the blue, an Englishman with a posh accent was at my door proffering an invitation for lunch. From which bottle of Cutty Sark Single Malt had this genie been conjured?

I gaped. When I eventually found my voice—by which time he probably wondered if he should try another language—I said, "Sorry, but who are you? Do you live in this building?"

"Erm . . . yes, of course. I'm next door's Tom Bennet. I'm the husband."

Ah-ha! Both elusive neighbors had eventually shown. And bearing an invitation as well! Now how blessed was that?

Weekend travel plans with my students throughout September precluded me from accepting Tom's gracious overture. But I didn't want to close the door on a possible friendship. God knows how reserved the English were known to be.

I said, "How sweet of you! But I will be away on Sunday, I'm afraid. Could I take a rain check perhaps?"

"Right." He swiveled around to enter his flat. "Another time then. Cheers."

And with that, the man I would always think of as 'Next Door Tom' vanished. His unexpected visit and his generous invitation gave the lie to everything I'd ever heard about English reserve. And gradually, it was in Next Door Tom's flat that I relished some of the most memorable of the British meals I ate (say "et") all year. For, since all my stars were in happy alignment, in a past life, Tom, an IT consultant, just happened to have been a professional chef in the West End and it was during companionable evenings in their welcoming home with him and Brenda, a patent attorney, that I mustered the courage to put behind me the awful memory of Kristen's offal and dig with delight into that 1950's staple of the British Table—Liver and Bacon with Onions.

Two days later, my professional life in London began during Orientation Week. I sought out my modest basement office that offered partial views of wrought iron railings, lumbering red buses and stockinged feet. And I met my new English colleagues. If reading too much Enid Blyton in my childhood and P.G. Wodehouse in my youth had led me to expect to twist my tongue around names like Peregrine Polyps or Algernon Aching Toes, I was much mistaken. They had perfectly normal Western names like Dennis and Michael, Nancy and Martha. But I soon found out that men with perfectly respectable names were nicknamed in the most evil fashion imaginable.

"I'm Potty," said one of the doormen ("porters"), as he inspected my identity card.

"Excuse me?"

"I'm known as Potty. Because my name is Allan Potts, y'see."

A postman who was clearly a loser in the heights sweepstakes named Cornelius Shrimpton cheerfully answered to Shrimpy and a rotund maintenance man in my building named Colin Hodge was simply called Hog. As for British women, their nicknames had absolutely nothing to do with the names with which they had been christened. Over the course of a year, I met a Bunny, a Bunty, a Brandy and quite simply a Dee.

In my classrooms, multiculturalism reigned supreme. While the majority of my freshman Humanities' students were Caucasian Americans, a few were international from varied curves of the globe—Korea, China, Turkey, Greece, France, India, Pakistan and Canada.

In our corner classroom in the University of London's Birkbeck College with its wide wraparound windows, my students penned their first impressions of London. Unfamiliar vocabulary foxed them ('quid' for pounds, 'cheers' for thanks, 'Tube' for the subway, 'spuds' for mashed potatoes). All that rain! they grumbled ("whinged"). Milk that turned in minutes—even in the fridge! Don't they use preservatives here, they questioned. And Jeeeze! The cost of living! Those prices!

Meanwhile, my afternoon Sophomore Seminar class on the UK's Anglo-Indians met in a room at Bedford Square with high ceilings, brass chandeliers, deep dentil moldings and a fireplace! Audio-visual equipment clashed incongruously with the room's Georgian elegance. Outside, a magnificent staircase punctuated with Robert Adam plaster-work curled downwards. How cool was that? Such a far cry from the plain dry-walled concrete cubes we called classrooms in New York City.

Mind you, Bedford Square Gardens didn't remain merely a view. On an unexpectedly fine morning, after dreary days of intermittent showers, I made another one of my fondest More Perfect Life fantasies a reality—I taught a class in a sun-drenched garden overlooked by ter-raced housing one of which had once been occupied by India's reform-ist Raja Ram Mohan Roy.

Then, a week into my new academic life in London, administrative staff invited me out to dinner. Ooooh! My spirits soared. A chance to eat a professionally-presented meal in the company of other human beings, in a nice restaurant, with linen napkins and a tablecloth! Oddly enough, my ventures into the fascinating business of discovering English food were intrinsically associated with making new friends. And perfectly palatable too were my medallions of veal served with potato gratin and roasted asparagus that, wonder of wonders, remained recog-nizable. But it was when my colleagues suggested I opt for a favorite English summer dessert ("pudding") on the menu, that I made the acquaintance of Eton Mess. Now here was something about which English chefs could justifiably boast—a lusciously-layered concoction of fresh and stewed strawberries, cracked-up meringue and fat clouds of whipped cream served in deep parfait glasses. It carries the distinction of being the only English 'pudding' that isn't served swimming in its own pool of super-sweet custard!

"Why Eton? And why Mess?" I ventured to ask my new colleagues as I relished my pudding.

"Eton because it was reputedly first created there and Mess because when the carefully crafted layers blend, the effect is rather a mess, you see."

"There" meant the super snobby boy's boarding school near Windsor-on-the-Thames that has produced most of Britain's Prime Ministers.

"A very special public school," I was told.

"Ah, a public school. I'd have thought a place so exclusive would be private." I said.

"Well, it is, really. It is a private school."

"I thought I just heard you say it is a public school."

"Yes, but public schools *are* private schools."

It would take me a while to wrap my mind around the Mess. Wasn't it George Bernard Shaw, another Bloomsbury luminary, who had said that England and America are two countries separated by a common language?

Back in my building, I met the concierge of *Bishop House*, Aren, who said, "Welcome Please. Let me know if I can help you, yes?" His accent sounded Eastern European. "I'm from Armenia," he said. "Been in London twenty years."

Aren was truly God-sent. *Bishop House's* built-in Handy Man surveyed my flat, set my heater on a timer and nailed a full-length mirror to my bedroom door. Most significantly, he introduced me to my flat's built-in security system which, I hoped, would sooth my anxieties. Through the use of a sophisticated electronic device, I could press a button to reach him in the lobby where he was available all day. When the buzzer in my flat sounded, I could press another button that allowed me to receive images of callers standing outside the building's main door on the street below. If I did not recognize visitors or did not wish to let them into the building, I simply did nothing further. But, despite owning high-tech safety gizmos, I remained cautious and concerned about my seclusion. Oftentimes, I experienced more than a twinge of unease.

I turned lights out at night with a prayer on my lips. When scary thoughts assaulted my mind, I rebuked myself. You no longer live in a three-level house in the remoteness of Connecticut woods. You are now in the thick of London. Fifty flats surround you. You own an electronic security system. You can reach Aren at the press of a button. There's another flat, a step away, adjoining your door, occupied by perfectly nice neighbors. Someone *would* hear you if you were to scream! There's an office building across shinning a million kilowatts inside your flat. Enough already! Begone Phobia!

The dressing-down I gave myself helped hugely. Although I still felt ill at ease during those early nights, daylight unfailingly brought renewed confidence. I awoke each day with a strange lightness of being. I felt unbound, completely free, to pursue the kind of life of which most married women in their fifties can only dream: the luxury of time and a dramatic city in which to spend it.

Before long, my flat's unadorned walls and functional furniture began to feel unusually serene and, pack rat that I was, the idea of Minimalism appeared oddly de-stressing. In the closet, my carefully-weeded clothing felt strangely liberating. Who needs stuff? With three pairs of trousers, three cardigans, three blazers, three T-shirts, and three pairs of shoes, I became crowned Queen of the Capsule Wardrobe, Mistress of Mix 'N Match because I owned an abundance of scarves. My unhindered mind turned towards work as I registered at local libraries, prepared lectures, and made lists of Anglo-Indian contacts to initiate field inquiries.

I was grappling with the newness of another academic year and my solitary September when the US credit crunch left the globe reeling. All hell broke loose when Lehman Brothers collapsed in America and the UK was gripped by the Bradford and Bingley debacle. I blew a giant bubble around myself to remain isolated from the planet's depressing meltdown. My world, in its novelty, still felt like an unending adventure I was determined to keep effervescent.

Confronted by leaden skies and slick streets for endless days in a row, it seemed pointless to mope about the weather. This was, after all, London and Londoners, worth their salt, got on with it, notwithstanding the gloom. The stack of laminated library membership cards in my wallet grew bulkier and my ego swelled as I enrolled at the Senate House Library of the University of London, the library of the School of Oriental and African Studies and the grand-daddy of them all, the British. It might have poured buckets all of September, but my spirits were not dampened as I checked out two birthday presents, both Frommer publications, from Dot: *24 Great Walks in London* and *Best Day Trips from London: 25 Great Escapes by Train, Bus or Car.* I resolved to

return home, a year later, having ticked them all off their Tables of
Content pages. Six items became permanent fixtures in my backpack:
camera, Tube map, Central London bus map, Oyster Card (for travel
on local public transport), credit card and cell phone (which I soon
grew accustomed to calling a "mobile"). And as my conquest of the
capital commenced on foot, I lost track of the number of miles I
trekked per day. General enthusiasm to comb every last nook and niche
of the city made me oblivious to distance—or to the toll all that pave-
ment-pounding would take.

Aren confirmed that our building did not house a gym for the use of
its residents. It would have been convenient, no doubt, to work out on
the premises—especially since I had taken to ardent eating. But, considering that I was located in the heart of 'The City'—a mile-wide
radius that comprised the financial nucleus of London—and surrounded by some of the capital's tourist highlights, I would walk my way
to Twiggy proportions. Having lived in coastal Connecticut's countryside for years, I'd grown accustomed to over a one-hour schlep into
Manhattan. It boggled my mind that all these museums, theaters,
churches and art galleries, could be reached on foot in less than fifteen
minutes.

On weekends, I accompanied my students on day trips to Mustn't
Miss Tourist Sites; but by the enthusiasm they managed to muster to
participate in them you'd think I was dragging them off to the Gulag. I
footed it out and courted adventure on the soft clay of the river bed
along the Greenwich Foot Passage, delighted at having discovered a
nineteenth-century engineering marvel—a tunnel under the Thames'
bedrock that connects its two banks. Estimated mileage logged that day:
five.

On other weekends, we piled into a bus ("coach") towards the stones
of Stonehenge where my American students, city-raised, became far
more fascinated by grazing sheep than the mammoth sarsen and blue-
stone rocks associated with ritualistic druids. In traversing the ancient
structure among which Thomas Hardy's star-crossed protagonists had
awakened in *Tess of the D'Urbervilles*, I logged more mileage: Another
Five. But, it was when we arrived at the Georgian city of Bath that its
compellingly golden streets, constructed in honey-colored Cotswold
stone, really did me in. On the coach back to London, I calculated
another fifteen miles on my personal pedometer. My calves felt like

stone columns, but I wasn't about to let them stop me exploring. During September's last weekend, I sauntered off to St. Albans to spend the day amidst a Gothic cathedral and among higgledy-piggledy houses from a previous century. Back home, I soaked my throbbing feet in Epsom Salts after logging in another ten miles. Such determined walking tours, alone and in company, finally wore me out.

As the month dissolved, I became acutely conscious of two things: One, I was being lulled to sleep much more easily at night. Falling darkness no longer filled me with dread; sleep, although sporadic, was satisfying. Two, I was frightfully foot sore. From my upper thighs to my calves from the arches to the balls of my feet, I could feel the strain of all that unaccustomed trekking. I had found my rhythm in a city that was both new and familiar. Although I had not even set up or begun conducting field-research with Anglo-Indian 'subjects', I felt entitled to a spot of recreation. Refusing to be cowed down by a bit of discomfort, my mind turned towards the Continent. Budget airlines such as Ryanair and Easyjet with hubs at Stanstead airport put out regular online news bulletins announcing "offers". This was exactly what I had hoped my More Perfect Year would be—fulfilling work assignments punctuated by bouts of solo travel.

It was time to acquire a few inexpensive air tickets and check out Hosteling International's website for Youth Hostel reservations. And it was in Catalonia, a part of Spain I'd never explored, that I would launch my year-long European travels and begin rubbing shoulders with the idiosyncratic. Little did I know as I lost my heart to Gaudi, that I would be rubbing shoulders with hip-gyrating cross-dressers in a youth hostel or facing the disastrous development of debilitating health issues.

5

AFFLICTED

Barcelona did me in! You know what they say, right? When it comes to misfortune, it never rains, it pours. Well . . . somewhere in mid-November, misfortune brought a damned deluge.

London was still snoring when I awoke at 5:00 a.m. the day after my return from España, to catch up on work-related email. Swinging out of bed, I stumbled almost to my knees for I saw proverbial stars when my feet hit the floor. The pain in my soles was crippling. Searing in its intensity, like flames of fire, it licked my soles, shot past my heels and crept into my calves. The arches in both my feet had turned heavy—like solid concrete arcs. I had never experienced such a weird affliction.

Several minutes later, when I took a few frightened steps forward, the pain eased slightly, but not enough to allow me to walk normally or even stand upright. I hobbled like a three-legged gnome to the bathroom. There was no denying the fact that I needed to seek medical attention immediately. But where? Or how? A newcomer to the UK from the USA, I neither knew physicians nor even the location of the nearest doctor's office. To add insult to injury, I had my very first interview lined up later that morning. Pinning down human 'subjects' for my field research on Anglo-Indians to actually grant me dates had been slightly less challenging than sending Armstrong to the moon. There was no way I was pulling out of my commitment. Bewildered, I assessed my options.

Despite the burning pain that wracked my feet, I was determined to keep calm and carry on—as every Brit has been instructed to do in the face of crippling warfare. I was going to set mind over matter. It was just foot soreness. A natural outcome of my frantic Scottish wanderings with Hubs and all that rambling on Las Ramblas in Barcelona—not to mention at least three of the 25 Great Walks in London that I had ticked off my to-do list. Nothing a good application of Ben-Gay wouldn't handle. If I denied the pain's existence, it would simply go away.

I wish!

Still blanching in physical agony, I staggered on to a bus and into *Boots* pharmacy on Oxford Street. I needed painkillers and I needed them fast. Scouring the shelves, I found nothing familiar. No Ben-Gay or Iodex. No Icy Hot or Moov—none of the tubes or jars of ointment had recognizable or even pronounceable names. A painful consultation with a pharmacist followed. He scribbled something unintelligible, told me to buy an ankle brace and go directly to my GP. It seemed too much of an effort to explain that I did not have one. Clutching at a tube of Nurofen (Ibuprofen in disguise), I stumbled straight into the offices of NYU at Bloomsbury to consult with an administrative assistant who had functioned as Chief Consultant On All Matters Foreign. Where could I find immediate relief? Who'd write me a prescription for morphine? Over-the-counter pain-killers would hardly do the trick.

"You need the A and E." said my Gal Friday at NYU-London when I sought her help.

"The what?"

"A and E. For Accidents and Emergencies. You'll find them at Euston hospital. You need immediate relief."

"Hospital?" I repeated, alarmed. She was obviously over-reacting. Merely a family doctor would do, wouldn't it?

But in the end, I took directions on where to find the nearest A and E and limped towards it, pain making every movement unbearable. And I lost no time cancelling my interview appointment.

"Planta . . . what?"

"Plantar Fasciitis," Zorba the Greek pronounced.

Actually his name was Dr. Pericles Gavalas and we were not in Athens but at the ER or what Brits call the "A&E" in a fluorescent green skyscraper visible for miles—the University of London Hospital at Euston.

"But . . . "

"And there is nothing we can do for you here. Go and see your GP."

"But . . . " I was crestfallen. "I don't have one."

"You don't have a GP?" He stared. "Where are you from?" I interpreted the subtext contained in his tone. What he'd meant was from which planet?

"From America. I'm working in the UK for a year."

"Ah, well, then you'll just have to get one."

Just get one. I'd just get out there, say "Abracadabra" and conjure up a GP.

I stumbled out of his clinic ("surgery"), miserable. How did I even get this Thing? This Plantar Thing. Was he sure? Could he be positive? He hadn't even touched a foot. Didn't even take a look at my throbbing instep.

He'd only asked one question: "So what's the trouble?"

My measured response had been just as brief. "It's my feet. The arches. Excruciating pain. I feel as if they've collapsed."

A firm diagnosis had been delivered after I'd pronounced thirteen words. No MRIs, no CT scans, not even an X-ray! How impressive was that? Good, old-fashioned medicine is still practiced in the UK—the kind the USA had abandoned.

I limped home in the darkness, ankle in a flannel brace, flyer ("brochure") on National Health Service Registration in my hands, my mind racing. London had done me in. Poor ignorant me. All the time I thought I was merely foot sore, I'd been battling a serious orthopedic condition. Once home, Googling provided all the answers. Incessant walking had worn out not just some serious leather, but my very soles. Arches under my feet had shrunk pathetically causing tendon inflammation. Although, strictly speaking, excessive walking does not cause PF, walking in unsuitable shoes does—only those with high supportive arches can prevent its onset. If only I'd known! For the first time since I'd arrived in London, I went to bed in tears as I conveyed Zorba's diagnosis to Hubs on the phone. What's that they say about Man Proposing, God Disposing? I had proposed to do so much on my feet during my Perfect Year of Action and Adventure. But my Boss Above had disposed of each proposal in the most efficient manner possible.

The next morning, I was online filling registration forms to identify a local Internist or what Brits call a "GP" for General Practitioner. Next-

Door Tom recommended the Holborn Medical Center where a nice chap called Steven yakked on about "procedures" and "proper channels" when I called for an appointment. I needed to register at their surgery before a GP would see me. To register, I'd need proof of UK residence. Armed with Camden Council tax papers and my Virgin Media TV license and bill, I shuffled to Lamb's Conduit Street to prove my residency in Holborn and to fill forms. Many forms. Mostly in triplicate. In those few minutes, the origin of India's obsession with bureaucratic red tape dawned on me. We'd acquired our penchant for form-filling from the Brits.

Half an hour later, I was called in to see the very dishy Dr. Nigel Bentley, G.P. a Hugh Grant Wannabe. When did physicians get so much younger than I? Or so cute? If I hadn't been in such a state, I might have batted my eyelashes at him.

He confirmed Zorba's diagnosis. It *was* Plantar Fasciitis. A second opinion, instantaneously delivered without even examining my feet. Brilliant, as his fellowmen would say. This NHS thing couldn't be half bad. Now if only he would suggest a line of treatment, I could be up and running (OK, only metaphorically) in a few days.

That's when the prophecies of doom began. A few days? Perish the thought, smirked Bentley. I would need complete foot rest.

"How complete?"

"No more walking. Not even standing!"

"For how long?"

"Two whole weeks at the very least."

What the . . . .??? I stared at him, crushed as he issued instructions. I could only leave my horizontal position to use the toilet ("loo").

He was kidding me, right? I had classes to teach. I had interviews to carry out. I had official documents to peruse in the library. I hadn't travelled a thousand miles from home to request a leave of absence. Plus, I had personal goals. To complete all of Frommer's *24 Great Walks*. I had booked tickets to travel to Greece when Hubs arrived at month's end for our Thanksgiving break. Month's end? What was I talking about? My Ryanair ticket to Berlin at the weekend was burning a hole in my handbag! I even had a confirmed bunk at the Youth Hostel near Potsdammer Strasse! Clearly, Barcelona hadn't completely turned me off youth hosteling.

The doctor intruded, "Is that clear?"

"Er . . . Y-y-es."

"Really clear?"

"Crystal."

"Next," he snarled, "exercises. Here are a few easy ones to do until your number comes up on the waiting list for physiotherapy."

Waiting List? Why couldn't I see a physiotherapist . . . like Now?

"Ah. It's obvious you're from America. No instant gratification here, I'm afraid. Under the National Health Service, plantar fasciitis doesn't count as an Emergency, you see."

I didn't see. It was unfathomable that I'd have to wait until a specialist became free and it could take months. Now if I had a torn aorta . . . it'd be a different story. Meanwhile, I could wallow in pain all I liked.

"Could I see a specialist faster?"

"You can choose to go the private route."

"Private route?"

"Well, you can pay to see a specialist, but they are costly. The NHS offers free treatment which is why you need to wait till your turn comes up."

"But I'm fully covered by global insurance. From America."

It was his turn to look askance. "Global Insurance? From America? Why didn't you say? Then you don't need the NHS at all! You can see a physiotherapist immediately. You can go to any specialist you like. You'll need to pay upfront, I think, but your insurance company will reimburse you."

One compelling question simply had to be asked although I dreaded the doctor's response. "What is your prognosis? When can I expect to resume my normal life again?"

When his answer reached my ears in a seemingly muffled buzz, my sense of dejection escalated. "There is really no cure for Plantar Fasciitis. We can treat it, but only time—a long time—will heal it, really. Any affliction of the ligaments or tendons of the feet takes ages to heal."

I was close to tears. Mercilessly, he continued. "Attacks also vary in intensity. Your condition appears particularly virulent. And you have it, rather unusually, in both feet. This is not going to be something you will get over in a hurry. Get used to completely changing your lifestyle and your routine."

So there I had it. Homebound and bedridden. No cure available. Long-term treatment based entirely on exercises and foot rest. A dismal prognosis overall. All at once, my proposed Perfect Year had just become Nearly Perfect. I had never felt more alone. Or more afraid. Or more grateful for American medical coverage.

Finding the right private physiotherapist was the most urgent priority.

"Could you recommend a good specialist, please? I'm a foreigner here, you see . . . " Had I just said "you see"? I was a little stressed, so you could forgive me for talking British.

He could. He also recommended I join the queue for consultation with a physiotherapist allocated by the NHS. Then, as and when my number came up, I could dispense with my private consultant and use state-funded facilities. Sound advice, to be sure, but in my disturbed frame of mind, I could see no silver lining to the accumulating dark clouds.

I turned towards home clutching a letter addressed to Central Health Physiotherapy on Chancery Lane, right opposite the building in which I lived. He'd suggested I go there immediately. But first, I filled out a prescription for pain medication in the pharmacy next door and remained a pill-popper for two weeks running.

Meet Morgan Wintner. Pretty, spritely, Kiwi. My New Zealander Physiotherapist Number One gave me a brisk blissful calf massage and demonstrated a series of plantar-stretching exercises. In a couple of weeks, she decreed, I would feel much better.

"Could I get to work the day after tomorrow?" Since all my classes were scheduled on a single day in the week, it stretched on until dark; but missing that day would mean missing several contact hours with my students.

"If you take a cab to and fro . . . maybe," she said. "It is imperative that you restrict walking or even standing to the absolute minimum."

Coping strategies were urgently called for. I would not miss a class if I could help it, but I would postpone or reschedule interviews and research sessions at the British Library. As for my proposed travel plans, it seemed foolish to even inquire about them when medical opinion was so firmly opposed to any unnecessary movement. I banished thoughts about Berlin at the weekend and inquired hesitantly about getting to Greece at the end of the month when Hubs would arrive to join me.

That sounded like a plan, she smiled. If I rested in bed for two whole weeks and did all my exercises, I just might sail upon the Aegean in four weeks' time.

And what about continuing with my *24 Great Walks* book?

"Take the Tube," she said dryly. I didn't realize it then, but my walking days had just come to an inglorious end. I was deeply saddened at the prospect.

Just try to stay off your feet as much as possible was Morgan's parting shot as she filled out an appointment slip to see me again in a few days for more massages and more exercise routines.

By the end of our hour-long session, my wallet was lighter by 75 quid. A steal, really, all things considered. In America, I'd have had to see an internist, an orthopedist, a radiologist and a physiotherapist before even receiving a diagnosis and would have become poorer by several hundred dollars.

Profoundly distressed, I did battle with my fraught emotions all the way home. Being bedridden meant losing precious time—time I had intended to spend working—teaching, conducting field surveys, reading official correspondence in the library. My year-long work visa meant that I could not extend my stay in the UK even if I wanted to continue my scholarship beyond that limit.

I was furious with myself for being so foolish in having overdone my walking routine so mindlessly. I was sorry for myself for having no one in London to fuss over me. If I could scream with frustration right there on the traffic island at High Holborn without being taken for a lunatic and marched to the nearest asylum, I would gladly have succumbed to the temptation. Instead, it was more prudent to unleash my inner Zen Master. Breathe. Breathe deeply. It was time to snap out of denial and get real. I took stock of my condition and cancelled my Berlin bookings. No *knodel* near the Brandenburg Gate just yet, but if I wasn't too naughty, I could possibly partake of *moussaka* in the shadow of the Parthenon.

I was ready to drown in a Bucketta Tea.

Between seeing my Gal Friday at NYU, Pericles Gavalas, Nigel Bentley and Morgan Wintner, I'd been away from home almost all day, tottering all over London on my inflamed arches like a mutilated ex-serviceman. I'd reached home, climbed into a sweat suit and into bed making sure my phone and laptop were at arm's length. My bedside table developed into a landing strip for all sorts of minutia—pen, notepad, bottle of water, medication, ointment. It was a good time to start work on yet another item on my London To-Do List—Read All Seven Harry Potter Books.

Did I mention that I was in unspeakable agony? I can, therefore, be forgiven, I hope, for missing Dot's calls. I had turned off my cell phone as I'd prepared for my doctor's appointments and, with all the bad news hurled at me all day, it had completely slipped my mind to turn it on again. It seems she'd tried calling countless times. No, she didn't leave a message because she had something really important to share with me, person-to-person.

Swollen with self-pity, I fell asleep, only to awake at twilight to the jangling of my landline. I made a painful lunge towards it. In the throes of my melancholia, Dot's announcement that she had become engaged brought welcome diversion. Her boyfriend, Colin, had proposed. At that moment, caught in a blur induced by morphine-strength medication, all I could wonder was, when would the wedding be? I really did want to be a part of it all. Dot was my only child and this was the only wedding I'd go through from start to finish.

There was another little surprise tucked somewhere into my phone conversation with Dot. Colin would be joining us on a proposed family trip to Bombay in December to meet the parents—not Dot's, of course. Us he'd already met—and knew well. Mine. In India.

Oh, happy day!

Oh horrid night! I had a hard time falling asleep. PF had provided the mental distraction I needed to take the edge of my worries about being alone in my flat after nightfall. So when I thrashed restlessly throughout the night, it was not from anxiety about my solitude but because Dot's news gave me pause. How was it possible that the time had come for my daughter to exchange rings at an altar? Only yesterday, she had been the quietest little baby with the largest eyes in the world staring trustingly up at me. Dot woke up at least nine times every night for a whole year! But she was walking on her own two feet at ten months and talking, nineteen to the dozen, long before her second birthday. Memories flooded my mind as I lay awake and looked back on her life and mine. And now she was engaged to be married. I was joyous.

After two days spent rooted to my bedroom, I took a cab to Bloomsbury to teach my classes. Good job I'd retained the business card Mahen, the Sri Lankan cab driver, had given us at Heathrow upon our arrival. Duty dictated "Jump" and I said, "How High?" The show must go on and all that. I felt obligated to carry out the most compelling of my responsibilities—teaching.

Thankfully, my flat was located only a twelve- minute walking distance from my campus at Bloomsbury. Had it been further away, I'd have spent a small fortune on taxis. By this point, most of my office staff had become aware of my affliction and remedies were bandied about with aplomb. Everyone knew someone who knew someone who had PF—which made me wonder if I was the only person on the planet who had never heard of the affliction, much less how to spell it! "Keep your feet raised—at least a foot higher than your body—when you are stationary." "Hot fermentation of your calves twice a day will help." "Wear orthotics." I'd never even heard of them. They turned out to be rubber inserts stuck into footwear to create elevated arches and were available at any pharmacy. "No, not rubber inserts. Make sure they are gel ones." "Stretch, stretch, stretch . . . whenever you are on your feet, stretch." "Roll a bottle or a can with your feet for five minutes at a stretch. Make sure its icy cold—straight from the freezer!" And so on and so forth, *ad infinitum*, till I thought my head would explode.

From the ridiculous to the sensible. The most practical advice came from my Dean who happened to be visiting London from New York for a series of meetings. "Allow me to let you into a little secret," he whispered. "Buy a monthly Bus Pass. It is simply the cheapest and easiest way to move around the city." Not only was he right but his advice was most helpful. As the months went by, red double deckers became my London lifeline. PF made me a pro at using Journey Planner—Transport for London's beautiful website that custom-designed routes from point to point. I soon acquired expertise in reading bus maps that enabled me to chart out my routes and make transfers or connections with the confidence of a trickster. No more endless walking through Tube tunnels every time I needed to make a connection.

I spent two wretched weeks in bed on the brink of depression. Granted, I wasn't diagnosed with cancer, diabetes or heart disease. But an orthopedic condition with an uncertain prognosis that required two whole weeks of bed rest sounded pretty dire to me. I missed Hubs and Dot— even my parents in Bombay—like crazy. Stark white walls in my bed-room tightened around me like a vice as I tried to Think Positive. This was a good time to design my spring course syllabi—which I did. I could create a few travel pages for my website—which I did. I could get acquainted with British TV—which I did. I could make a scrapbook of photographs and memorabilia from my driving tour of Scotland with Hubs—which I did. My bedside table became crowded as a pair of scissors, glue, photographs and postcards jostled for space on it.

Filled with concern, Hubs called me daily when he awoke in Con-necticut at the same time that I was eating lunch in Holborn. Because they insisted on a daily update, I called my parents when I awoke at the same time that they were eating lunch in Bombay. Traveling telephoni-cally through time zones was not half an exciting as it might sound when all one discussed was doctors, remedies, debilitating pain and depress-ing solitude.

When the novelty of this laid-back (pun unintended) activity dimin-ished, I shamelessly solicited solace from my newly-minted English neighbors. NextDoor Tom waltzed in, saying, "So, ready to go danc-ing?" and then issued invitations to home-cooked dinners. Brenda, for her part, brought me her Harry Potter paperbacks. For the next few months, I dreamed of Postmen who looked like Owls, Hats that Whis-pered Secrets in my Ear, Luggage Carts that Disappeared into Solid Walls and I familiarized myself with a whole new vocabulary that in-cluded Monkshood, Mandragora, Muggles and Mudbloods.

Next I called every London acquaintance, friend and probable foe, upon whose number I could lay my hands. Like magic, pals came flood-ing in. By calling them, I had killed multiple birds with a single stone for they offered advice, remedies and company. To my enormous de-light, not only did they drop everything to visit me, but they swanned in bearing gifts.

"Here. This is what my favorite patient needs," said Megan, a class-mate from Bombay's Elphinstone College who'd served as lawyer to the British Government for decades. Rummaging through the enormous bag she thrust at me, I found flowers, a potted plant, a packet of a flat scone-like pastry called Eccles Cake, a carton of Long-Life milk ("Since you cannot leave your flat for a good bit"), and most thoughtful gift of all, the TV guide ("So you can cheer yourself up with some of our famous British humor.")

"Now just you let me know what else I can do for you. Don't let me hear you've been flouting doctor's orders," she said sternly, wagging her finger at me.

Another classmate from my high school days in Bombay, Binita, brought more food. As luck would have it, she worked for *Waitrose* which soon became my favorite supermarket chain. As if it were not enough that she'd schlepped typically English goodies all the way from Harrow where she lived, she marched right into my kitchen and yelled questions at me as I lay chained to my bed.

"Where can I find a knife? Do you like the crusts cut off your bread? Do you have any Cling Film ("Saran Wrap")?"

"What the heck are you doing in there?" I yelled back.

"Making sandwiches for you. For the next few days. So you won't starve during your convalescence."

Bless her! Forever after, I would associate Fig and Walnut Bread, cold pressed Ox Tongue and Stilton Cheese with Ginger with my convalescence in my Holborn bedroom.

It wasn't just my OBs (Old Buddies) who arrived to cheer me up, offer company and creative ideas for passing time, but BOBs (Buddies Of Buddies) who materialized from out of nowhere to aid my inactivity. Take Raynah, for instance, whom I'd met a couple of years previously on an earlier trip to London. She was the live-in partner of a former colleague of an old friend of Hubs'! As English as fine porcelain, she bundled me into a cab without so much as a by-your-leave.

"But the doctor and my physiotherapist said that if I get out of bed . . . "

"And I say I'm taking you for a decent dinner that's on me. No ifs or buts about it. Come along now. I don't have all night."

Tumbling into the first pair of pants I could find and squishing myself into a coat, I followed her docilely as she ordered a cabbie to take us to *Italian Kitchen* at Bloomsbury.

"Garlic bread for starters, Lasagna for a main, gelato for pudding," she pronounced. "Exactly what your doctor ordered. Now eat up. And I'm getting you a takeaway order too. Think you'll be able to reach a microwave at home?"

"Raynah . . . I have painful feet, but I'm not a cripple, you know. Not by a long shot."

NextDoor Tom and Brenda stopped by at least twice a day to find out if they could pick up groceries for me or share their daily newspaper. It was the beginning of my introduction to Tom's prowess as a *raconteur* for he left me most evenings doubled up as he waxed eloquent about growing up in a boarding school, narrated anecdotes relating to his time as a chef in a fancy West End kitchen, told jokes as he lapsed into effortless impersonations and imitations complete with sound effects and wild gesticulation.

As I nattered for chilly nights on end with my neighbors, OBs and BOBs—all of whom were either English or Indians who had become Anglicized from several years in the UK—I made another startling discovery. In less than two months, my vocabulary had undergone a sea change. I was speaking as I'd once done in India pronouncing words like 'class' and 'pass' with a heavy 'Ah' sound instead of the American 'Ae'. I no longer "took care of" something, I now "looked after it." I didn't "make do" in a situation, I "managed." When applauding my students, I'd stopped saying, "Good Job," I said "Well Done!" Young entrepreneurs were no longer "doing better," they were "coming up." I no longer said "lousy" or "weird". I replaced them with "dreadful" and "horrid", "ghastly" and "hideous". I banished "Great" and "Cool" from my vocabulary and replaced it with "Lovely." Oh . . . and every second word I uttered was "brilliant". I was speaking English the way my parents did, using British vocabulary and turns of phrase imbibed from Anglo-Indian education in Bombay's Catholic-run schools. Two decades in America had caused my Indian-English to metamorphose into a Yankee version of its original self. Yet, two months in London was all it took to restore the linguistic patterns of my Bombay breeding. If I had hoped to have a year of transformation, it was evident right away in my diction.

With nothing more productive to do than gaze at my bedroom ceiling, crushing guilt settled about my shoulders. I really ought to have been in the States to hear Dot's Big News from her in person. I really ought to be around to plan her Big Day with her. I really should be looking at her ring, turning her fingers over in my hand and admiring it. What was I doing a whole ocean away? Should I return to work in the US? Not possible as my teaching contract would not permit me to renege on it. Should I make a lightning trip back? Well, I was hardly in a position to fly across an ocean. The timing of my London assignment suddenly did not appear ideal at all. What's that they also say? Be careful what you ask for. I had asked for a single year of Aloneness. Well, let's just say solitary confinement in my bedroom while I writhed in pain was not exactly what I'd had in mind.

Despite misgivings, I arose, three times a day, from a stupor brought on by powerful pain-killers, to perform foot stretching exercises as instructed by my physiotherapist. These included acrobatic contortions worthy of Cirque du Soleil such as tracing figures of eight with one pointed foot while tip-toeing on the other, like the pre-pubescent Nadia Comaneci, the Rumanian gymnast, during an imaginary dance routine. Who'd have thought I'd come to London to stumble gracelessly through gymnastic motions?

I stuck to medical orders for all of one week not stirring from my flat except to get to work to teach. During my second week of mandatory convalescence, just when I thought Cabin Fever had slowly unhinged my mind, my physical pain eased considerably. If I didn't get out, I'd lose my mind. I sat at my PC and booked tickets left, right and center for anything theatrical upon which I could lay my credit card. I played bed-ridden patient by day, ravenous culture-vulture after dark in defiance of all medical orders.

One evening, I cabbed it to the Theater Royal on Drury Lane to watch the inimitable Dawn French and Jennifer Saunders, two of Britain's most beloved female comedians, in their last live show *Alive and Kicking*—Butt, I might add! But when I reached the entrance, I discovered that I had purchased nose-bleed seats, way up high on the fifth floor. Was there an elevator, I inquired? "Sadly, Madam, No. This theater was originally built in the Age of Elizabeth—the First, that is. Long before lifts were installed anywhere in London, I'm afraid," the usher said.

I mustered Herculean effort to climb each insufferable step up five Himalayan floors as I clung to the handrail for support like a drowning rat to a raft. As none of the theaters had elevators and my tickets were of the cheapest last-minute kind, buying them was really not that brilliant an idea.

Funnily enough, as exercises began to have an impact on the muscles of my calves, aches and pains developed in different portions of my legs. One day my knees felt like they'd turned to water, another day my calves appeared leaden, a third day piercing stabs of sensation coursed through my heels.

As for me? By the time Hubs arrived, I had a serious bout of Bedroom Boredom. Sipping hot mulled cider in his company, I found renewed optimism. As Aretha Franklin put it so inimitably, "I Would Survive." In his enthusiastic company, I planned our getaway on the Aegean Sea intending to push off soon on our Greek Odyssey.

6

AN AEGEAN ODYSSEY

Hubs roused himself in the middle of the night to discover that Obama had just taken Pennsylvania. As I surfaced from sleep, I heard his exultant whoops.

Barack Obama's victory was confirmed, that dawn, as we awoke in Greece. "He did it, babe," my Democrat husband shouted, sitting upright in bed.

Obama's name flowed copiously from the tongues of countless TV anchormen and women although what they said was, literally, all Greek to us!

"Obama ÆΩΠΞÓ. ÆΩΠΞÓ ÆΩΠΞÓ ÆΩΠΞÓ Obama. Obama ÆΩΠΞÓ. ÆΩΠΞÓ ÆΩΠΞÓ ÆΩΠΞÓ Obama".

We got the gist of it and celebrated with a band of local Athenians at breakfast. Much as we rejoiced that our preferred candidate had swept the polls, Hubs could not help saying, "What a pity we weren't around to vote in such a historic election." As for me, having stayed away from most American news—Mad Madoff's Ponzi Scandal, Folding up of Lehman Brothers, Sub Prime Mortgage Crisis—I felt breathless. Strongly propelled into the vortex of world reaction, I observed Greek responses to Obama's triumph with amusement. Though the seductions of Greece would take the edge off his regret at being so far away from home at such a significant time, Hubs voiced his immediate need. "Do you think we might find a newspaper somewhere in English?"

Easyjet had whizzed us off to Athens's balmy clime at the start of our week-long voyage in early November. Hubs was wracked with nerves on my behalf and functioned as my crutch as we soldiered on towards the ancient Castilian Springs in Delphi where cool water flowed from a stony leonine mouth.

On the three-hour bus journey from Athens to Delphi, we made friends with a beautiful German woman named Ulrike and her Italian boyfriend, Giovanni. Though our interaction had been brief, I had taken to Ulrike immediately. Visually striking with a burst of bushy brown-blonde corkscrew curls, it was her soft voice I found instantly appealing. And her English was impressive. Our common interests in art history had drawn us closely together. A Berliner, born and bred, Ulrike revealed that she had been writing a doctoral dissertation on a Venetian Renaissance artist in Italy when she'd met Giovanni, a university professor of Modern European History.

"Berlin?" I said, wistfully. "I was almost there. It is my hope to visit Berlin before I return to America. If I can find cheap airfares again, I might soon be in Germany."

"Promise me that you will contact me if you plan to come to Berlin," she said and I agreed never for a second believing I would ever see her again.

Knowing Athens well from earlier visits, Ulrike and Giovanni had directed us for dinner to Monastiraki, a colorful warren of streets at the foot of the Acropolis. Would they like to join us? I offered an invitation.

Retsina, that took the roof straight off my mouth, started us off in a small *taverna* where we ordered a salad. Nowhere in the world does Greek salad taste quite the same way it does in Greece where volcanic soil imbues it with a deliciously distinctive flavor. Picking at pickled red onions, crinkled kalamata olives and red peppers, we sighed, satiated. And oh, that fresh feta. Saline-as-the-sea and sinfully creamy. A whole thick slab crowned each organic offering.

Drinks done, we penetrated the old crowded quarter of Plaka in search of dinner. Together, at *Cafe Konstantin,* in the shadow of the Acropolis, we got to know our new friends better as we sampled *medzes,* tearing at pita and dipping our fingers into communal bowls of assorted spreads. Grilled zucchini and green peppers, *tzatziki* (garlic flavored cucumber-yogurt dip), *spanakopita* (spinach pie with toasted pine nuts), *dolmades* (rice stuffed vine leaves), *gigantes* (lima beans in a spicy tomato sauce), *taramasalata* (fish roe in a cream cheese base), salty olives and cheese pie filled our grazing platter. With carafes of red wine and the simplest of desserts—thick yogurt anointed with thyme honey showered with toasted pistachios—we had ourselves a feast worthy of the Gods. At the end of our eating orgy, we felt as if we'd known our friends forever. We exchanged contact numbers and parted company while promising to stay in touch. How could I have known that I would meet Ulrike again, not just once but twice before my Year of Discovery was over and each time in a different city in Europe?

Setting sail, the next morning, upon the ink-blue Aegean Sea from Piraeus Port in Athens to tony Mykonos, our cruise promised to be uneventful. I gazed out at the Aegean's startling sapphire waters. This was what, in his epics, Homer had meant by "wine-dark seas". I looked at my dozing husband and thought how lucky I was that he was mine. Few husbands would have indulged their wives as fully as mine had done—letting me goof off for a year without guilt to live my dream. I glanced around at the smattering of bored fellow passengers for whom taking cross-island ferries was like boarding Tube trains. A few TV sets played programs in desultory fashion with frequent snatches in English of Obama's acceptance speech.

The rhythmic movement of sea-faring soon lulled me too into a medicated stupor. We ignored occasional announcements in Greek that meant little to us and when our ship came to a stop on a busy island, off we hopped, pulling our wheeled cases ("strolleys") with us, to wait in glaring sunshine for the proprietor of our hotel, Phillipose, to show up, as promised. When ten minutes had passed and most of the passengers who'd disembarked had disappeared towards waiting vehicles, I pulled out my mobile to call him. Something just wasn't right.

Watching from the corner of her eye, a Greek woman approached me and asked, "Tinos? Mykonos?"

"Mykonos," Hubs and I replied in unison.

She became alarmed and shook her head violently. "This Tinos. Tinos. No Mykon . . ."

We didn't wait for her to complete her sentence. Omigawd! We'd alighted on the wrong island.

Meanwhile, our ferry was belching belligerently as it prepared to sail away to Mykonos. Hubs and I had already hit the ground running. We waved frantically as we panted and prayed that we'd make it on time to re-board. (Please, God, get us back on that %#@!!% ferry!) And then, rapturous relief as we just about threw our toes on the gangplank before it was hoisted up and away.

Back on the deck, we stooped like Marathon runners at the finish line, clutching our bursting chests and aching tummies. We'd almost been left behind on tiny Tinos! Only the Greek Gods knew when the next ferry would sail in and then away to Mykonos. We could have been marooned out there for at least a week! In ordinary circumstances, there'd have been a lot of finger-pointing between us. Like "Weren't you listening for announcements?" and "Well, wasn't it you who dozed off?" as we did the sort of thing long-time married couples do.

Instead, we remembered that we were on a second honeymoon and our sense of humor kicked in. Such mishaps, we decided, were part of our travel adventures, as we went in search of a cold beer.

An hour later, disembarking on deserted Mykonos, we found Philli-pose, true to his word, awaiting our arrival. Our hyper inn-keeper tre-bled as chauffeur and tour-guide. After settling into his empty *pensione* overlooking the harbor, we walked along the five minute stretch of unspoiled beach leading directly to the *Chora* (say "hora"), a maze of narrow streets whose brightly-painted balconies reached out to kiss each other. Hubs' eagle eye descended upon an internet café and, be-fore I knew it, I was being shepherded firmly towards its air-condi-tioned interior. Protests rose to my lips when second honeymoon deco-rum resurfaced and I acquiesced, smiling. We were able, finally, to catch up with *The New York Times* online and become part of interna-tional US election euphoria. It was infectious. As Democrats who'd nurtured an aversion to Dubya throughout his two excruciating terms in office, we joined the world in waving Republicans out of the White House. How appropriate that on such a historic day in American elec-tion history, we were in the very cradle of Democracy on a remote outpost in the spectacular Cyclades.

And then, just as we emerged from the cybercafé in blinding sun-shine, who should I bump right into, but Wayne, one of my students! Now what are the odds that I would leave my boisterous bunch of international teenagers behind in London only to run right into one of them on Mykonos?

Why was I so excited to see Wayne? Shouldn't I have resented the presence of a student while I was on vacation? Hadn't I come away with my husband precisely to escape them? But then it came home to me. With my real small family so far away in the States, my students in London had become my family. We'd all been in the same boat together as we'd embraced the British capital as home. On the coach and in cafes during weekend trips, I'd bonded with them, establishing, in the process, the kind of closeness I'd never experienced with the hundreds I'd taught during many years in New York. Running into Wayne so unexpectedly was like finding a long-lost relative.

Next thing I knew I was inviting Wayne to join us on our excursion, the following day, to the little-known island of Delos, a short sail from Mykonos. If all Wayne had intended to do was sunbathe for a week in Greece, I was going to sneak a little educational excursion into his itinerary!

We arrived at the ferry terminal in Mykonos, the next day, to board the inappropriately named *Delos Express* that skimmed lazily over choppy waters. Archeologically most significant of the Cyclades islands and considered, by Grecian decree, to be the earthly headquarters of the Gods, no one is allowed to be born or to die on sacred Delos. It had remained empty of habitation for centuries. Visitors are carefully counted while disembarking, only to be carefully counted again before the last ferry returns to Mykonos, each evening, as no one is allowed to remain on the island overnight. Like Pompeii, an entire thriving settlement, it had lain buried beneath centuries'-old rubble. I felt like a character in a Homeric adventure as I shared the remains of a prosperous city dating back to three thousand years with Hubs and Wayne. As we strode upon the Terrace of the Lions, I realized that plantar fasciitis was doing all it could to prevent me from "drinking", as Tennyson had put it, "life to the lees"; but taking inspiration from his Greek hero Ulysses, I was resolutely forging on. Jason and his sturdy Argonauts could not have been prouder than I. Charcoal grey volcanic crags and stone-stepped terraces provided frequent rest stops and, with a lot of rah-rahs from Hubs, I took the mosaic ruins, as it were, in my stride.

Apparently not content with sitting pretty and soaking in the scenery, Wayne suddenly pointed to a mountain and declared, "I'm going to climb that mountain."

"*That* Mountain? What now?" Hubs and I chorused, as we surveyed a distant towering promontory.

But he was already on his feet. We watched as Wayne ran——and I mean sprinted—up, up and away to the summit of a looming slope until he was a mere white speck on the horizon. When he was up on the summit, as instructed, I took his picture with his powerful telephoto lens and was admiring my handiwork when he disappeared from sight.

We waited almost breathless as our eyes scoured the blue-gray mountain. Half an hour went by. Then a scary hour dissolved into the past. It had taken him less than fifteen minutes to sprint up the summit. Why on earth was it taking Wayne so long to get back down again?

Gripped with anxiety, I surveyed the horizon. Nothing. No one. Wayne had disappeared into the wild blue yonder. As always happens when the brain is suddenly expected to wrap itself around a crisis, mine began to imagine the worst. Had he lost his way on the route downhill? Had he tumbled down a ravine on the other side, out of sight of our eager eyes? Had he sprained or fractured his ankle and was he writhing somewhere on the ground in pain unable to support his own body weight? No, I chided myself—that's you, remember?

How were we to react? To whom could we turn for help? Other than Hubs and myself, there wasn't a living soul to be seen anywhere. If my students had become my family, then Wayne was my son and it was like a Den Mother that I was reacting. Unlike my reaction to Gisela's disappearance in Barcelona, Wayne's vanishing was not something I could shrug off and forget. This was my student. I felt responsible for him. Had I still been capable of racing after him to search, I would have done so. As it was, PF kept me rooted to my rock, unable to think straight.

Hubs volunteered to become a one-man search party. God knows what he was likely to find. I shuddered as he set out on his approach up the mountain while I stormed Heaven. I called upon every Greek God and a smattering of Christian saints for good measure to plead for Wayne's safety. Would he make history? Would Wayne become the first person in the modern era to spend a night on Delos? The idea did not bear consideration.

Then, after Hubs had also disappeared from sight, serious dread set in. I was entirely alone on a Greek island with not another creature stirring. Something contrary to claustrophobia gripped my insides and squeezed my belly. It was the endless wilderness surrounded by azure waves that alarmed me and my awareness of being the only human being on the scene almost brought on a panic attack.

Then, half an hour later, just when I thought I had become physically ill with worry, I saw two figures trudging slowly towards me.

When they were within touching distance, I threw myself upon them both and hugged them fiercely. Neither one had broken bones or dislocated limbs. As anti-climaxes go, this was one of the very worst I'd experienced. It had taken Hubs much longer to get to the summit since he hadn't torn up the way Wayne had done. And when he got there, to the very top, what had he found but a dazzled Wayne staring out at sea as if mesmerized, admiring the glory of the seascape while deep in tantric meditation. Wayne had spent an hour on a mountain top attempting yogic *asanas* and breathing deeply.

"Sorry," he said, sheepishly. "I simply lost track of the time."

"I almost had a heart attack," I screamed. "Did you not think we'd worry about you?"

"I . . . I..didn't mean to stay. It was the view. So awesome."

"You have just as good a view from here. I mean, what does all this look like to you? Peak Hour at Grand Central Station? "

"I wanted a bird's eye view."

Wayne was mortified, Hubs was knackered, I was . . . well, livid but also profoundly relieved. I'd wanted adventure—well, I was getting it, but not in quite the ways I had desired.

At day's end, our ferry operator, a latter-day Odysseus, did a rapid head count as we boarded the *Delos Express*. I still could scarcely believe that both Wayne and Hubs were actually on that boat as we sailed back to Mykonos.

We returned to our Mykonnian *pensione* overlooking the port and harbor to chill with Phillipose, who, in halting English, confided in us his favorite woes. "My maader . . . she wants go to market. . . . I her drive . . . not buying allthings same time . . . want go again . . . then again . . . it long climbing for me . . . but what to do? She my maader. . . . I not married," (hoarse chortles) "married to my maader."

Greeks! Even when speaking gibberish, I decided, they were the nicest people on the planet. Warm, unpretentious, natural.

The next day, we sailed into the sensational sunsets of Santorini. PF did little to stop me clambering over white-washed hills past turquoise-domed churches to the island's soaring cliffed tip where tourists had gathered to gape at the Aegean horizon.

Heading towards deserted black-sanded Kamari Beach, the next day, at the far end of our Odyssey, we realized just how kind, how generous and how spontaneous Greeks could be. After spending more than half an hour in the autumn sunshine awaiting a bus that never showed, we opted to hitchhike to the beach. Except that not a single vehicle was headed in the direction of Kamari. Giving up in despair, we crossed over to the opposite side of the street and stuck our thumbs out for a ride back to our hotel in Fira.

When an old farmer with sheep skins in his pick-up truck stopped, we squeezed into his little cubicle in the passenger seat. Needless to say, his English was virtually non-existent; but a few minutes later, when we saw the Kamari Beach bus go by, we groaned so loudly in unison that he understood what our original intention had been.

Not to be phased, he turned to us and said, "You want go that bus?"

"Yes . . . but forget it now . . ." I began, while Hubs said, "It's gone now on the other side anyway."

"We go after bus," said our farmer-chauffeur, exposing missing front teeth and instantly resolving to quell our disappointment.

And before we could say "Aristotle Onassis," he'd made a U-Turn right there in the middle of the narrow road and raced behind the public bus toward Kamari.

"It's okay, really. No need to risk an accident." I tried to communicate to him that we fervently desired to get away from Greece alive in two intact pieces.

"It stop. Soon it stop Messaria . . . you . . . bus" he made a sign with two fingers of legs climbing stairs.

Still almost speechless with astonishment, we got his drift. A few minutes later, the bus arrived at the tiny village of Messaria where a neat queue waited to board it.

"Now . . . now . . . you go bus," he said, leaving us with mere moments to thank him profusely, charge towards the bus and board it.

Ten minutes later, I was eating chestnut yogurt while seated in an abandoned boat on Kamari Beach in the shadows of volcanic elephant leg-shaped cliffs while Hubs took a lone walk along the surf to do his good deed for the day—picking up litter washed ashore. I gazed wistfully after him. I'd dreamed of romantic beach walks with my husband, fingers linked, sand between our toes, never dreaming that PF would keep me stationary.

For the rest of our stay, violently blood-stained sunsets at Fira and Ia (say "Ee-ah") were counterbalanced by superlative meals that taught us why the Mediterranean Diet has its rave reputation. Each evening, Hubs massaged my aching calves as I stretched, toned and flexed my plantar fascia. Did I worry that there'd be a price to pay for this wanton wandering? Far from it. Touring Greece with my husband was a once-in-a-lifetime opportunity. There'd be time enough to atone for my traveling sins when I returned home to Southport.

7

ACQUIRING ENGLISHNESS

By the time Hubs and I returned from Grecian gallivanting, we'd missed a mighty significant date on the British calendar—Armistice Day that occurs on November 11, also known in the UK as Remembrance Day. But, for at least three weeks before its arrival, I had adopted that most British of patriotic customs—the wearing of a red paper poppy in my coat lapel.

A week before we'd left for Athens, Karina, my American colleague at NYU who'd also arrived with me from New York to teach for a year, had asked, "What's with that thing you're wearing? I see everyone here walking about with it." She'd pointed to the lapel of my fall blazer as I'd walked into the basement office we shared.

"My poppy," I replied with pride.

"Your poppy?"

"Yeah. Do you know the poem by John McCrea written in 1915?"

"Er . . . I don't think so, no."

"In Flanders field the poppies blow. Between the crosses, row on row . . . Every British school kid can recite the poem by heart."

Poppies have been the Remembrance Day flower of choice for at least three generations of Brits whose ancestors saw action on the Western Front during World War I. Every year, when frosty mornings herald the arrival of early November, red paper poppies pop up on the pavement to be sold by vendors as fund-raising vehicles for Britain's war veterans. The choice of flower has to do with the fact that the digging of trenches during the Great War, contributed to the propagation and spread of wild poppies in the killing fields of the Somme and the Marne. When they grew by the thousand in the wide-spread fields of Picardy in France and Ypres in Flanders, they appeared to flow like the blood of fallen soldiers.

As for me, the adoption of a British ritual associated with the Great War had much to do with honoring memories cherished by my own beloved Mum Edith. On a visit to my home in the States from Bombay, a few years previously, having viewed a succession of floats decorated profusely with poppies at a Veteran's Day Parade in our little New England colonial town of Fairfield, Connecticut, my mother had revealed to me that, as a student in a boarding school in British India, she and her classmates had made crepe paper poppies each autumn to raise funds for British troops on the Front. More than sixty years later, making a monetary contribution to the same fund-raising spirit somehow made me feel closer to my Mum.

Armistice Day, marked as Veterans Day in America, is still a big noise in the UK and memorial ceremonies to remember war victims bring members of the Royal Family out to the Cenotaph on Whitehall, a monument designed by the predominant Edwardian architect, Sir Edwin Lutyens, who'd also designed the city of New Delhi. "At the eleventh hour of the eleventh day of the eleventh month", two minutes' silence descends all over Great Britain as the Queen and sundry members of her progeny stoop to the monument's base to place reverential poppy wreaths to honor the dead as military bands play the Last Post hauntingly. Although Hubs and I were in Greece when Armistice Day dawned, the significance of the build-up to the holiday was not lost on me. Belief in the soundness of the adage "When in England, do as the English do" had led me to purchase my own poppy for a pound's contribution.

Back in London, after our Greek vacation, Hubs and I hopped off a bus to pose for pictures at the Cenotaph and in the yard of Westminster Abbey where thousands of tiny wooden crosses adorned with paper poppies created a poignant scarlet carpet that brought a concrete lump to my throat on a nippy fall evening. My regret at missing the solemnity of the occasion in Britain was intensified when NextDoor Brenda said, "We missed you. We had our own little private neighborhood ceremony with wreaths laid at the small Lutyens war memorial right outside our building on High Holborn. You Americans would have enjoyed that."

Acquiring Englishness was something we Americans would do enthusiastically that autumn.

It is time to introduce that most rural of British pastimes into the
picture—the thrill of the chase. But lest your imagination stirs you in
the direction of a ruddy Englishman seated on a horse preceded by his
pack of beagles while clad in a traditional red jacket—misleadingly
known as "hunting pinks" (don't even ask!), banish the image. Our
family friend Karim Khan—Khan Saab to us—once Hubs' boss during
his banking days over three decades previously in the Middle East, is a
study in British paradoxes. Impeccably attired in Saville Row suits with
a Brycleemed coiffeur and a pencil-thin moustache, he is also petite,
brown, and a Muslim who keeps every Ramadan fast. This product of
Pakistan via Dubai, Miami, Cape Town, New York, the Cayman Islands
and London, has traversed the world, picked up local hobbies—with
the kind of ease associated with picking seashells on the seashore—and
added them to a persona that defies easy national categorization. After a
decade in London, the favorite hobby horse of this citizen of the world,
was game shooting and he would introduce us to his passion in the
poshest of English interiors and over the classiest of English meals—
Afternoon Tea in the Palm Court of the Ritz.

The British have a twisted way with words. Just as a scarlet jacket is
referred to as a hunting pink, High Tea is, in fact, the lowliest of British
meals. Despite its lofty name, the latter was, in fact, associated with the
humblest of peasantry and is almost defunct everywhere in the UK
today. Once upon a time, when it was frequently consumed, it was a
rustic meal eaten by farmhands after a hard day's toiling in the fields
and always included one hefty meat course such as a game pie or
roasted leg of lamb. Today if it is tiny finger sandwiches, melt-in-the-
mouth chocolate eclairs and Battenberg Cake you're after, Afternoon
Tea—not High Tea—is what you crave. In the UK, it is the meal most
associated with delicate paper doilies, svelte socialites and wannabe
aristocrats strung with pearls.

Khan Saab suggested we meet in the lobby of the hotel at Green
Park. Did I mention it was the Ritz? Where anyone in trainers and jeans
is told by a top-hatted, tail-coated concierge, in the politest of terms, to
get lost? Where the décor is classy and music, produced by creatures
plucking strings on harps, ethereal? Where soft-footed, white-gloved

waiters ply you with unlimited helpings of three solid courses starting with the most savory and graduating towards the sweetest?

Controversy in such surroundings is kept to a minimum—the most raging debate converges around whether cream or jam goes on your split scone first. Oh and don't dare request anyone to pass the 'jelly' or allow your pinkie finger to protrude! You need to check in all your Americanisms at the ornate gilded doors of the Palm Court and savor the offerings quietly—so leave your multi-decibel American voice at home too. Wear a jacket and a tie if you are a male of the species and feel free to bring out your Mikimotos and spikiest Jimmy Choos should you belong to the fairer sex. As for yours truly, guess what happened to me whilst in the midst of the upper crust? I was born and raised in India where *kadak chai* is synonymous with mother's milk; but it was The Ritz that made a tea drinker of me that afternoon. Before I could say "Darjeeling" I was buying *Fortnum and Mason's* tea assortment from the upscale gourmet shop next door and as soon as Hubs returned to the States, my own daily tea-time cuppas began to be consumed by the potful.

Suitably attired, we sat down with Karim Saab to Afternoon Tea and a natter that also offered a built-in education in yet another traditional aspect of British life. Much to our astonishment, our dapper friend turned out to be a country squire in disguise. A sedate banker during the week, he was a passionate game bird shooter at the weekends and during the 'season' kept himself out of mischief by stalking partridge, pheasant and wood cock. In fact, he revealed that a friend had roped him into a "syndicate."

"Another Pakistani?" I asked, still awash in ignorance of the sport.

"Oh no no no. Englishman! Cent per cent Englishman. This is not the sort of club your average Pakistani would join. Even though, mind you," he said, "*shikar* is an old aristocratic Indian and Pakistani sport, is it not?"

Neither plantar fasciitis nor Hubs' departure from London stopped me from getting ahead with work assignments. While the pain in my arches was at its worst first thing in the morning, exercises and massages plus regular private physiotherapy sessions enabled me to continue with the routine tenor of my life provided I kept walking to the minimum. To make up for time lost convalescing in my flat while bedbound, setting up appointments with elderly Anglo-Indians became a top priority. And it was with a couple called Helen and Donald in Norwood that my forays into the idiosyncrasies of elderly settlers of mixed racial descent began.

I was fully flexible in my own availability, but pinning my respondents down to an interview was a feat more challenging than getting a camel through the proverbial eye of a needle. My teaching schedule ("timetable"), carefully planned around a single day of the week, allowed me to say, "I can carry out interviews at your convenience. Except for Thursday, I can work around your schedule."

If I expected Helen to be a little biddy with oodles of time spent twiddling her thumbs, I could not have been more mistaken. It would appear that she was solely responsible for running the universe for her calendar was chocobloc.

Amazingly, after playing hard-to-get on the phone, two days later, Helen had sent me an email wondering "if I'd care" to join Donald and her "for a meal". I never really knew what to make of such antiquated phraseology. Was I expected to accept gratefully? Or decline gracefully?

It was at the front door of his modest suburban dwelling that Donald greeted me. Thick glasses occupied his entire face. Large teeth broke into a welcoming smile. Salt and pepper-haired Helen, petite and proper, wore a severe olive-green suit—clearly perceived as appropriate attire for a formal meeting with an academic from America. Pearls were strung around her neck. Sensible penny-loafers, polished to a shine, added to the no-nonsense manner in which she moved about. She settled me down with a cup of coffee and a biscuit on a tired sofa that had borne the bottoms of her visitors for decades. Clusters of photographs of children and grandchildren littered living room tables. Like their home and its furnishings, she and Donald had seen better days; but they were not about to wear their diminished lifestyles on their sleeves. Can't grumble. Can't complain. Stiff upper lip and all that. Retirement had brought fixed incomes, mainly through modest government pensions, but appearances must still be kept up. Think Audrey Forbes-Hamilton in *To The Manor Born*. Helen might have lacked Audrey's aristocratic lineage but she possessed every last affectation of Britain's landed gentry.

When the interview began, Helen spoke primly, hands held in lap. Donald shared a funny episode with me and chuckled. They'd been married close to sixty years and completed each other's sentences.

"We thought you'd appreciate a simple Indian meal . . ."

". . . so we cooked you some doll."

Doll? Was Barbecued Barbie on the menu? Anglo-Indians were notorious for anglicizing Indian words. They had cooked me *dal*, the Indian term for stewed lentils, but on their tongues the word had been transformed into a little girl's plaything.

Later, Donald said, "We were not sure what sort of information you wanted . . ."

". . . so we were hesitant to grant the interview," finished Helen.

They spoke the kind of English that was in fashion between the two World Wars--that is to say, like the Edwardians. They said, "By Jove!" and "Fiddlesticks!", "Goodness Gracious!" and "Oh Lordy!"

We paused for lunch. "We cooked you Chicken Korma . . ."

". . . with Yellow Rice. Bet you're only eating sandwiches these days."

"Would you care for a drop of sherry?" asked Donald, then proceeded to pour me exactly that amount. A drop in a thimble-sized stemmed glass. Just enough to whet my appetite for their home-cooked rice and curry.

After lunch, it was time for dessert (say "pudding"). "Some ice-cream, perhaps?" asked Helen. "We have . . . let's see . . ."

". . . vanilla and strawberry," finished Donald

I scribbled copiously as they recalled their immigrant journey by steamer from Bombay to the docks of Southampton, of early days of hardship in post-World War II England, of racism and rejection from employers and landlords as they sought jobs and rental accommodation. I left with a stack of notes containing valuable data for sociological analysis.

By the end of the interview, my frosty hostess had thawed towards me. "Before you take your leave," she said.

". . . please write down your phone number." That was Donald. "We might think of other Anglos you can call. Oh . . . and you must come to our weekly luncheon club meeting. We'll introduce you to a lot of our Anglo friends there."

Awwright! That was exactly what I'd desired. The more 'Anglos' I could reach, the more networking I'd do and the more networking I did, the more valid would be my scholarly findings. I'd take any help I could get.

Late November found me wondering how I would spend Thanksgiving—that most Yankee of national "holidays"—in Blighty. And there was a very American treat to which to look forward when I received an invitation to attend an evening of American classical music and folk songs at a rival institution—Boston University in London. And the sender of this welcome diversion was yet another BOB. The very English Director of BU's Study Abroad Program in London, Rupert Connors, was the buddy of a couple of my Connecticut buddies. He wondered when I called him on the phone to say Hello, if I'd like to attend a recital by his Music majors attached to London's Royal College of Music. Wanna bet? There'd be no stopping me. How could I pass up the opportunity to enjoy holiday tunes in a gracious old mansion called *Boston House*, furnished in colonial American style, in the middle of London?

The concert ended on a rollicking note with the most spirited Yankee melodies churned out by a talented lot of American students who seemed to feel the kind of homesickness with which I could empathize as Turkey Day approached. As my invitation had included dinner "at a somewhat inexpensive place", the *Langan Coq D'Or* in upmarket Kensington provided the ideal venue to network with a lovely group of music-lovers and fellow-invitees. Hubs' departure had left me bereft and overly eager to compensate for his loss by reaching towards new friendships. I chose the Pan Roasted Partridge simmered superbly in red wine *jus* with smoked bacon and whole chestnuts.

In keeping with the conventions of his homeland, Rupert did not suggest I package my leftovers. Sorely tempted, out of force of habit, to request a "doggie bag"—that other crass brainwave of the Yankee diner—I stopped myself just in time as I recalled a piece of instruction issued by my new friend, the Bishop's wife, Celia Carrington: "Over here . . . it's simply not done. Don't ever ask for a doggie bag . . . especially not in a nice restaurant."

I wanted to let fly a mental wail and decided that, in these circumstances, the dining customs of Yankee frugality were certainly preferable to the wanton waste of the British table.

Meanwhile, much as I focused on the food and the new friends I was rapidly warming to, I could not take my eyes of the mother-daughter duo who had been my immediate neighbors during the concert. The little lady whose elegant appearance was deeply reminiscent of the actress Helen Hayes in her later years went by the name of Hilary, while her daughter, soft-spoken with the most charming smile and the friendliest handshake, called herself Lorraine.

Having so disfavored me at the start of the evening by leaving me waiting for a bus that took forty-five minutes to arrive and make me shamefully late for the concert, Fate decided to even the scales at its end by locating the twosome in a residential building just one Tube stop away from my own. This allowed us to walk to the station together, ride the Tube to our respective destinations and discover that while Hilary had journeyed from Yorkshire to attend the concert, her daughter, close to my age, lived on a farm in Suffolk but had the use of a London *pied-a-terre* for occasional weekends—which would give us the excuse to meet again. Barely six Tube stops later, we'd formed the sort of newly-hatched friendship that would play a gigantic role in the course of my Nearly Perfect Year, although I was not to know it then.

I alighted from my train in Holborn with a song in my heart that had nothing at all to do with the musical concert I had just attended and everything to do with the new friends I knew I would always cherish. It was impossible to see Lorraine that evening in the role of knight in shining armor. But it would be only a few months later that she would scoop me up on to the broad back of her gleaming white steed in my hour of distress.

As Turkey Day grew imminent, my colleague Karina and I made plans to be perverse. We would spend Thanksgiving evening consuming that most British of meals in the last of the traditional 'chippies' in Covent Garden.

A Vermillion poppy pinned to my jacket, Afternoon Tea at the Ritz, sherry before luncheon, a concert in Kensington and making plans to eat Fish and Chips at Thanksgiving. How quickly I was becoming "Cent Percent English"!

8

HALF A MONTH OF MOOD SWINGS

On the morning of Turkey Day, all hell broke loose. Not in London, but on the other side of the world.

I intended to savor three relaxing hours before leaving my flat for a mid-morning appointment at St. Paul's Cathedral with Bishop Andrew and Celia Carrington who had invited me to join hundreds of fellow-Americans at an annual Anglo-American Thanksgiving service. The aroma of percolating coffee permeated my kitchen as I reached to switch on the telly. Within seconds, I was left, as my Brit colleagues would say, gobsmacked. My mind could make so little sense of the assault of images that all I could do was stare at the screen in disbelief.

Lone gunman barging his way through gleaming marble lobby. Panic-stricken screams in background. Guerrilla sniper swinging from cable, rifle slung across shoulder. Regiment of soldiers firing intermittently at iconic building from behind wall of sandbags.

Wasn't that the five-star Taj Mahal Hotel in Bombay?

Throngs of people running helter-skelter in insane circles. Shattered windows. Smoking cars. A bloodied hotel lobby. It *was* the Taj.

Mayhem prevailed as guests were held hostage. But by whom?

And at *Leopold Café* on active Colaba Causeway in the old colonial nucleus of a city, someone had opened fire on innocent patrons enjoying sips of frosty Kingfisher lager.

Next, a horrifyingly familiar railway terminal. Eerie. Completely emptied of its multitude of humanity. Women in sarees crouching to take cover behind Victorian Gothic walls. Wasn't that Bombay's Victoria Railway Terminus?

Confusion, chaos, carnage everywhere.

It *was* Bombay! And terrorism had struck it seemingly from out of nowhere.

I burst out of my self-imposed bubble on what the people of India would forever refer to as "26/11"—Thanksgiving morning—to confront terrorism in the city of my birth. I watched, horrified, coffee turning icy in mug, as the railway terminal I had known as Victoria Terminus, was besieged by a mob of terrorists. Every brick of that venue held special significance for my family members and for me—as they would for anyone who had grown up in Bombay. I had come halfway around the world for a second tryst with terrorism—albeit vicariously—through broadcast media. I ached for the comforting presence of Hubs and Dot across the pond. I pined for a glimpse of my ageing parents and my loving brothers—all in Bombay. Instead of being enveloped in their reassuring arms, all I was surrounded by were stark bare London walls. I had never felt more alone or more homesick for those I'd left behind.

Seeking reassurance, I desperately dialed my folks in India. Their own horror at the ongoing saga of extremist activity only a few miles from their apartment made the voices of my family members unrecognizable on the phone. I finally understood how wracked by fear and worry they might have been when I had found myself in the thick of 9/11 terrorist activity almost a decade previously in New York. It was a relief to find out that my nearest and dearest were unhurt; but the city I will forever know as Bombay was being blasted possibly beyond repair. Then, as if in slow motion, they gave it to me: the news that a neighbor down the street who worked at the Israeli Consulate—which attackers had also struck—remained missing. Words exchanged across telephonic static contained only more reason to worry.

When I had witnessed a similar catastrophe, eight years previously, it had been on a Manhattan sidewalk as the Twin Towers had tumbled, while clutching the hands of students with tear-smeared faces. When I had walked forty blocks uptown from our NYU Manhattan campus to Grand Central Terminal, many hours later, to board my train home to Connecticut, I had been in a crowd of several thousand ash-coated escapees, trooping, shell-shocked, through New York streets devoid of traffic. When I had last mourned so publicly in the Big Apple, millions had mourned with me. But when I stuck my head outside my London window, it was business as usual on High Holborn. This time round, I would do my grieving alone for no one seemed in the slightest bit perturbed by the drama unfolding half a planet away. It was time to turn to prayer for comfort. Good job I was scheduled to be at St. Paul's later that day.

Security was tight at Wren's Neo-Classical portals. Police swarmed around the stairs and inside the Cathedral, closed to tourists that morning. My bag was searched, my body frisked, my motives questioned. I neither looked nor sounded like your standard-issue American with my brown skin and convent-educated Bombay accent. I had no business being at the Cathedral that morning. How could an Indian—possibly a non-Christian—have anything to do with America's Thanksgiving holiday, right? It was my first brush with racism in the UK—subtle, unintended, but present all the same. Seething from what I considered racial profiling, nothing was more comforting, when I was finally allowed inside, on that mournful morning than my fellow-Americans belting out "America the Beautiful" to the accompaniment of United States military bands. The service marked the fiftieth year since Americans in London had begun celebrating Turkey Day in Wren's Baroque interior. Robert Tuttle, outgoing United States ambassador to the UK, was present in the congregation amidst hundreds of expatriate Americans assembled on their national holiday. Sadly, neither the homily nor the speeches that followed made any reference to the tragedy in Bombay. In the midst of many thousands, I was isolated.

Over the next couple of days, as news flashes trickled in, the world learned that the young men, only very recently boys, who held a city hostage for days were terrorists from Pakistan programmed to slaughter in cold blood. It took the force of India's army to subdue and annihilate them, but the victim toll had climbed steadily and, by the time the ordeal was over, the lives of nearly 200 people had been snuffed out. That this would happen on Thanksgiving Day was incomprehensible. I dreaded the moment I would receive confirmation that the missing neighbor was no more; but, thankfully, she had been found, safe and sound if profoundly shaken, among the Israeli Consulate's personnel that had been released.

Then, excitement—albeit of a different kind—entered my life once again after the telly led me to yet another royal sighting. News anchors announced the State Opening of Parliament when Queenie journeys formally forth from her home at 'Buck House'—British slang for Buckingham Palace—to Westminster in a Cinderella coach drawn by handsome horses to formally declare Parliamentary proceedings open for yet another season of civilized debate. Traditionally, crowds, kept in control by members of the armed forces, line the pavements of Whitehall and Parliament Square aching for a glimpse of the monarch.

Since my flat was merely minutes from the venue, I decided, on an impulse, to make a beeline for the Houses of Parliament for a possible royal sighting—notwithstanding the fact that it was an unusually chilly day, even for November. Bundled into my warmest cashmere cardigan and down coat, I found myself on a busy London street surrounded by thousands of onlookers who shared the exact same objective. Squaddies pranced around on horseback, bobbies plied their beat keeping overly-enthusiastic tourists at bay, helicopters buzzed about cloudless skies as Queenie's carriage appeared, preceded and followed by assorted members of her entourage.

As in Scotland, so here too in London, excitement was palpable—only here on a much grander scale. From where I gazed, camera at the ready—for photographs were not banned on this occasion—about five hundred yards away from Whitehall, I stood the tiniest chance in hell of catching a glimpse of royalty. Yet, to my enormous good luck, for some inexplicable reason, her golden horse-drawn coach came to a sudden standstill, affording me a distant but very lingering look at a snow-white head of hair encircled by a gleaming tiara, a white-gloved hand and a benign smile for Her Maj was attired in full regalia to deliver her Speech from the gilded Throne in the House of Lords. I joined in the satisfied gasp uttered by every bystander as she and her faithful consort, seated right beside her, slowly drew away.

A second sighting of the Queen and the Duke of Edinburgh! As unexpected as it was exciting, this adventure sent my sagging spirits soaring—and all because I had made the impulsive decision, that very morning, to leave my flat and sally forth to see them in the flesh rather than on the small screen. A few minutes later, she was at the Sovereign's Entrance to the Houses of Parliament, where, in one of the most baffling traditions of English protocol, she was expected to humbly seek permission to enter—a gesture, deriving from the Magna Carta of 1215, that symbolizes her inability, even as ruler of the land, to interfere with the goings-on in Parliament. That evening, on TV, as I watched the Queen deliver her ceremonial address to her Lords, I kept pinching myself—the better to believe that I had personally seen her arrive in grandeur.

A couple of days later, still dazed by the continuing uncertainty of events in Bombay, I felt the urgent need to beat a retreat from the confines of London to find autumnal refuge in the Thames-side village of Barnes. In the swift and sudden descent of darkness, the placid upscale settlement glowed softly. A few yellowed leaves still clung to trees as if some magical sprite had shaken a bag of gold flakes over them to lend holiday sparkle. As part of one of Frommer's *Great Walks in London*, I entered the Roman Catholic Churchyard of Mary Magdalen to find the lichen-covered grave of Richard Burton. No, not the Welsh actor-husband of Hollywood siren Elizabeth Taylor, but the one who gave the world the English translation of *The Arabian Nights* based on far-flung travels in the Middle East. Set in—get this—a concrete Bedouin tent, there was a ladder at the back and determined to catch a glimpse of his mausoleum, I climbed it to peer inside a tiny window to find him lying besides his wife, Isabel Arundel.

Anxiety induced by inexplicable terrorism and the Burton-Arundel gravesite rendered me morbid. What if something were to happen to Hubs or my beloved daughter while we were apart? Would I ever forgive myself for leaving them to their own devices while I marched forth all over Europe? Hubs had his eye on the global financial debacle as it affected retirees in America. Dot was pushing forward with wedding plans. An ocean apart from both, I nursed my own anxieties about Bombay's misfortunes.

Alone with my thoughts, I became aware, that I was the sole occupant, at twilight, of a vast graveyard. And yet I did not feel the slightest urge to leave. Connecticut Rochelle would have hurried homeward in panic glancing shiftily behind her shoulder every few seconds. London Rochelle walked calmly towards the bus-stop having had an empowering epiphany. I had lost my timidity. My irrational dread of solitude was fast becoming a non-issue. I no longer jumped at the sound of my door bell. I'd stopped creeping about at home on tiptoe after sundown. I moved freely from one tiny room to the next in my flat without wallowing in worry. In less than three months, I'd made progress in triumphing over one troubling aspect of my past life. I had conquered my fear of domestic singularity, slowly but surely.

But even as I tried to conquer emotional gloom, I had a physical setback. No matter how much better my feet felt, they protested each time I provoked them beyond their limitations. After a hiatus from manic walking, I had resumed pavement-stomping on a tentative note, but my forays into Barnes only aggravated my discomfort. Gone forever, it seemed, were my days of mega walk-abouts. The morning after by exploration in Barnes, my left knee rattled like a bag of bones. Lucky Richard Burton. He never had to cope with a collapsed plantar fascia, I bet. On the other hand, the knee constriction was possibly a result of new exercises private Physiotherapist Number One Morgan had prescribed. They were challenging, created a burn in my left knee and could well be producing adverse reactions. Who could be sure? My moods swung like a pendulum on steroids as I tried to come to terms with my disability.

That same sorry week, as if determined to explore newer pastures, I boarded a National Express bus ("coach") on a frigid November morning to re-discover the university town of Cambridge that I'd last seen twenty-two years previously. I felt as if I'd strayed into a photograph as I strolled along The Backs on the banks of the Cam. Punts glided unhurriedly by, their occupants well enshrouded in raspberry wool blankets. Coppered leaves burnished the landscape and rattled underfoot as I roamed through college quadrangles eloquent with stories. Black-gowned students zipped by on bicycles hurrying to dinner in aged halls. In the fast-fading light of a frosty evening, I hurried also to the Bridge of Sighs to pose for pictures at the very same spot where, as a visiting grad student, I had once stood and smiled for another camera one long ago summer while sporting the big hair of the 1980s. On the cusp of winter, the university town seemed different. Its sights remained unchanged. Only my mood had mellowed. Age made all the difference to my perceptions. My outlook appeared to have grown deeper—more philosophical—softly tinted by a quarter century of intervening experience.

Later, fighting melancholia caused by terrorism, continuing troubles with PF and nostalgia for long-lost friends with whom I'd last visited the city, I trooped into the candlelit interior of King's College Chapel to attend Evensong. Long before the choir struck its first high note, I raised my head to admire the splendid fan-vaulted ceiling that Christopher Wren had so admired. Had someone told him where to place the first stone, he'd remarked, he could have built it himself. In pin-drop silence, in a sacred space filled with candle-bathed softness, the Chapel's renowned choristers lifted their voices and transported me to the Gates of Paradise.

When a week later, London got into the festive spirit, I responded resolutely. I was going to plunge headlong into Yuletide in Blighty.

"The questions is," whispered NextDoor Tom to me, "do we stand for the Hallelujah Chorus?"

I was back in London, listening to another choir in another church. Within the grand confines of St. Paul's Cathedral on an icy evening in December, Tom and I prepared to be serenaded to the stirring sounds of Handel's *Messiah* as Brenda was tied up with a legal commitment. I had expanded my social circle by introducing one set of new friends to another. When NextDoor Tom and Brenda hit it off with Bishop Andrew and Celia Carrington, we often made a companionable fivesome. Seated in the first row, at the very feet of thundering drums, I squirmed in excitement and saluted the Lord quietly for bringing my new friend Bishop Andrew into my London life. As one of the head honchos at St. Paul's, he frequently allotted us privileged perches.

Whatever did Tom mean? "The custom of standing during the *Hallelujah Chorus* was started by King George II as he listened to the *Messiah*, you see," Tom explained in his posh public school accent. "And when the king rises, so do his underlings. Since then it has been customary for the audience to get to its feet at the end of the second movement. I bet we'll be standing."

Hmmm. Had Georgie-Porgie's gout acted up as the choir mouthed its first "Hal?" Or did he merely need to stretch his pudgy pins? I was still pondering these possibilities, when another Cathedral bigwig climbed the pulpit and announced, "Incidentally, Ladies and Gentlemen, we will stand for the Hallelulah Chorus." Tom gave me the All-Knowing Nod as the priest reminded us that rising would provide the opportunity to reach into our pockets to contribute generously to circulating collection baskets. I saluted the Lord again for endowing his Anglican ministers with such an unfailing sense of humor!

When the last note of the concert hung suspended in the wintry air, the three of us walked home together—Tom and I and his tightly rolled umbrella. I stepped straight NextDoor for a natter with Brenda while Tom produced the very epitome of 1930s home-cooked British Comfort Food—Liver and Bacon. Now lest you say "Ee-yew", may I remind you that he was once a West End chef? Brenda poured us chilled *isewein* to round off the evening by which point I was staring at my empty plate, barely believing I'd just polished off a doorstopper of a hunk of liver. I'd ignored my aversion to offal and tucked in. And it was scrumptious.

Right on cue, in late December, our Almighty Dollar came splendidly into its own. After floundering for months to regain its title as King of Currencies, it emerged victorious at Christmas. Tudor *Liberty* and Restoration Age *Fortnum and Mason's,* Victorian *Selfridges,* Edwardian *Harrods,* contemporary *John Lewis,* and up-to-the-Minute *Harvey Nicks* offered retail therapy from grading-induced headaches and the sadness prompted by the catastrophe in Bombay. I slid off towards Piccadilly and Knightsbridge in historic Routemaster buses, older in age than I, taking pictures with rotund conductors flushed by frost as I lugged home ruby *M&S*, emerald *Harrods* and turquoise *Fortnum* shopping bags. I made endless lists, then, as the song suggests, checked them twice. My buys grew weightier with each dying day of the passing year as I gift-shopped for family and friends across the Atlantic and in India—for I was going home to Hubs and Dot for Christmas in Connecticut, then winging it off for some urgent emotional recuperation in Bombay's maternal bosom.

Determined not to miss a beat, I searched Visit Britain's website for holiday ideas. Eat hot mince pies in Covent Garden's Festive Market, it said. I did. Alone. Go to Shoreditch in the East End to one-of-a-kind Geffrye Museum that decks its halls in boughs of holly through the ages. I did. Also alone. Go ice-skating at Somerset House, it said. I did. Still alone. Under the domed jade roof, I joined seasonal revelry while clutching a warming glass of citrus-toned, cinnamon and clove-laced mulled red wine and watched wobbly ice-skaters land on their behinds.

But before I left Blighty to its own Christmas devices, there was one urgent item on my To-Do List that needed ticking off. How could I ever let December in the UK pass me by without experiencing that most English of seasonal traditions—the Christmas Panto? Weeks in advance, while we were still in Keats's season of mist and mellow fruitfulness, I'd made reservations to see one of my favorite British actors, Simon Callow, play Captain Hook in Britain's most beloved pantomime *Peter Pan*. Freed from adult inhibitions, like all the six-year olds in antiquated Richmond Theater, I clapped my hands, stamped my feet and balled out until I was hoarse at the 'baddie' hidden behind the rocks. "Where is he?" asked Peter. "Behind you," I yelled with the same enthusiasm as the midget audience. When we trooped out of the theater, I thought, did I just do that? Never in sedate Southport would I have reacted with such few inhibitions. London offered the kind of anonymity that allowed me to metamorphose into someone I was having a hard time recognizing.

A month previously, in mid-November, I'd received the thrilling news of election to the position of Senior Associate Member at St. Antony's College, University of Oxford—an honor that granted me affiliation with the college and entitlement to its research facilities. Had I lucked out or what? All that remained was a trip to the college office to tie a few loose ends before my summer stay at St Antony's became a Done Deal. And then, when I discovered that the famed Ashmolean Museum was due to close for a year of extensive renovation, there was no time to lose. Before you could say 'Elias Ashmole', I'd booked a coach ticket for an amble among the city's Gothic spires.

I was deposited on Oxford's High Street on a particularly vicious day—cold, grey, rainy, a far cry from the sunny vistas of my youthful summer memories of the city. I charged off to spend the morning in the museum whose highlights had been gathered into one gallery as it reorganized itself. What a treat! But despite spending leisurely time studying its oldest and most valuable item, the Alfred Jewel that had inspired an episode is my favorite *Inspector Morse* detective series and *The Hunt*, a brilliant medieval painting about the vanishing point by Paolo Uccello, that inspired an episode in the *Inspector Lewis* series that followed, something seemed missing. I simply couldn't put my finger on it. What was it that held my excitement at bay? I thought I'd be exhilarated to return to the city in which I'd left a part of my heart, a quarter century previously. But no.

Three important meetings, that afternoon, paved the way for my summer stay in the university town. A lunch meeting in St. Antony's cafeteria ("buttery") with a sponsoring faculty member tied up loose strings. My Anglo-Indian field research, still on track in London, would be supplemented by examination of official documents in Oxford libraries when summer arrived.

Next, Norham Road in North Oxford to check out accommodation possibilities for international scholars in a sprawling Victorian Gothic manor. Ela Lonsdale, retired Oxford don, stooped with age but slim as a reed and regal, gave me the Grand Tour of her spacious English home—all silver heirlooms, sepia family portraits and weathered wooden furniture. Not half bad. But why was I still morose?

My last meeting was scheduled with Lina Derwent, an administrative aide who'd once handled my summer stay at Exeter College during my graduate student years. Lina who had ascended the bureaucratic ladder welcomed me warmly, barely able to hide her amazement at our reunion after such ages had elapsed. The mousy Indian grad student she had once known who had been too timid to say shoo to a spider, had evolved into a professor at NYU and, come summer, would be a Visiting Scholar at St. Antony's. How had that even happened?

Then, casually, softly as if dropping a tissue, she dropped her bombshell.

"You simply must participate as a guest lecturer in our coming summer program," she invited. "I know we'd all love to have you back!"

I stared at her, aghast. What were the odds that I'd be invited to return as a professor to a graduate literature program in which I'd once been a student myself? Was I agreeable? Er . . . not only was I agreeable, I was eager. I almost exulted, "Show Me The Contract!" There was not a minute to waste setting wheels in motion. Lecturing at Exeter College in the summer would be one of the highlights of my Nearly Perfect Year. My gloominess lifted a tiny fraction.

By the time semi-darkness had wrapped itself around the city, I decided, for old times' sake, to visit Exeter College where my love of Oxford had been born. Was it nostalgia, as I walked past the Porter's Lodge at the entrance, that gripped me with the most fervent longing for my Oxford friends of old scattered around the world? As I strolled through the Fellow's Garden, I remembered every single one of them. We'd sprouted a few pesky wrinkles, all of us, like moist beans do when soaked overnight. And though I'd attempted to turn the clock back by returning to my student days, it was futile. I had to reconcile myself to sad reality—I did not feel like a student anymore and never would again.

And then it dawned upon me with scary certainty—it was the presence of my friends, long disappeared but never forgotten, for whom I'd ached as soon as I'd alighted from the coach on The High that rainy morning. A lone tear of self-pity slid down my cheek as I recalled our collective lost youth. No, you cannot really turn back the clock. At fifty, I could only dwell upon the gift of friendship with which we were all endowed during those idyllic months and feel blessed by its anointing.

It had been a month of mood swings. Fear when my birth city was traumatized by terrorism followed by the thrill of another royal sighting. Elation at election to Oxford as a senior researcher followed by disappointment over continued setbacks with PF. Unabashed Yuletide jollity in London accompanied by a yearning for close friends from a previous epoch in my life.

It was time to return to London to scour *el cheapo* fares and youth hostel websites for another budget bed-down. And it was in Belfast that I had my next hair-raising adventures.

9

TROUBLES IN NORTHERN IRELAND

Belfast! In the winter? What, you might wonder, was I thinking?

What I was thinking were the Giants Causeway and Londonderry. I was seeking political enlightenment on "The Troubles", as the Protestant-Catholic conflict is known. No, seriously. This was going to be a trip about getting to grips with Northern Ireland and when Ryanair offered a £5 one-way fare to Belfast (yes, seriously) plus a BOB named Irene Donovan—a Bombayite married to a Irishman—materialized in Carrickfergus, my travels were a no-brainer. So what if the country was shivering under mid-December's North Sea blasts? I bundled up and was on my way. To yet another youth hostel.

An infinite improvement upon Barcelona's Las Ramblas, the one in Belfast, thankfully, had gender-segregated dorms. In a six-bedded room with bright blue counterpanes, comfortingly thick blankets and (big bonus this, huge) an attached bathroom in our suite. I met Janie—tall, dark curls, heavy glasses, hoodie—and Mathilda ("Call me Mattie")—pretty, long blonde hair, jeans through whose torn windows her knees played peek-a-boo. They were Aussies from Melbourne, spending a year in the UK on work-study visas. I took to them instantly and jumped at their offer to share a giant pizza—barbecue chicken, piping hot. We downed it with lukewarm Cokes as we huddled in our dorm. They explained that since Australia is part of the British Commonwealth, it has reciprocal agreements with the UK to permit students under twenty-six the opportunity to travel and work for a year in the British Isles while experiencing a different culture. Cool!

"Except that this bloody recession has dried up all the bloody jobs," grumbled Janie.

"And British employers feel obligated to employ their own rather than someone from Oz," said Mattie. "Still, I'm lucky. I'm a programmer . . . so there are a few jobs around for me."

"Wish I were a bloody programmer." Janie, a dog groomer, cursed her lack of opportunities, her mouth full of pepperoni.

In the midst of their moaning, Esmeralda arrived from Brazil to occupy a bunk in our room. If she'd turned around for a second, she'd have seen a string of male hearts that had collapsed in her wake all the way from London.

"Hi," she said, blinking sultry eyes around us, "Call me Esme, okay? I traveling in Europe to improve the English."

I blinked. Janie blinked twice. Mattie couldn't stop blinking. "The English? In what way?"

"I am talking to everyone nice things about me cunt . . . ree."

"Bloody hell," said Janie. "Best of luck to you, matie."

"Is anyone going to bathroom? I am desperate wanting for a shower."

"Be our guest," grinned Mathilda.

"It's all yours," I said, suppressing a giggle.

She was in the shower when her love-lorn paramour followed her into our room. "I am Pablo," he said, "Mehican student from Mehiko. Where is the Esme, please?"

Mouths stuffed with pizza, we choked, quite incapable, between the three of us, of getting a syllable out.

"Okay, maybe she be down filling the papers. I came back again . . . soon," he promised.

Esmeralda emerged from the bathroom, blue from nape to heel. "There is not the hot water. I am taking cold shower in this winter. Imagine . . . " She shuddered.

"Oh yeah, I forgot to tell you," said Janie, matter-of-factly. "Hot water is available up to 10 a.m. . . . if you're lucky."

Esmeralda looked as if she could cheerfully strangle Janie.

"Your Pablo was here," said Mattie casually.

"What?? Pablo?? Oh no!! You are sure it is Pablo?" Esmeralda put away her shower gel and said, "I must hide. Quickly at once."

A drama was clearly about to unfold. I cleared up our litter. Janie and Mattie climbed into their top bunks, to watch the fun as if from balcony seats.

"He was in London with me. He has following me here. I think he wants to love me, you know."

"To love you? You mean, he wants to make love to you?" That was Janie.

"Or maybe she means he's in love with her," said Mattie helpfully.

"Yes, yes, how you are saying it? He's already loving me? But I don't want to love him. I must hide. Now."

She was surveying our tiny room looking for hide-and-seek options when Pablo walked in. Fully exposed, she screeched and flew into his arms. "Pablo!!! *Meu amor! Mi amor!*"

"I think that means My Bloody Love!" said Janie.

Meanwhile, Pablo had clasped Esmeralda and covered her face with kisses. Mattie laughed hysterically. I was dumbfounded. Janie pulled out her camera. This was too priceless not to be videotaped.

After an eternity of sighing and kissing, they drew apart. Pablo said something none of us could figure out. Esmeralda responded, he said something else, then disappeared.

Esmeralda sighed. "We are speaking the Spanish. He is not speaking the English well like me . . . or the Portuguese."

"Where'd he go?" Janie asked.

"To improve the Gaelic, maybe?" snorted Mattie, wiping tears off her eyes.

"No, no, he is wanting bed, here in our room."

"WHAT???" We combined forces to do battle. "HERE?"

"NO Bloody Way," shouted Janie.

"Okay, then we will go out. Maybe you know some clubs, yes?"

"To club Pablo with, yes," said Janie under her breath.

"This is a female dorm," I explained in patient professorial fashion. "Pablo will be given a bed in a male dorm."

"But maybe if you all . . . go . . . leave somewhere?"

"NO Bloody Way," shouted Janie again "What bloody cheek!"

"Okay, okay, then we will go out. Maybe not come back."

"Now that's a plan!" said Mattie.

Esmeralda dug about in her backpack and produced a make-up set. The whole darn kit and caboodle. We watched, riveted, as she worked with foundation, blusher, eyeliner, eye shadow, mascara, lipstick, lip gloss, squinting and scowling with each application. She climbed into golden Jimmy Choos (honest, no kidding!) and as she metamorphosed into a supermodel from the runways of Rio, she chattered. "Okay, first we will eat the dinner. After that," she turned to us and shrugged, "who knows?" She left us in a cloud of cologne.

Not long after, the three of us switched lights off and hunkered down for the night. It wasn't more than an hour before someone snapped on the light. I awoke with a start to see Esmeralda and Pablo murmuring by the door. I waited for a few minutes hoping their exchange would be brief. Maybe a long goodnight kiss and he'd be gone.

Meanwhile, Janie had awoken. "What the bloody hell is goin' on?" she demanded.

"It is Pablo," Esmeralda whispered. "He see the empty bunk. He want this room."

"Didn't you tell him we said No Way? What's the bloody time?"

Time for me to enter the fray, methought. Against my better professional judgment, I attempted some damage control: "Now look here, Pablo, if you don't mind, we really don't think . . . "

"Just tell him to fuck the hell off!" screamed Janie to Esmeralda.

That he understood. "You fug off," Pablo screamed back, red in the face. "You all go fug off."

And he turned around and fugged right off. To Be Continued, I thought, as I turned back to sleep.

Esmeralda refused to speak to us for the rest of her stay. One gooseberry she could easily have taken on. Two, a challenge. Three was, most certainly, a crowd.

The next morning, when we awoke, Esmeralda was still asleep her face streaked with smudged mascara. She was alone in her bunk bed or pretended to be. Either Pablo was hiding under the covers or had well and truly vamoosed. We'd never find out as we never saw them again. That was the thing about staying in youth hostels. Bizarre characters came buzzing into your life; but then they left, just as swiftly, and you never ran into them ever again. Usually.

Roller-coasting from one hilarious experience and on to an inspirational one seemed to be the pattern of my days in Northern Ireland. Things looked up again when I met Irene Donovan—not just a BOB but a BOBB—Buddy of my Buddy from Bombay—who arrived at the youth hostel to pick me up for a day's excursion to her neck of the Celtic woods.

"What's this place like?" she asked, glancing around the lobby and suppressing a shudder. She was a petite, pretty, very compact package wrapped in the mahogany skin of India's Keralites.

"You want dramatic travel romance?" I replied. "You've come to the right place! Just get your butt into a bunk and grab some popcorn."

Clutching my elbow as we crossed the street to her car, she laughed and said, "In this country, we say bum."

Irene drove me along the coast to her home where I met her Irish husband, a forest ranger named Declan and her beautiful children, Siobhan, twelve and Rory, five. Five minutes into our meeting I felt as if I'd always known her. There really is such a thing as an instant connection. Either you 'click' with someone or you don't and I was certainly going clickety-click with Irene. We stopped at Ballygally for lunch. I was starving and ordered a horse—well close enough. It was one of those Irish Sunday Roast Dinners, so enormous it could feed an army.

As I exclaimed over them, Irene told me how to make the Roast Potatoes on our platter. I inhaled them hungrily. Wwrrfff! And then they were gone! Oh yes, the Irish sure know their spuds. Only they can get potatoes to cooperate so fully—perfectly mealy on the inside, golden, crispy crust without. What's the secret?

"You have to parboil the potatoes, y'know," Irene began. "Then drain off the water and while they are still in the pot, you hold the lid tightly and shake them violently, y'know. Some people score the potatoes with a fork to make them crispy when they first go into the oven. Pour some oil in a pan and place it in the oven first. The oil has to get hot—and I mean smoking. Then when the parboiled potatoes hit them, you hear the sizzle. That's what gives you the crust. Leave them there for about a half hour to allow the insides to cook. And serve straight away. Straight from the oven."

I gaped. Such a culinary production!

I met Declan and the Donovan children later than afternoon. And what were the first words the very Irish Declan said right after we were introduced?

You got it! "Cuppa Tea?"

To conclude my rambles in Northern Ireland, I'd booked a day-long coastal trip by a company called Paddywagon to Londonderry from Belfast with sundry stops in-between. Janie and Mattie learned of my plans over breakfast and decided to tag along. In bleak weather—meaning roaring wind from off the wild seas and icy needles of rain—we climbed the hexagonal shaped basalt rocks that frame a portion of Northern Ireland's coast known in legend as the Giant's Causeway. After steak and ale pie and a barrel of Guinness at a 'local', we hit the road again passing those legendary forty shades of green. Before we reached Londonderry (say "Derry" unless you want to be attacked by the IRA), the rain stopped.

"We've arrived in Derry," announced our driver, stating the obvious. Our walking tour guide Patrick (of course!) would be along in a minute to lead us, he said.

Patrick ("Call me Paddy") Hannigan was stocky, ruddy, radical. "Stay close by me, mates" he said, "I'm going to show you all the sites." And he did mean sites—not sights. An underground member of the IRA (Irish Republican Army), Paddy was an out-and-out rebel. Too young to have actually lived through the bloodiest battles of the 1980s, he was, nevertheless, one of those Neo-IRA activists still obsessed with liberating the Catholics of Northern Ireland from Protestant British royalist tyranny. Decades of gory struggle had ended with an uneasy truce achieved through Sein Fein's Gerry Adams who had brokered a deal that always seemed on the brink of being scuppered. Yet, almost a decade had passed since the last significant upheavals. Today, Derry extracts tourist currency in clinging on to venues where milestones of the conflict were laid.

Paddy's heavy Irish brogue led us to spots associated with Bloody Sunday when scores of Derry's youth initiated a peaceful march against British rule in the 1980s that ended in violence and bloodshed. In his commentary, he called Prime Minister Thatcher "Maggie" and described her as "a monster." He said she'd left his brothers to rot in jail while they were on a hunger strike in prison. "May she burn in hell someday," he said. Yes, he would take questions and No, he didn't accept the Queen's rule in Northern Ireland and, and yes, as an adult, he had learned to speak Gaelic fluently and no, the friggin' English didn't allow his parents to teach him Gaelic as a kid.

"We are the rebels of tomorrow," he declared, as we stood at a Celtic Memorial Cross to the dead. "These are the true heroes of Northern Ireland," he said, pointing to names engraved in stone, "not those morons in friggin' Stormont." He meant the Parliament in Belfast. More detailed accounts of bloody heroic struggle followed. Patrick didn't edit the gory details. I glanced at my fellow-passengers. Janie'd lost her tongue somewhere along the way. Mattie was brushing away tears.

An Australian, traveling on his honeymoon with his new wife, said, "That's radical, man. You want to start more Troubles? What about the peace process?"

"In your dreams, bro," Patrick replied. "Ireland for the Catholics. We are Irish and we are Catholic and if you don't want to be a Catholic in Ireland, you can go to friggin' England, okay?"

"Mind your tongue!" said the Ozzie. "I didn't fork out all those euros to listen to abuse."

"You tellin' me how to conduct this tour?" said Paddy, getting more belligerent by the minute.

"I'm telling you I didn't think our tour would throw in an attempt to brainwash participants. You'll want to stop now."

"Or else?" said Paddy, advancing towards Ozzie.

Janie might have stopped speaking, but I'd stopped breathing. The last thing I wished was to see our walking tour turning into a Bloody Monday!

"Or else I'm getting off this tour now. And complaining to Paddywagon. They got to get their guides' heads examined."

"Are you threatening me?" asked Paddy becoming puce.

"I'm telling you to do your job. Be a guide. Save the propaganda for your next political rally."

Ozzie then turned to us. "What do the rest of you guys think, eh? Am I being unreasonable? He's been feeding us blobs of baloney all afternoon."

"Baloney?" said Paddy. "Which bit of my balo . . . er, my commentary . . . was untrue?" He challenged us collectively.

Put on the spot, most of us shifted uncomfortably. I did not wish to get dragged into their fracas.

"Say something," provoked Ozzie. "What are you guys? A bunch of Wooses or what?

His new wife had the good sense to step in. "Honey," she began. "Don't you think it's moronic?"

But she never had a chance to finish. "The only moron is the one right here in front of us," said her husband, sticking his finger at Paddy.

"Who're you calling a friggin' moron?" asked Paddy.

"You, pal. You got a problem with that?"

"You bet I have," said Paddy, reaching way up high and depositing a solid blow on to Ozzie's jaw. There was a sickening thwack as Ozzie staggered back clutching his face. His wife shrieked and hurled herself at him.

They did it. They had actually come to blows. A tour about Irish violence had turned violent in front of my disbelieving eyes.

Ozzie recovered and approached Paddy menacingly. "You want a fight? Right. Bring it on."

Paddy would have to be demented to rise to the challenge. He was no taller than five and a half feet while Ozzie towered over him at well over six.

"No!" his wife screamed. "Stop it right now, the two of you." She glowered at her husband and continued. "If you don't end it this minute, I'm leaving. Right now." And she turned and stalked away. Which was why she did not see the ringing blow that her husband gave Paddy who apparently saw stars as he sank to his feet. We watched in horror as Ozzie turned calmly away, dusting his hands off as if in some B-grade spaghetti Western flic and followed his wife. Paddy tried valiantly to get off the ground but the wind seemed to have been robbed right from his sails. Other members of our tour group disappeared like greased lightning, none wishing to get involved. It took Janie, Mattie and me to lift him off the ground and steady him on his feet. He was crimson and although mentally he itched for more, it was clear that he was outdone by Ozzie's larger girth. The Aussies were nowhere on the scene as our coach made its subdued way back to Belfast.

So I'd wanted to find out if Northern Ireland was still wracked by religious divisions, yes? I'd wanted to see the impact of The Troubles, right? I'd wanted to find out how far the national psyche had been affected by the mood of loss and mourning, correct? Well, I asked myself, had it been grim enough for me? Had I learned enough? Later, Janie, Mathilda and I drowned our shock in Magner's cider at *The Crown*, Belfast's oldest pub.

While flying above the Isle of Man en route to London, I decided, Okay, not all youth hostels are the pits. This one wasn't too bad if you could discount the Esmeralda drama. Plus I'd made two good gal pals. On the other hand, there was no privacy, no hot running water and a never-ending pantheon of weirdos.

Then I'd get home to Holborn, take a look at my credit card statement and discover that I'd paid less than a hundred dollars for five nights in the center of a European city. I'd shrug off the inconveniences and think, how can you possibly beat that during a recession? And where on God's earth would I find roomies to provide such unfailing built-in entertainment?

Youth Hostels were far from my mind as my thoughts flew across the Atlantic to sleep in my own bed and shower in my own bathtub as I prepared to spend Christmas in Connecticut.

10

A TRANSNATIONAL CHRISTMAS SEASON

Christmas was a week away when I stepped out my Holborn door for the ride to Heathrow and the long haul across the Atlantic. New York was still snoring when Hubs picked me up at Kennedy where typical crystalline rain of a North Atlantic winter lashed the city. Icy driving conditions had me on edge all the way from Queens to Connecticut when I forced myself to burst out of my British Bubble. How happy I'd been within the little globe of my own making at High Holborn. Hopefully, given the global fiscal crisis, getting back Stateside would not be too traumatic.

By the time, our car was turning into our driveway at Holly Berry House in Southport, Connecticut, a precarious skating rink over which it needed coaxing to reach our garage door, I was ready to have a memorable Christmas. There had never been any doubt that I would leave London to be home in Southport, our picturesque New England sailing village, at Christmas—hence all the frantic Oxford Street, Piccadilly and Knightsbridge shopping that had preceded my departure. But the sheer elation I expected to feel at finding myself back home after five whole months away was dampened by jarring global goings-on as well as the sense that newly-evolved Minimalist Me had become a stranger in her own *milieu*. Was this what London had done to me in just one semester?

Christmas Day dawned laundry clean and crispy white, our garden held firmly in a snowstorm's glistening grip. Had I dreamed of a White

Christmas, I couldn't have been more delighted. For the first few moments on awaking, my eyes still firmly shut, I had no idea where I was.
The surrounding silence of our Southport village was complete and
added to my sense of bewilderment. Was I in London? Or Athens?
Barcelona? Or Belfast? I'd lost track of time and place and distance.
Opening one eye, very slowly, I spied our navy blue comforter draped
tightly around me and knew then that I was home in Connecticut. But
for those few elemental seconds, the sense of being suspended in obliv-
ion was the strangest in the world.

By the time they staggered in through the front door in the late
afternoon, laden like Santa with bulging sacks, I couldn't wait to see my
newly-engaged daughter and her handsome fiancé again. Peach Bellinis
were sipped after Dot and Colin extricated themselves from warm
hugs, a hundred kisses, a gazillion giggles. Colin focused on swallowing
malaria pills as he prepped for his trip to Bombay less than a week
away. In a nod to my British sojourn, I flambéed *Harrod's* pud carted
across the Atlantic, poured over the molten gold of brandy butter,
clutched at silver pennies concealed in each boozy wedge and sighed
contentedly.

On Boxing Day at dawn, we drove out again into the ice-skating rink
of our Connecticut driveway to board a flight at Kennedy airport. For
the second time in a week. I'd be airborne over the Atlantic, winging it
away with Dot and Colin to Bombay.

Less than twenty-four hours later, I was on the other side of the globe.
How marvelous to be gifted, during my fiftieth year, the opportunity to
return to my childhood home where so much of my past had been tied
up! My parents' flat in the upscale Bombay suburb of Bandra is a shoe-
box, tiny even by Manhattan standards. At best, a tight squeeze for us
all, it would be cruel and unusual punishment to subject Colin to a
sardine can for his first visit with Dot's grandparents. Stepping in handily was my friend Farhad who offered us an empty studio flat he owned
nearby. Clearly God-Sent.

Only Farhad, unwittingly, made one big error—and I mean, massive. Playing it strictly by the rule book, he'd informed the building
authorities that a "foreigner" would be occupying his studio for two
weeks. That did it! Barely six weeks after the worst terrorist catastrophe
had hit their city, Bombayites had become paranoid about foreigners—

and who could blame them? After all, it was a bunch of foreigners, albeit from Pakistan, who'd infiltrated their city and terrorized it. According to newly-enacted tenancy laws, foreigners were scrutinized and vetted. The building authorities flew into a panic. No keys could be handed over to Colin, they decreed, until we obtained written permission from police headquarters in Central Bombay!

Yeah right, said Dad. Getting police permission for anything in Bombay was akin to Edmund Hilary attempting to conquer Everest while afflicted by PF in both feet! It was not happening! But because we didn't want to give up without trying, off we went on a hair-tearing, nail-biting journey the likes of which Kafka could never have conjured in his worst nightmares.

Dad and Colin, Dot and I were dispatched from pillar to post on a wild goose chase. We brooded for hours in musty bureaucratic corridors of police precincts, at the mercy of underlings, awaiting big guns who never showed. It was little short of gruesome. Finally, after three days of disappointment had tested our stores of patience to their collective limits, wisdom dictated we drop all plans for Colin's move into Farhad's studio as we scrunched him into my parents' flat. Somehow.

I turned my thoughts towards healing my feet. London doctors had convinced me that there was no treatment for plantar fasciitis in allopathy. Homeopathy, however, had just the thing. And, as so often happens in Bombay, networking unearths Someone who knows Someone who introduces you to Someone who cured Someone of Something.

So, my cousin Bella took me to Dr. Anita Nair. She was a homeopath of thirty years' experience by whom Bella's entire family swore.

I was frankly skeptical. How could tiny white sugar pills sooth the ravaged ligaments of my soles when the miracles of modern Western medicine had nothing to offer? Still, I made the pilgrimage to her modest little dispensary where I met Dr. Nair who asked me the most unexpected questions.

"What's your favorite form of exercise?"

"Taking long walks . . . but that's what gave me this condition in the first place."

"Correction," said Dr. Nair, sternly. "Walking didn't give you this problem. Walking with the wrong kind of shoes brought it on. You'd have been fine with well-supported arches."

I left with a bottle of six months worth of medication to swallow while in London.

Bummer! I'd expected to start 2009 with a miraculous overnight recovery.

My detour to Bombay during my Nearly Perfect Year in London offered the opportunity to sail on waves of nostalgia. By the time I hugged my doting parents goodbye to board a Jet Airways flight back to Heathrow, my Indian heart had been warmed by the generous hospitality of immediate and extended family. We had been treated like royalty, plied everywhere with foods to pacify the gods and affection as only close relatives can dole. As an immigrant in the West, how much I had missed that tender feeling of being enwrapped in the close embrace of family! I packed my memories into my baggage knowing that they would sustain me through several more months as a Singleton when I disembarked in London leaving Colin and Dot to continue their flight to New York.

My dawn landing at Heathrow in the middle of January found London engulfed by uniform arctic greyness. The capital seemed scrubbed of every tint and hue. Oh, but was I buzzed about being back!

At High Holborn, my concierge Aren gave me a hero's welcome in the lobby. How oddly like home my little flat felt! How great it was to nestle once again in my enveloping private cocoon! I couldn't wait to settle into my solitary life after Bombay's crowds and craziness. In three months, that coming April, I'd have spent twenty years as an immigrant in the West. And how much like a Westerner I'd become, I marveled, after two decades in America. I had actually begun to crave Space—a concept unheard of in India. Yet, simultaneously, I missed my Bombay family sorely.

Wasting little time, I hit post-Christmas sales at *Harrods* and *Fortnum's* with the zeal of a seasoned shopaholic. Winter also brought incredible travel bargains from budget airlines upon which I swooped, pronto.

The new year's first month ended on a historic note as I watched the investiture of a new President on TV. My students invited me to Inauguration parties but I preferred to mark the unique moment in time *toute seule* in the privacy of my High Holborn haven. Then, feeling much too lonely on such a landmark evening—for the time difference had already brought darkness down upon London as Obama took his oath in Washington D.C.—I had both Hubs and Dot on the phone with me as we rejoiced together, able to watch events unfold simultaneously. I clicked away at my TV screen hoping to memorialize the moments, knowing that, in years to come, I'd proudly say I was lolloping around the telly in my London flat when America put a black family in the White House. I might have deliberately blotted out the run-up to a US election, but I was a proud expatriate American as I watched its ultimate results.

And then I went to Berlin.

Remember Ulrike? And Giovanni? The lovely pair Hubs and I'd met in Athens? Remember Ulrike making me promise I'd contact her if I was ever in Berlin? Well, I did. Truth can be stranger than fiction. I had another youth hostel at Potsdammer Straße in mind but Ulrike responded immediately and generously when she offered an alternative housing possibility. My own private place in her friend Anneke's studio. I leapt at it. My head did not need examining after all.

I arrived at Schonefelt airport in Berlin after 9:00 p.m. on a frigid night. I've always abhorred arriving in a strange city after dark, especially when I cannot speak the local lingo and my German was restricted to *Jah! Jah!* Anneke's empty apartment was slap bang in Charlottenburg in the city's upscale West End. This would be a definite improvement on youth hostels, I thought, grateful for the arrangements. Alighting from the S-Bahn (the local railway network) at Hallensee, I found myself on a cobbled street called Halberstädter Straße just off another cobbled street called Sessener Straße (how I loved these names—and saying them!). And by the time my stay in Berlin was through, I felt as if I had strayed into half a dozen Hollywood classics.

Just when I'd started to believe I'd conquered my groundless fears of being alone, they resurfaced to haunt me, close to midnight, on the antiquated street, lit with the dimmest of lights, much too few and far-between for my comfort. Dread came rushing back to tap me on my shoulder and make me as skittish as a colt at the knowledge that there wasn't another soul in sight. As I dragged my trolley along the cobbles, the clattering echoed eerily, while my plantar protested at being subject to the torture of bulging uneven stones on which I trod.

Shivering under sub-zero temperatures, I reached the building where, to my enormous relief, I found Giovanni who gave me a tour of the warmed apartment, although, truth be told, there wasn't really very much to show. It was the sort of bohemian space customarily occupied by the concierge in European *film noir*. One large room filled with books and bookshelves, old armoires and a writing table formed the main living space. A thick mattress on the floor was a make-shift bed. Giovanni forgot to point out one crucial detail—a large wicker basket containing bed linen and duvets. Because I resisted the urge to snoop around in someone else's space, for the next four nights, I huddled under my own down coat that doubled up as a blanket, cold, uncomfortable, uneasy. A youth hostel bunk bed in Potsdammer Straße appeared deluxe by comparison—at least I'd be toasty at night!

Before he left, I turned to Giovanni and asked, "So, where's the bathroom?"

"Ah," he said, using almost all the English he could boast. He led me to the basement downstairs, reached by descending a spiral wrought iron staircase, where I found a single old-world, claw-footed bathtub and a wash basin overlooked by a curtainless window. Much as Giovanni assured me that no Peeping Tom could practice his voyeuristic skills during my cleansing rituals, I remained unconvinced. Bath times were stress-filled episodes in attempting to remain undetected by passing perverts.

"And where's the toilet?" I asked, alarm growing by the second.

"Ah," he said and handed me a key. Only then did it dawn on me that the toilet, a tiny private cubicle really, was half a mile down a lonely dark hallway that twisted and turned past a few other apartments and an ornate wrought-iron elevator like the one in Alfred Hitchcock's *Charade*. It didn't help to recall vividly, at exactly that moment, a scene in the film in which at least one character is found murdered in said elevator! God forbid if I needed to use the facilities in the dead of night. Wild pachyderms, I knew, would not drag me there. Before he departed, Giovanni handed me another key—to the building's imposing main door that opened out into a vast hallway with a great big marble fireplace.

I was convinced then that I wasn't completely over my fears of domestic solitude and deserted dark spaces. Not by a long shot. As I snuggled under my down coat reading a Harry Potter paperback until my eyelids drooped, I tried to think comforting thoughts while praying that fatigue and jet lag would combine forces to lull me to sleep.

In the clear light of day, my surroundings were evocative of old German films starring Marlena Dietrich. Hesitantly, I parted curtains to peek at cobbled grey streets, shiny as glass, under overcast skies. Through five long days and nights in Berlin, I did not see the sun at all.

Descending on tenterhooks into the basement kitchen in the morning, I found Audrey Hepburn winking cheekily, Cary Grant smiling raffishly, Shirley McLaine and Sophia Loren posing sexily and John Wayne leering at me with hands on cowboy hips from life-size black and white posters. Anneke, I later learned, completed Film Studies in America and was in love with 1950s Hollywood classics.

Parts of Germany had still dwelled behind the Iron Curtain when I'd backpacked across Europe, more than two decades previously, as a grad student in England. This time round, the city was my oyster as I rode in buses up and down Kurfunstendamm (say "Ku-damm") and Unter der Linden, took walking tours through former East and West Berlin in the bitter cold, condensation billowing around me with every breath. Being a history-buff, I never met a museum I did not love and Berlin provided plenty into which I could escape the biting cold. Indeed the entire city was a living museum for, at every turn, reminders of its eventful past, from its squat Soviet-era buildings to its antiquated trams, brushed by me.

But every evening, upon my return from the Pergammon Museum or the Gemaldegalerie after gawking at treasures like the Ishtar Gates and the wonders of Vermeer and Caravaggio, the prospect of making my way from the bus stop to the building was a stupendous challenge I felt determined to conquer for the cold had left the side streets empty. On the second evening, I made certain I reached my apartment before sundown so a blue-grey twilight could illuminate my path to the building's front door. On the third evening, I lingered outside longer but still got back before darkness settled over the cobbles. But, by the fourth evening, I resolved to look fear in the face. I'd become accustomed enough to the neighborhood and the building to get a grip. I deliberately returned home just a little later each evening—still never sighting another soul—until advancing darkness and silent streets no longer bothered me. It was one more positive step I took in the war against my own inner demons. I drew the line, though, at visiting the facilities in the middle of the night!

The next morning, my fifth one in Berlin, just when I was brushing away crumbs from the packaged chocolate croissants I had consumed at breakfast and draining the last dregs of my instant coffee concocted on a pre-war gas cooking ring, I heard a key jiggling at my front door as someone attempted to enter. My blood ran cold. Who was it? And what did he or she want?

The jiggling continued but the intruder could not enter as I had very firmly latched the door and secured the chain. Realizing that there was no way he could enter, the caller rang the doorbell.

I was petrified. Was it a Peeping Tom? Someone who knew I was alone and ill-at-ease on my ownsome amidst these strange surroundings? I shuddered. The bell rang again. It was time to confront the caller.

I opened my front door a tiny slit, keeping the security chain on, to see a gruff-looking man, swarthy skinned, mustachioed and overweight. Middle Eastern, I'd guess, by the looks of him.

"*Fraulein . . .* " he began. A string of unintelligible words followed. He held up the key he had used to try to get in and to indicate that he was no intruder.

"*No speken ze Deutsch,*" I responded in some bastardized version of what I thought was German.

"English?" I offered.

"Eengleesh. *Nein. Nein.*"

He glared at me and said, "*Francais?*"

"*Oui, oui. Je parle francais,*" I responded in relief.

But he only stared back blankly.

We gazed at each other, the conversation going nowhere from that point onward, until he said, suddenly, "*Moment*" and hurried away.

He was back in two ticks. This time he brought along a burly white woman with a flushed face, clad in a plastic apron and carrying an assortment of cleaning paraphernalia.

Ah-ha. This was the cleaning crew. But why hadn't anyone told me about them? And was it safe to allow them inside? What if I was being taken for a jolly ride by a pair of thieves disguised as cleaners well aware that I was a foreigner in a strange *milieu*?

"*On va nettoyer . . .*" began the woman, a French speaker but, going by her accent, clearly not a native one. Eastern European perhaps. The man behind her nodded enthusiastically.

"*Pouvez-vous venir apres Dimanche?*" I began. I would be gone by Sunday. Would they return then, I inquired.

"*Lundi? Mais non. Nous sommes tres occupé tous les jours,*" she huffed, annoyed. Nope, not Monday. They were busy every day.

"*Alors . . . demain peut-etre?*" If they appeared tomorrow, they would leave me time to find out who they were and if it was safe to allow them inside.

"*Demain? Ce n'est pas possible. Aujourd-hui,*" she declared firmly. Negative again. It would have to be today. Here. And now.

I still stood steadfastly guarding the door to prevent their entry, my mind racing. Whom could I turn to for confirmation? Ulrike was not in Berlin and I had not thought to take Giovanni's number. Somewhere in the apartment, he had left Anneke's number for me, but she was in the Black Forest apparently, ensconced in her mountain lodge. I was nonplussed.

"*Depechez-vous,*" said the woman, brusquely. "*Allez. Maintenant.*" I had to hurry.

Merde! Only in Berlin, crossroads of modern-day Europe, would one find a Turkish man named Bayram and a Polish woman named Antonia speaking French to an Indian woman from Bombay in a studio that belonged to a German named Anneke who thrived on American classical cinema. The perils of globalization. And as I contemplated the paradoxes of my situation, I undid the security latches. They bustled in, clearly in a hurry and annoyed by my vigilance.

Before I could protest further, Antonia was shoving me aside and bamboozling her way in. Bayram followed resolutely. They set to work, the two of them, while I watched bewildered. What if they stripped the apartment in the process of airing it out? I resolved to watch them like a hawk. But when she disappeared into the kitchen-cum-bathroom down the spiral stairs and he plugged in the vacuum on the upper level where I stood, I was at a loss. Obviously, my frugal belongings that reposed in my backpack close to my make-shift bed on the floor needed protection, but I could not be in two places at the same time. Probably the most valuable items I owned were my passport and credit card and they were in my cross-body handbag, on a nearby table. I refused to let those documents out of my sight.

There was nothing else to do but remain glued upstairs while he moved light furniture around to hoover the carpet. As he worked, he muttered. Occasionally he shooed me from one side of the room to the other as he snorted like an angry horse. My presence was clearly considered an intrusion. Only the lack of linguistic comprehension between the two of us prevented our encounter from becoming verbally abusive.

Meanwhile, I could hear Antonia downstairs. Pots and pans were banged about as she neatened countertops. From time to time, they shouted instructions at each other. About a half hour later, I heard water running downstairs as she whooshed it around the bathtub. Meanwhile, upstairs, he began dusting. Tabletop items—framed photographs and paperweights—were shifted around as he worked with aerosol furniture polish and a duster. I had to commend the thoroughness of his endeavors as he fluffed and dusted and blew. The tangy fragrance of lemon assailed the apartment. When he was done dusting, he moved to the windows to swish each glass pane with a liquid window cleanser, moving his duster around in concentric circles till each one sparkled.

Half an hour later, he joined Antonia downstairs, leaving me with no choice but to follow him down the wrought-iron staircase. She had been as thorough as he had, using sweat equity to make the kitchen spotless. She tsked and tsked again when she saw me, pointing to my recently-consumed breakfast and indicating that she wanted me to clear it up. He scrubbed the bath tub while she polished the faucet and the mirror at the wash-basin. I hurriedly closed up the package of croissants, moved my coffee mug to the enamel sink which had been so perfectly polished I was loathe to ruin it. The kitchen too smelled refreshingly clean, lavished clearly with an abundance of liquid cleansers.

Another half hour later, they were done. Not a thing was out of place. Both upstairs and down, the apartment shone like a centerfold in an interior decorating magazine.

Then, quite suddenly, he turned to me, snarled *"Fraulein"*, held out his hand and kept twisting his wrist. I stared clueless.

Antonia intervened. *"Le cle, s'il-vous plait, madam?"* The key!

"Quel cle?" I said.

"Le cle pour la toilette." She rolled her eyes. *"On va nettoyer le toilette maintenant."* Of course! They wanted the key to the toilet outside so they could complete spitting and polishing.

"Ah, d'accord. Bien sur."

The desired key changed hands and the pair disappeared down the hallway taking their mops, brooms, pails, cleaning products and vacuum cleaner with them. It had occurred to me by then that Anneke probably had some kind of arrangement that brought them to her studio on a regular schedule to clean it. If only I'd been told I'd have been more prepared, less apprehensive.

Twenty minutes later, they returned the toilet key to me and as Bayram muttered, Antonia said, *"Au Revoir"* and they parted company with me and drove off to their next cleaning appointment.

The studio in Charlottenburg was empty once again and as soundless as a cemetery. But for the delicious fragrance that lingered for the next couple of days, there was no sign of their occupancy.

On my last day in Berlin, Ulrike returned from Munich. We had a very fond reunion and a non-stop chinwag before she volunteered to show me more atmospheric pre-war parts of the city in the extreme East End called Prenzlauer Berg. At the *knodel* and *spatzel* dinner to which I treated her that evening in a lovely rustic restaurant filled with the fragrance of roasted meat, broiled potatoes and grilled cheese, I finally feasted on local and regional Bavarian cuisine—a relief from the *wurst* sandwiches and Richter-Sport's rum and raisin chocolate on which I'd survived.

How did it work out with Anneke's apartment? Ulrike wondered. I recounted, my escapade with the cleaners, my chilly adventures in the studio and my lack of blankets or comforters to keep me warm at night. Probably because she took pity on my sleep-deprivation, she offered to spend my last night in Berlin with me in Charlottenburg. Yeeeessss! I mean *Jaaahhhh!!*

Back at Anneke's, she threw open the armoire and a mammoth wicker basket in the living room to expose dozens of down duvets and blankets hidden in them. Darn! Why hadn't I been impolite enough to snoop around? Under their warmth, I slept the sleep of the dead that night while Ulrike shared my double mattress on the floor. At dawn, while Berlin remained swaddled in sleep, I walked with her down those cobbled streets for the last time to the train station to board the one that dropped me off to the airport for my return flight to London. As we kissed goodbye, we knew we'd see each other again in Italy, as Ulrike had promised to attend a lecture I was invited to give in the spring at the University of Padua.

Astride the Berlin Wall I had stood with one foot in former East Berlin, the other in the democratic West. I had been photographed at Checkpoint Charlie with actor-imposters masquerading as pre-World War II Yankee soldiers. With every step I had taken, I became re-acquainted with Berlin's compelling mid-century past. But evocative as these experiences were, none made history more real and alive for me than actually living in Anneke's apartment in a building and neighbor-hood that might well have housed Jewish tenants during those menac-ing times as I was confronted by a menacing couple who made their living in the newly-unified Germany as cleaners. Each glacial evening, when I turned the key in the door, a la Sally Bowles in her Nazi-ravaged garret in Christopher Isherwood's *Berlin Diary*, I was whisked back to that Hitlerian era when flappers made cabaret the preferred form of entertainment.

I returned to London wondering what else lay in store for me. I never knew on which floor the elevator of life would set me down for the next close encounter of a weird kind. So I almost wept with relief when Samantha barged into my life.

11

FREEZING IN FEBRUARY

"So, what do you think? Did Charles ever really love Diana?" asked Samantha Prescott who entered my life in London not like a breath but a whole whooshing breeze of fresh air bringing with it a personality to match. She was yet another BOB introduced to me in cyberspace through a New York-based mutual friend named Amelia. Beautiful, funny, friendly, warm, confident, thirty-something, I warmed to my young friend the instant I laid eyes on her. Imagine, if you can, my joy in finding a single, female, fellow-American, car owner, also afflicted with wanderlust who just happened to be as heart whole and fancy free as yours truly? I hadn't prayed for a soul mate and kindred spirit in London, but she was another example of God's ceaseless munificence.

Samantha arrived from New York for a year through a posting with the famed British tea company for which she'd worked as a marketing whiz kid in Manhattan. Still a tad nervous about negotiating a stick shift car on the other side of the road, she took a couple of driving lessons before sallying forth in her spiffy, company-provided, nautical blue Lexus. Within weeks of her settling in Wimbledon, London, I placed myself in her shaky chauffeuring hands as she surrendered herself into my navigational ones. Together we made a formidable team each weekend as we hit the motorway, sometimes in fair weather, but mostly foul.

It was when she discovered my avid love of British History that she began to ask me the most impossible questions, probably believing I had insider information—such as the one about Charles and Diana. Another time, she asked, "So how did Albert feel about being a mere

Prince while his Victoria was Queen?" And my personal favorite, "Was Elizabeth the First really a virgin?"

In Sam's company there was never a dull moment. My weekends looked up distinctly after she staged her appearance.

Our first destination together was Rochester in the Garden of England, Kent. Astride the Medway that flowed sluggishly in an unsightly shade of yellow, Rochester sat brooding over its lengthy history on a miserable day when it bucketed down, not in sheets, but in an annoyingly persistent drizzle. It was uncomfortably cold as we huddled into bulky coats and headed straight to the High Street for a heartily traditional Sunday Roast at The King's Head pub . I became convinced that I was destined to make friends with Sam when I discovered that we shared an uninhibited appetite for food and owned the same book: *25 Daytrips from London!* Don't great minds think alike?

And then, one weekend later, I was with Samantha in the town of Battle in Sussex when it began—the Mother of All Snowstorms. On a Sunday so bracingly cold we layered like Eskimos and still felt like ice-cubes, I battled the Mother of All Winter Colds and headed for the Hastings coast.

We'd just finished touring the barren field on which England's most significant battle had been fought in 1066 when William the Conqueror of Normandy in France had met the Anglo-Saxon King Harold and trounced him. Samantha turned to me and asked, "Did you just feel that flake?" holding out her hands to collect powdery deposits that dusted our locks to give us the appearance of wigged QCs.

I had indeed. With dread. We had a long drive home and neither of us fancied sliding on the motorway. Twilight and a full-blown snowstorm had fallen over arguably England's most historic town as we drove home in terrified silence.

More than an hour later, as the outskirts of London appeared vaguely through our windshield darkly, I gazed fearfully at glacial skies that forewarned a mammoth blizzard.

Snow fell throughout that night. On Monday morning, High Holborn was a sugar-dusted fairy tale lane. Enchanted, I stuck my camera out the window to capture images of beautiful medieval Staple Inn, slumped under what appeared to be thick white royal icing.

I snozzled my way through a cold the same week England had her worst blizzard in twenty years bringing normal life to its knees. Ever conscious of the call to duty, however, I set out, a hoarse whisper, having pulled on my snow boots, to teach my classes, thinking nothing of braving large flakes and the crusty white build-up.

At his post in the lobby below, my concierge Aren was dubious. "You really want to walk to Bloomsbury in this mess?" he asked, gazing wondrously at swirling flakes.

Shrugging off his concern, I stepped up to my knees in a deep snowdrift outside the door to our building, unable to fathom what all the fuss was about. I hadn't lived in New England for nearly two decades without learning how to cope with winter's vagaries, had I?

But only a few feet down the street, I was baffled. Walking in the snowdrifts of these streets was a far cry from treading well-plowed ones in Manhattan. Where were London's snowplows? Why were the pavements still snowbound? Why hadn't shop owners shoveled their doorways? Apparently, they didn't own shovels! Where had all the red buses gone? And the black cabs? Off the roads, that's where!

Walking gingerly on PF-afflicted feet, risking slippage with every step, I arrived at the entrance of NYU at Bedford Square to find a group of students seated glumly on the steps. Their relief at seeing me turned quickly to disappointment on discovering that I did not possess keys to unlock the main door. Security staff, it appeared, hadn't been able to get to work as Tube lines had come to a grinding halt.

With six inches of snow? No way. Though flakes had long stopped falling, schools were closed, nation-wide. What? Why? Was this London or Vladivostok?

Far from giving in to their Inner Kid on this freakish impromptu playground, Londoners trudged as if shell shocked. They had clearly never seen anything quite so awesome. They stepped carefully in their trainers—none possessing snow boots—over slushy sidewalks. They took pictures of snow piles on their own doorsteps.

A few minutes later, I received the news from one of the few administrators whose phone number I happened to have saved in my mobile. In the distant suburb in which she lived, she had appeared incredulous on finding out that I was outside our building expecting someone to show up. After making a few calls herself, she phoned me back to confirm that the university was declared closed for the day. So as the

UK sorted itself out on one of the most frigid days in its memory, I stayed cocooned at home, nursing my cold, swallowing warming medicated lemon-honey concoctions and stirring soups I concocted with zeal—gingered carrot and butternut squash with orange.

Imagine how ecstatic I was when my doorbell rang that evening and NextDoor Tom invited me to join him and Brenda for that most British of fish dishes, kedgeree. I was there is a heartbeat bearing my soup. I drank rivers of cider before we tucked into an Anglo-Indian mélange of boiled basmati rice, smoked haddock and peas, lovingly brought back to Blighty in their tiffins by former Rajwallahs. It was beastly outside, but indoors I nestled deliciously with my friendly neighbors who provided sustenance that took me back home to my Mum's kitchen in India and her 'khichdi' as we indulged in the color of turmeric and the flavor of cumin.

I waited out the blizzard that, somewhat unbelievably, made global headlines for it had closed Heathrow airport and disrupted international air traffic. Dodging February's wintry bite closeted in heated museums. I met strange characters in red buses into which I escaped winter's merciless blasts.

Living alone for a year often meant doing the American thing—getting into friendly chitchat with strangers. Barney breezed in, one grey afternoon, nearly falling over as he breaststroked himself into the seat beside me and instantly struck up a conversation at the heated upper deck's picture windows.

"Everyone thinks I'm mad," he began gruffly, "but I'm only a paranoid schizophrenic."

Yeah, like that was a big consolation. Next thing I knew, he proudly extracted a small glass phial out of his back pocket and showed me the cocktail his medics had prescribed so he could stay functional.

"I need to take these as injections," he said. "They allow me to feel normal. They really work. On my bottom."

Me: "Hmmm." (TMIP. Too Much Info, Pal.)

He: "Oh and so's my wife. Paranoid, I mean, but she's worse. She doesn't take her medicine and she goes wandering about." His spit flew into my face.

My heart bled for the poor man. He shot rapid questions at me while slurping coffee in great big gulps out of a paper cup.

Once again, I'd stepped outside the box. Abandoning my inhibitions so completely was not something Pre-London Rochelle would ever do. Yet, rather like having picked up Brendan, the hitchhiker in Scotland, my impulsive exchange with Barney was quite obviously the result of finding myself in an alien environment in which such odd encounters seemed like the most natural things in the world. Or perhaps it was simply that being alone so much, I had begun to crave conversation with anyone at all.

When we arrived at Kensington, I rose from my seat, politely wished him goodbye and proceeded to alight from the bus, only to discover, to my astonishment, that he followed me out.

"I'll come along to the Museum too," he said. "You can show me your favorite bits."

Once inside, I attempted to lose him but Barney was an assiduous stalker.

"OK," he said, "so, where do we begin?"

"If this is your fist time here, why don't you take a guided tour?" I suggested, gently. It was clear to me that Barney was lonely, craved company and wasn't going to let me out of his sight. In my own self-imposed solitude, it was something with which I could empathize. Having found me on the bus, he had latched on and would cling on for dear life. I had to find a way to shake him off without being unkind.

"I don't like guides," he said. "They talk too fast and they glare at me when I ask questions."

"Right," I said, "let's begin in the Cast Courts then, shall we?"

I led him to the vast gallery that contained some of the world's most recognizable sculpture: *Trajan's Column* from Rome, the main doorway of Chartres Cathedral in France, Donatello's *David* from the Bargello and Michelangelo's *David* from the Academia, both in Florence. Barney looked enthralled. Then he asked, "Why are all these foreign things here?"

"Well, the idea was to bring the world to Londoners who did not have the opportunity or the means to travel. In this one room, you can travel all around the world and see some of its greatest sculpture," I said.

Barney didn't seem convinced. "Why isn't David wearing his trousers?" he asked.

"Well . . . that's how Donatello and Michelangelo chose to portray him."

"But Donatello's given him this fancy hat. Why not a nice pair of slacks as well?"

I was beginning to realize how impossible it would be to shake Barney off, when a thought struck me. I could send him off to another section to explore on his own.

"My actual favorite places here are the Jewelry Galleries upstairs," I said. "Would you like to go there yourself and see diamonds, emeralds and rubies as large as hen's eggs?"

"That big?" he laughed uproariously. "Hen's eggs! Really?"

"Close," I said. "I could spend a whole day in those rooms. I think you'd like those."

"Does the jewelry belong to Queen Victoria? Were they gifts from Albert?"

"Not really. But there is some really fab Victorian jewelry there."

Just when it seemed as if I was well and truly stuck with him, he said, "Nah! I've had enough. Too many foreign things in this place."

"Well, what would you expect? This is a museum, you know." I was beginning to get a tad impatient and I was afraid it would be reflected in my tone of voice.

"It's the V and A," he said, solemnly. "I thought it would be full of things that belonged to them."

"To whom?"

"To V and A! Victoria and Albert! Like the name says."

Duh me!

But just as suddenly, before I quite had the chance to say Bye, he turned away and said, "That's it for me. If this museum does not have things that belong to Victoria and Albert and if I cannot see things from my country, I'm not interested."

And with those haughty words and that decidedly firm opinion, he simply shuffled off leaving me to look at the back of him in bewilderment.

A patriotic paranoid schizophrenic stalker. I had become a Weirdo Magnet.

And then five minutes later, I met Jennifer Helton, Highlights tour guide, who seemingly moonlighted as a medico. When she noticed that

I was not only the sole visitor taking her tour but that I looked for a place to squat at every object to which she led me, she asked if I was ill.

"Just afflicted with plantar fasciitis," I said, thinking that it sounded far more dreadful than it would seem to an onlooker and would involve a lengthy explanation.

"Oh, I had that," she said, breezily, "and I know how to cure it."

Oh yes? When the entire medical world was convinced that no cure existed, I had to bump into someone who had it down pat. What were the odds?

And so it happened that in the V&A, I met a fellow docent afflicted with PF. Was that meant to be? Perhaps. Because when her excellent tour was over, she turned to the topic of my obstinately afflicted feet.

"How long have you had it?" she asked.

"About six months."

"No improvement since it began?"

"Well . . . it often starts to feel better. But then I get impatient just hanging around and aggravate it by going on yet another trip. Or taking another long walk. Or another guided tour in a museum. I haven't really given my feet a complete chance to heal."

She nodded sagely, then revealed her secret.

"Alternate bathing," she said, lowering her voice to a whisper as if conspiratorially.

Alternate bathing? What in heaven's name could she mean?

It turned out that Jennifer's physical therapist had recommended she soak her inflamed foot tendons in a basin of the hottest water she could tolerate for a minute, then immerse them immediately in ice.

I stared at her as if she was out of her mind. Chinese torture would have to be more pleasant.

"I know. I know," she said with inexplicable confidence. "I know it sounds ludicrous. But just you see. It will work like a dream."

By that stage in the game, with PF reminding me repeatedly that walking would never feel comfortable again, I was willing to try anything. If someone had told me to stand on my head and try to touch the ceiling with my big toe, I'd have willingly given it a shot.

So, as soon as I got back home, I knuckled down to it. After all, I hadn't much to lose. If it was simply unbearable, I could abandon it after the first try. But if I felt the slightest twinge of relief from the persistent dull ache that had invaded my feet, it would be worth the effort.

The first time I tried the technique, I sincerely believed I would die of a heart attack. When I plunged my feet into a basin of ice cold water, the shock to my system was so intense that I felt my chest heave. Bear in mind that this was the middle of the worst winter England had seen in two decades. The next plunge that followed immediately in near-boiling water was no less traumatic. But amazingly, after the first two appalling plunges, my body adjusted and I actually felt less stunned by the contrasting temperatures. There appeared to be some logic to it too. Nerves in the feet were so shocked by the treatment that they grew temporarily numb—leading the patient to believe that pain had ceased, when, in fact, it had only been dulled.

Never one to give up in a hurry, however, I stuck with the treatment for weeks on end, faithfully soaking my feet, morning, noon and night in alternate basins.

By this time, Morgan, my Kiwi Physiotherapist Number One, had left me high and dry for an extended stay in New Zealand, having assured me that there wasn't very much more she could do for me. Just stick with the exercises, she'd said. After her departure, I was prepared to try anything that would rid me of my affliction. Meanwhile, I faithfully adhered to the homeopath's directives as Dr. Naik's pills found their way into my mouth.

And then, five whole months after patient waiting, my turn finally came up for Physiotherapy in NHS pecking order at UCL Hospital. The sluggish wheels of socialized medicine had taken their time to arrive at my name on the Waiting List. I met Physiotherapist Number Two, Paul (whose surname I never did get), a tall, handsome and very friendly chap who spent an hour making notes about "my history." He instructed me to walk across the room and pronounced me more flat footed in my right foot than my left.

"Would you recommend that I wear night splints?" I asked him, hopefully, having read about their efficacy on the Internet.

He dismissed my suggestion with a guffaw and said, "Just keep with the stretching exercises." He presented me with an elastic band for foot workouts and put me through the paces.

I had become almost acrobatic at contorting my body in an attempt to stretch the muscles of my legs. But to deal with new exercises, yet again, I felt hard pressed to keep up.

"Could I have a printout of the exercises?" I asked.

"'Fraid not," he said. "Computers are on the blink, you see."

No, I did not see. In fact, I felt baffled. But I also felt consoled when he said, "Don't worry. I am writing you a referral to a podiatrist."

"A podiatrist? Do I really need one?"

"A podiatrist is the answer to every plantar fasciitis sufferer's dreams."

Two weeks later, when I returned for another appointment, Paul had disappeared, taking my "history" with him. He'd been transferred, it appeared, to another hospital, apparently a not-so-uncommon occurrence in the annals of the NHS. Physiotherapist Number Three, Coreen Curran, replaced him—younger, chunkier and far less friendly. It seems I was doomed to see a new therapist every time I went to Euston Hospital for a session. Not only did the NHS offer no choice in medical practitioners but I was deprived of the continuity of treatment that comes from sticking to the same professional. My "history" was recounted all over again. I felt like a stuck record as I provided it. More copious notes were made. More frantic pressing of my feet occurred. More exercises were recommended.

"Could I get a print out, please?"

"Sorry," said Coreen, "our computers are out of service."

What? After two whole weeks? How could their systems function with such dinosaurs? I began to have second thoughts about socialized medicine. It seemed to have, like the patients it treated, some good days and too many bad ones. When I vented, my English colleagues simply said, "Welcome to the NHS."

And then, the bombshell dropped.

12

HOMELESS (OR VERY NEARLY)

By mid-February, a freak ball came hurtling out of left field that quite suddenly, and in a manner more shocking than the occurrence of plantar fasciitis, brought me to my knees. I was rendered homeless—or would soon be. The economic downturn upon which I had resolutely turned my back whirled around to bite me on the butt. Drastic budget cuts in New York brought me notice via email from NYU that, by the end of May, I'd need to vacate my darling Holborn flat. I'd expected to stay put through the summer doing library research; but with the entire world tightening its belt, NYU felt compelled to stop paying my rent as my contract did not require me to teach in the summer. Aarrgh!!!

Left with less than three months to find alternative accommodation, my spirits dipped and settled somewhere in the region of my inflamed soles. Even in the most idyllic of havens, harsh Reality had found ways to intrude. I was aghast and temporarily disoriented.

Breathe in, breathe out, breathe in, breathe out. I tried to recall every coping mechanism I knew—yogic *asanas* and soothing mantras, comforting prayers and Benedictine chants—then settled for a freshly-brewed cup of Darjeeling. Thank-you, Ritz Hotel, for making a tea-drinker of me! Britain's panacea for all ills slid down my throat comfortingly. When calm returned, I thought: Heck, Bring it on! It would become one more London adventure to write home about—The Hunt to Corner Central London Housing on a Shoe-String Budget. March, I decided, would get me going. I was more determined than ever to find the most economical summer housing possible. How grateful I was that those knuckle-cracking escapades in youth hostels had hardened me sufficiently to the inconveniences of shared dorms and communal bathrooms. Being far from fussy, I was sure I'd find something suitable in London for June and July.

That evening, I turned to my laptop with yet another mission. My colleague from New York, Karina, also sailing in the same soon-to-be-homeless boat, had recommended a website for international scholars on an overseas sabbatical. I began enthusiastic scouring of it and found some encouraging possibilities.

Then, as in the most enlightening comic books, a bulb lit up in my brain. Nothing worked like personal connections. Networking they called it—and I was about to ensnare a number of folks in one such net through the Net. So, with hope in my heart and a prayer on my lips, I sent out a joint email (what Brits call a "Round Robin") to all my new London friends—I sought their assistance in hooking me to home-owners looking for a temporary tenant. My needs matched my modest budget—a single furnished, safe and clean *en suite* room in a Central London location for the months of June and July. Could they help me?

It was time to reach out to The Big Boss upstairs. He'd never let me down. Meanwhile, I scoured cyberspace.

It was through the Web, not long after, that I made contact with a property-owner who ran a hostel in Kilburn. I introduced myself on the phone, but on discovering that I was a fifty-year old professor from New York, he balked.

"Nah! Get a grip!" he said. "Hostels are not for someone like you."

"But I've used hostels throughout my life and frequently during the past six months—all over Western Europe. I'm pretty accustomed to them."

The nice-sounding Englishman who answered the phone in response to the number he'd listed on the internet and who argued fiercely with me went by the name of Oliver Sacks. As I tried to convince him to check me out before jumping to conclusions, I almost added that most folks found me rather more youthful than my fifty years would suggest; but this declaration sounded vain even to my ears.

"Yeah," he said, "but not for two whole months, see? You'll hate it, I promise you. You'll have no privacy and will be irritated by noisy youngsters."

"Well, at least let me have a look at what's on offer," I said, hoping to comparison-shop. "May I come and take a look?"

"Certainly, but . . . what you need is a single room to yourself. Not a dorm with a bunch of kids who come and go as if through a revolving door. I warn you . . . you might be disappointed."

"I don't think so," I said, fervently. "My needs are meager and my budget is modest." I didn't need to disclose that I preferred to spend my pound sterling on travel.

Was I still in denial of my advanced years? Still determined to prove that I could rough it out with the best of the young'uns?

I managed to convince Oliver to show me his premises and, two days later, he picked me up at Kilburn Tube Station. As I'd expected, he seemed visibly surprised when he saw me.

"Alrighty then!" he said by way of greeting. "I think I might have to eat my words. I have to admit I had steeled myself for some fussily-dressed, overweight matron pushing senility. Now I think you might just fit right in."

"I take it that you think differently now about renting to me?"

"Well, let's not jump the gun, yeah? How about we take one step at a time? Why don't you take a look at my place first and then we'll talk . . ."

He drove me for a few minutes past neat single-family homes with neater front gardens. Oliver was well-spoken and wore a friendly smile, a snazzy leather bomber jacket and shades. He was one of those flamboyant, obviously well-off businessmen that most women my age would find irresistible.

When we arrived at his hostel, I discovered that my space would be confined to a single narrow bed with an accompanying steel locker in a room that would be shared with five other women possessing identical beds and lockers. Though this would be a massive comedown from the space I occupied at Holborn, what more could I possibly want? Plus, the price—and, more importantly, my attitude—were right.

"I think this will do," I told Oliver approvingly.

"Bollocks!" he insisted, Then, kinder, "Trust me. You're not like my massive Mum-in-law, and by the looks of it, you would fit in with my other lodgers. But you can do better than this."

"Ok, tell you what," I said. "how about this? I keep looking and if I cannot find anything better, I'll get back to you and we'll talk."

"Done deal," he said as we shook on it.

I rode the Tube back home brimming with confidence. Oliver's place convinced me that I would not be homeless in London in the summer. In the event that nothing better turned up, his hostel remained a concrete fall back option.

As I lay down to sleep that night, I marveled at my newly-minted tenacity. Pre-London Rochelle would have been a bundle of nerves, agonizing, day and night, over the uncertainty of future housing. Just six months on my own had endowed me with quiet confidence and supreme serenity.

What a change had been wrought upon my temperament by my Nearly Perfect Year!

Meanwhile, by early March, the Carringtons had become dear friends having cemented ties with me over pucca cuppas at *Amen Court* and regular events I attended at St. Paul's Cathedral, in their company, thanks to complimentary tickets they offered. Bishop Andrew was extraordinarily well connected to the Anglican ecclesiastical network. One evening, they invited me to their home for dinner to suggest accommodation possibilities. How heartwarming it felt to see a Bishop knead his own gluten-free bread on his kitchen counter as his proud wife looked on!

"That's amazing!" I said. "I have never baked my own bread. Would you share your secrets with me?"

"Well," he laughed. "This isn't all I can bake. I must get you to try my cakes and biscuits someday. This man does not live by bread alone, you know . . ."

Companionable good humor was commonplace in their welcoming home. On such evenings, I became privy to the family life of the English clergy—a notion as alien to my Catholic upbringing as a snowstorm in Madras. Celia had begun to regard me as a favorite sister and not having one myself, I warmly embraced the idea of an adopted one; and when her boys called me "Auntie," my feelings of fitting snugly into this family picture were strengthened.

As Celia laid the table, Andrew offered the idea of an introduction to an Anglican clergyman called Reverend Tristan Huddle who ran an international "club" in posh Kensington. "Club" was something of a misnomer, for it was basically a hostel for international students.

Later that week, I met a joyful Samantha who, coincidentally enough, had also been flat-hunting with the idea of moving from Wimbledon to Richmond to allow her to hit the highway more conveniently on her daily driving commute to Andover near Salisbury.

"So, I found a flat in Richmond, Woo-Hoo," she said as I stepped into her Lexus in Wimbledon at the start of yet another one of our Sunday excursions—this time to West Sussex to see the medieval towns of Chichester and Arundel. She'd spent a month of weekends traipsing with assorted estate agents through flats of varied provenance and was overjoyed at eventually finding something that fit her generous corporate budget but exacting New York standards. On another glorious drive into the country, I gave her an update on my own home search.

"Look at it this way," she said. "If push comes to shove, you can always use my couch. It won't be in Central London, but hey . . . "

"Yeah right! Thanks for the offer, but seriously . . . more than one week of my things littering your living room and you're going to want to pay me to leave."

When I made an excursion to tony Kensington's International Club, it yielded more optimism. Surrounded by multi-million-pound homes reserved for the rich and famous, Rev. Huddle's International Club was a delightful place—bright, breezy, neat as a pin. It helped that I'd chosen a rare golden London day when Nature, sensing the imminence of Spring, was stirring quietly in Georgian square parks. As I walked past homes that exuded the whiff of wealth, I heard a chorus of birds twitter in the trees.

I took an instant liking to the facilities and could so easily see myself ensconced in one of the *en suite* single rooms or in the lounge with my own laptop on my knees or on a wooden Lutyens bench in the back garden in the summer with a book and a cold Coke.

The Carringtons had come through splendidly and I was grateful. Oliver Sacks had been correct. I'd found a place in a far more desirable neighborhood preferable to the hostel he ran. Weren't the three golden words of home-hunting Location, Location, Location? Spiffy Kensington was where it was at. And I was game to give it a whirl.

I abandoned all worry and turned to work with a vengeance. Housing possibilities had popped up like sheltering umbrellas in a rainstorm.

But, three weeks later, despite Samantha's advice that I retain patience, I started to feel concerned again about spending the summer in a hostel. Yes, I could well settle for the kind of places I'd been shown by Oliver and Rev. Huddle. They were perfectly acceptable, of course, but all the while I kept hoping for my own flat or a room of my own in one.

So I had palpitations, the next morning, when I received an email from my new friend Lorraine who lived in Suffolk but had frequent stays in her London *pied-a-terre*. Indeed, Lorraine came up trumps with an offer that said: "You might already have found something suitable for the summer, but just in case you haven't, Charles and I were wondering if you'd like to consider the spare room in our Farringdon place which doesn't get much use at all. Not sure if this will work for you but if you think it might, you can come round the next time we're in London and take a look at it."

The offer of Lorraine's flat was so unexpected that I hyperventilated as I stared at my screen, bug-eyed, for several minutes. All I knew was that her 'place' was in Farringdon. But Farringdon was only three blocks from Holborn which I knew like the back of my hand. It was a no-brainer. No matter how modest Lorraine's place turned out to be, I would swoop on it if only for its easy access to the British Library where I'd intended to spend most of the summer. I could not wait to stroll to Farringdon to check it out.

Spring semester, beginning end-January, had brought a change in my schedule as I met new students. The city of London became our classroom on Mondays as I taught two advanced Writing courses designed around its multi-culturalism. Meanwhile, persistent networking, linking me with a large number of Anglo-Indians also caused my field research to progress at an accelerated rate and brought me invitations to meals at their homes.

Until the end of my year in England, I remained confused by British meals. Hoping to clarify concepts, I turned to NextDoor Tom who, as a former chef, was, I believed, well qualified to enlighten me. I should have known better. His sense of humor got the better of him as he explained, tongue firmly in cheek, "Well, in terms of British terminology governing meals, it all depends on who you are. The Toffs—meaning snobbish upper crust—and Proles—meaning working class folk, short for Proletarians—have Breakfast and then Elevenses. Then the Toffs have lunch or luncheon served by their butlers. Proles have dinner. Toffs have tea at five o'clock but their children might have high tea at six, if Mummy and Daddy are going to the theatre. The Proles, like the children of the Toffs, have tea at six when they get back from down the pit. Mummy and Daddy Toffs have dinner at eight o'clock. Proles have supper at nine o'clock and a sandwich and a cup of tea and perhaps a slice of cake, if that's okay, Mother. Then they go to bed to up for the six o'clock shift. If Mummy and Daddy Toffs have been to the theatre they might have supper in the interval with champagne, of course!"

Confusing enough for you? I seriously wish I hadn't sought guidance.

"Lorraine!" I exclaimed. "This is fantastic!"

I had arrived in Farringdon to meet Lorraine and, for the first time, her husband Charles Carson. The lift, that whisked me upwards to the third floor, opened directly into their flat! That's when it hit me like a ton of tumbling bricks. This was not the dinky little teensy-weensy London pad I'd expected. The whole entire shebang was the Carsons' alone. As we walked deeper into the living room, I eyed its leviathan proportions with a shock and saw that this was what New Yorkers called a loft!

A few moments later, I was shaking hands with Charles—tall, lean, handsome, smiling. I hoped I wasn't too flushed in the face from pure exhilaration at perceiving the first-rate art collection that my practiced eye took in as they graced the walls. Easily recognizable Andy Warhol's multi-hued versions of *Marilyn Monroe* shared space with self-portraits by Maggie Hambling and seascapes by Suffolk's Mary Potter. All the while I was thinking: Is this vast football field really going to be my temporary home? Never in my most vivid fantasies had I seen myself anywhere so expansive.

Pepped up on peppermint tea, Lorraine led me to the "en suite spare room" she'd offered. I took in a double bed and twin night stands as she expressed the thought that "it wasn't really up to very much." What? Was she, as they say in the UK, taking the Mickey? I wouldn't really be occupying this immense, impeccably decorated, art and sculpture-filled cavern, would I? It was inconceivable.

A few more logistical details were ironed out before Charles said, "Feel free to try out some of the wine in our kitchen . . . on an odd evening when you have friends over, for instance, you might want to open a bottle." It just so happened that the Carsons owned a vineyard in Tuscany—in addition to their 800 acres of Suffolk farmland—and were

keen for me to try out the vintages they produced. I had died and gone
to Oenophile Heaven.

The last offer was an example of their repeated generosity. Charles
and Lorraine were truly the answer to my most fervent prayers. All that
remained was the tying up of a few frayed ends before my move, two
months later, into their loft at *Sweden House* became a done deal.

I could leave for Norway, the following morning, with a ponderous
weight lifted right off my mind. I'd found myself an unbelievable home
for the summer. Not even Samantha's American pushiness and her
enviable corporate housing budget could beat a space like mine, bang in
the swanky center of The City, overlooking the aquamarine domes of
Victorian Smithfield Meat Market. My TV set looked down upon a
living room filled with alabaster urns, medieval stone busts, a walnut
wood Moghul chest inlaid with ivory and a whole whale's skeleton. This
place was the stuff of which a museum docent's dreams were made.

My Boss Upstairs had come through magnificently. I felt deeply
indebted to Him and to my brand-new friends.

With the practiced ease of airline crew, I embraced a new routine that
involved packing as lightly as a feather in a wheeled backpack ("strol-
ley"). Cashmere kept me toasty through weeks of winter travel. I had
also learned that just a single extra sweater thrown into a backpack
could double your airfare on a budget airline. Ryanair, for instance,
lured you in with laughably reasonable fares then piled add-ons (read
penalties) for traveling with anything weightier than a G-string. With
minuscule-sized toiletries stashed in plastic bags, I breezed in and out
of airport security lines and arrived, in due course, in Norway.

It was still freezing in London when I pushed off to Oslo, where my
education in global maritime history began. Knowing nothing more
about the country than its stereotypes—open face sandwiches and gorgeous Scandinavian blondes—I had few expectations. But with Ryanair
practically giving away seats on its Oslo flights in winter, I would have
needed my head examined had I foregone the opportunity. No marks
for guessing that, in the Land of the Midnight Sun, I intended to stay in
yet another youth hostel.

That famed Midnight Sun remained elusive, but long before we
landed at Torp airport, fluffy layers of cloud parted to reveal bird's eye
views of spellbinding fjords that appeared like white feathers around

Norway's coastline. Hazy outlines of scattered islands lay as if submerged under a thick padding of ice.

Every little vignette on the drive to the capital was worthy of a Christmas card. Toyland cottages scarred the terrain in three distinct colors—ivory, ochre and burgundy—draped like modest maidens in pallid shrouds amidst clumps of conifers. Bare white land masses with boat slips at their edges soon revealed themselves to be snow-covered lakes. I was taken back sharply to the aching beauty of my coastal Connecticut winters as I watched the stark Norwegian countryside slip past our window.

"Welcome!" said the pretty Norwegian receptionist who spoke perfect English.

"Would you mind placing me in a quiet corner?" I said as she checked me in.

"The hostel is almost vacant," she responded. "I am going to put you in an empty room for tonight but I can't guarantee it will stay empty all four nights."

No bizarre suitemates for tonight at least, I thought with relief, as I changed, settled in my bunk and pulled out *Harry Potter*.

Famous last thoughts! I was savoring my solitude in warm silk PJs, that first evening, when I heard someone outside my door.

"Knock Knock," said a deep commanding voice.

"Who's there?" I asked, feeling like a four-year old.

"Steve."

"Steve Who?"

Absurd as I thought this sounded, it was sane compared to the exchange that followed.

"Steve Sandburg." Okay, so at least this wasn't a juvenile riddle.

"May I help you, Steve?"

"Can you open up? I feel kinda weird talkin' to a door." He sounded verifiably American—probably a Midwesterner in Norway to dig up his Scandinavian roots.

"That depends on what you want here." I recalled Pablo's passion for Esmeralda in Barcelona and added, "This is a Females Only Room, you know."

"Well, okay, er, can I borrow some soap for my shower?"

"Soap? From whom? There isn't anyone else in this room."

"Er, from you . . . Can you lend me your soap?"

It was asinine. Why was I even having this conversation with someone I couldn't see behind a locked door?

"How do you even know I have soap to spare? Why didn't you bring your own?"

"Well, y'know these airlines nowadays. All these rules about toiletries. I just thought I could . . ."

"What? Freeload?"

"Er . . . okay" He'd heard the edge in my voice. "No worries . . ." His voice faded away.

But I wasn't finished with him yet. "Has it occurred to you" I asked, "that every occupant of this hostel probably dealt with the same airline regulations? How come it didn't stop me bringing along my own soap?'

Silence on the other side of the door. I should have saved my breath. Jerk, I thought. I'm glad you've made yourself scarce.

At breakfast, I tasted, rather tentatively, a traditional brown cheese called *geitost*, delicious on crisp breads for which the country is known. I also experimented with herrings every which way—in mustard sauce, tomato sauce and pickled with onions. Delish!

The ten-minute trek from the bus-stop to the youth hostel, each twilight, involved a climb up a sheer incline, a slippery sledding slope in winter, true, but crawling with tiny-tot sledders and tobogganers whose delighted shrieks echoed among the surrounding hills. As I huffed and puffed up the hill after an exhausting day spent seeing the sights, I was rewarded for my pains by saffron and mustard sunsets. As the hills slumbered, as if under a diamond encrusted comforter, my nights acquired an ethereal quality.

Through my explorations in the city and on the Bygdoy peninsula, I learned so much about Norway and its maritime expertise. It was in Bygdoy that I came face-to-face, unexpectedly and for the first time, with Oscar, in his residence at the Kon-Tiki Museum—the golden statue, I mean, awarded by the Academy of Motion Pictures each year. A documentary film made in 1954 on oceanographer Thor Heyerdahl's *Kon-Tiki* expedition had earned the award. After I took a picture with Oscar—the icon standing proudly in a glass case, one of the highlights of my year—I saw the award-winning film.

On my last morning in Oslo, melting snow falling in great bitter drops splattered my face and formed mini-stalactites around the eaves of urban buildings as I trudged to the Museum of Applied Art to see the eleventh century Baldishol Tapestry considered one of the country's finest treasures. My disappointment knew no bounds when I discovered that the museum did not open until noon on Saturdays.

Living alone in a foreign country, as I discovered within the next half hour, induced me to do the sort of things I would never conceive of within the familiar boundaries of my regular life. But when I got to the museum, it was closed. Refusing to allow my plans to see the Tapestry unravel, I snooped around the side of the building to find a basement entrance manned by a lone guard.

A short, stunted conversation later, he firmly reiterated, in crippled English, that the museum would remain closed until noon. What, I wondered, would get me in? Were I twenty-five years younger, I might have contemplated batting my eyelids. At fifty, I knew better than to indulge in light-hearted flirtation. Begging might just do the trick. Just one teeny-tiny super-swift peek, I pleaded.

"The museum is electric," he said. "Fully dark. You no see nothing." Even were he willing to let me in, I could trip up the security system with a single wrong move. Clearly, he was throwing his most effective obstacles in my way. But how was he to know that I rarely take No for an answer?

"Well, can't you lead me there?" I persisted.

It's worth noting that were Hubs with me, we'd have turned tail ages before the conversation reached this point. Being on my own, however, I pushed the boundaries, unwilling to give up.

"I alone am here," he said. "Cannot leave. I lose job if take you. Sorry Madam, sorry."

Crestfallen, I assured him that the last thing I wanted was to see him unemployed. Defeated, I turned to leave when he suggested, "Why you no wait? Twelve 'o clock I open for you. Or you come tomorrow?"

"I leave for London this afternoon and then go on to America. I will never be returning to Norway again. It's now or never for me," I said, sadly, as I walked off.

Was it the mention of the magic word "America" that opened doors—literally? I will never know. Good job I don't know his name for he'd get into boiling H2O for the risks he took in departing from routine and escorting me to the third floor where the tapestry is displayed in a glass case.

As in scenes from *The Thomas Crown Affair*, we rode gingerly in a secret Staff Only elevator in near-darkness, walked through forbidding doors that he opened with secret codes and, with the aid of a flashlight, found our way to the elusive object of my desire. As if my eyes had settled upon the Holy Grail, I encircled the tapestry reverentially, transfixed by the fragment of exceptional workmanship, pinched myself to ensure I really was there in the flesh, not seeing it in some fantastic dream.

I had braved hell and high water to cast an appreciative eye over the vivid duo portrayed by a loom—an exquisitely-wrought Druid pair. How worthwhile it had been!

When he'd permitted me to get an eyeful, in respectful silent, the guard and I made the reverse journey back to the entrance.

How does one repay a Nordic guard for so monumental a favor? I hadn't a clue. Other than pressing his hands warmly and thanking him not just with words but with eyes brimming with unshed tears, I could do little.

"No problems," he smiled. "You happy, yes?"

Not just happy, I thought. Ecstatic. Indeed, I felt victorious. If I'd been looking for a good example of the manner in which my year alone had coaxed me to live beyond the pale, take calculated risks and dare to do the unspeakable, then here it was, knocking me on the head.

On the flight back to London, I couldn't help thinking that my little adventure had made that scrap of fabric, Norway's greatest cultural treasure, far more significant to me than the better-known masterpieces for which the country is reputed. These included the much-coveted painting *The Scream* by Edvard Munch and Gustav Vigeland's sculpted wonders in the expansive city park named after him.

Back in London, spring fever set me prancing like a lamb on steroids. I was determined to ignore physical limitations induced by plantar fasciitis and push myself to achieve set goals. I was in Canterbury with Samantha, at the ornate West Gate, the one through which pilgrims over the centuries received their first sighting of Thomas Beckett's grand Gothic cathedral, when what seemed like disaster struck. Stone-faced saints and winged cherubs watched as my trusted camera fell from my hands on to the stone pavement and broke. My heart broke with it for my camera had been my third arm, indispensable on my travels and just as 'handy.' I'd taken at least 3,000 photographs by this point in my unusual year.

Then gazing up at the heavens, Sam asked in despair "What's with this country that it is unfailingly awful on a Sunday?" She had a point. It had poured in Rochester, snowed in Battle and remained overcast in Canterbury, so God knows we had ample reason to indulge in what the British called "whinging". As East Coast Americans accustomed to sub-zero temperatures but incandescent sunshine all winter long, we made the joint discovery that the sun remains firmly locked behind cloudy leaden doors throughout winter in the British Isles.

Well, at least Spring was decidedly in the air although the sun played persistent peek-a-boo on our next trip to the South Downs. When it did make a guest appearance, it gilded glorious Sussex in the warmest shades that lifted our flagging spirits no end.

That afternoon, after roaming through medieval Chichester, Sam and I drove on to Fishbourne Roman Palace to see the remains of a Roman villa with its impressive original mosaic flooring, and finally, to Arundel where the turreted towers of its fairy-tale castle perched high on a mountain, took our breath away. We stopped, for good measure briefly at Petsworth *en route* to London as the sun set over a spectacular salmon and aquamarine evening sky. We finally saw small spurts of sunshine that lit up the dormant countryside with a burnished glow. With a little bit of luck, we'd see the rest of the United Kingdom at its cheerful best.

Kinder, gentler March temperatures also meant new NYU student field trips and I turned to focus on the first one to Hampshire that took us to Winchester and Portsmouth.

Winchester is poised in a southwest corner of England. Medieval ardor is responsible for the creation of yet another remarkable Gothic cathedral, the nave of which is supposedly the longest in the country. Being a devotee of Jane Austen, I found the author's grave of particular interest as Jane had spent the last few weeks of her short life in a modest home not far from the Cathedral—immortalized in a song from the 1960s—where she was buried in accordance with privileges granted by her Archdeacon brother. I touched the brass memorial on her grave with sentimental fondness, a tribute to an author I adored, pleased to find it touchingly decorated with fresh flowers. Later, my students and I climbed a short hill to the only surviving remains of Norman Winchester Castle—its Great Hall to see the item that for ages was thought of as the Round Table of King Arthur and his Knights.

In the coastal city of Portsmouth, my maritime edification, begun in Oslo, continued that same afternoon. There, seeds of research projects were sown in the minds of my students as we roamed through its Historic Dockyard. I was squeamish on several occasions and admired their forbearance as I learned more about English seafaring in one afternoon than I had in my entire life. My knees constantly threatened to buckle under me as the guide dispassionately disclosed little-known maritime facts. Such as: Sailors were "hard-pressed" or forced into sea service in the eighteenth-century! Snatched from local taverns while in a sodden stupor, they awoke on the high seas, as forced laborers, hundreds of nautical miles from home. How unspeakable the idea of deck-hands catching rats in galleys to supplement their frugal shipboard rations that consisted exclusively of live 'biscuits', squirming with maggots, and salt-preserved meat! How "sucky" (as my students would say) the thought of onboard "surgeon-barbers" sawing off injured limbs with instruments that belonged in a carpenter's toolbox at a time when anesthesia was unknown! Sailors—even teenage boys—were flogged repeatedly, for the most minor misdemeanors, with a cat 'o nine tails—a whip that divided itself into nine smaller ones, each with a hard metallic nugget at its tail-end! How vile to be told that a mixture of salt and vinegar was then deliberately rubbed into mangled backs to prevent infection. The sado-masochism of long-ago captains and bosons made me unsteady on my feet (and not from PF!) and relieved that we live in far more compassionate times! All this and more I discovered on an excellent guided tour of the *H.M.S. Victory* in Portsmouth Harbor on whose deck Admiral Lord Nelson had fallen during the Battle of Trafalgar in 1805.

March also brought me the thrilling news that Dot had received the green light from her job in a Belgian telecommunication company in New York for a visit to London in May. I lay awake at night just thinking of all the fun we'd have together. It would be the Mother-Daughter Trip of a Lifetime—the last one she would take as a maiden with me. With Spring hiding around the corner, its armful of flowers was sure to bring city parks alive. Daffodils were dancing in their thousands as the end of March see-sawed offering wintry days and near-spring ones. I became increasingly conscious of the paucity of time. With less than two months at my disposal in Holborn, I focused on accomplishing every last item on my To-Do List, one of which was viewing the Changing of the Guards at Buckingham Palace.

Wait! What? Is it true that I had never witnessed this most clichéd To-Do Item of every first-time tourist to London? Indeed! I who had, by this stage, been to lesser-known spots such as the Geffrey Museum in the East End and Kyoto Garden in Holland Park—which became my favorite corner of the city—had never seen the pomp and pageantry associated with squaddies parading down The Mall culminating in the studied steps accompanying protocol within the front yard of the Palace. But it was just as well I hadn't viewed the ceremony previously.

For, around this time, I also made the discovery that the guards at Buckingham Palace wear a winter uniform that is a lot different from their usual red summer jackets. It was as good a time as any other to hotfoot it to Pall Mall with my injured camera in tow to shoot pictures of the troops in their long Kremlin-like grey winter coats.

I could hardly wait to inch towards the spring-time joys of Easter when Hubs would return to join me in London. I didn't expect my solitary days to be filled with anything more exciting than work as my year in T'Smoke drew to a close.

13

OPERATION HUSBAND HUNT

In the UK, winter seems in a mighty hurry to melt into spring. Bulky gray cloud cover that settles like a winter duvet over the British Isles, rises as if shaken out by a fairy godmother. Moods lift miraculously as sunlight floods Great Britain. Londoners, grown stir-crazy by confinement, elbow their way along Thames's bridges. Tourists, chattering in polyglot tongues, attempt to 'do' the sights in two frazzled days. Poor sods. Disgorged by coaches they sprout like mushrooms around Trafalgar Square, St. Paul's Cathedral and The Tower.

Bitten by the friskiest bugs of spring, Samantha Prescott thought it an appropriate time of year to launch Operation Husband Hunt. Determined not to leave Britain without an Other Half, she stepped out to delete a principal item on her Must-Do List—The Acquisition of a Spouse. But to find a husband, she first needed a boyfriend. The quest was on.

English colleagues at work put her through the paces: Avoid football matches like the plague, they said. That's where you'll find the riff-raff. Get to rugby matches, they said. That's where the posh lads lurk. Hang out in pubs at Canary Wharf—that's where the chaps with the big bucks chill.

Sam took their advice. Plus, being a child of the twenty-first century, virtually born with a cell phone in her fist, she trawled through dating websites on the internet and even posted a couple of Wanted adverts herself. Days lengthened into salacious nights during our phone sessions while she gave me a ball-by-ball commentary on the dating game.

Against my better judgement, I was roped in to provide match-making advice.

"I'm not really familiar with today's dating protocol," I demurred. "When I was last in the marriage market, Victorian rules of propriety and decorum had prevailed."

"But you have, like, experience," she said, making me feel like an octogenarian. "And instinct. And you're an Indian. You guys are all about arranged marriages!"

I was dubious about her last statement, but I said, "Okey-doke. I'll give it a shot."

The next evening, during a phone call, she said, "Guess what? I went out on my first date last night."

"Already? Great. And?"

"On the web, Trevor said he was like, a professional stylist. I thought he'd be the art director of a glossy magazine. Now don't you dare laugh. He turned out to be . . ." (theatrical pause) "a dog groomer."

Later that week, she sounded slightly more enthusiastic. "At the weekend, I'm meeting a chef who's also a foodie. What do you think I can chat to him about?"

"Ask him what his favorite wine is. Ask him what his dream menu would be. Ask him where he would recommend we eat in this city."

The weekend came and went. Sam couldn't wait to phone me. "Gary talked about eating all evening long."

"Sounds like fun . . ."

"It was . . ."

"Then why do I detect a trace of disappointment? What happened?"

"I could take it as long as he talked about, like, relishing frog's legs in Paris and snails in St. Tropez. But I nearly threw up when he talked about savoring, like, monkey's brains in Singapore and, like, mopani worms in South Africa."

"Yikes. But at least he's a globe-trotter... Just like you wanted."

"Yeah, right. Imagine traveling with him and puking over every meal. I don't think so."

She continued, "Next Saturday, my colleague is hooking me up with her cousin Arnold. He sounds half way tolerable. Tall, she said, and handsome and pure fun if I can get past what he does for a living.

"Why? What does he do?"

"I didn't ask. I thought it would be too, like, crass. Too American."

The change in season nudged me out of London to saunter in the spring countryside where pea green meadows came alive with trundling sheep. Elegant country estates awoke to spring life exactly as extolled by novelists like Jane Austen. When my American colleague Karina suggested I join her class on a field trip to Austen Territory in Hampshire, I jumped at it, double-quick. We visited her cottage and neighboring Chawton House, her brother's estate.

I returned home to Holborn from Hampshire to find a message from Samantha on my machine. When I got through to her home in Richmond, she said, "Yesterday was, like, a disaster."

"Okay, let me have the worst of it."

"I went to a friggin' rugby match. It was, like, freezing. I had no idea how to dress. I wore jeans and a hoodie and an overcoat."

"Sounds like you were warm enough,"

"As if," she said, angrily. "I should have worn thermal undies, carried gloves, a scarf and a hat. I didn't. And, of course, I wore boots. My heeled ankle booties."

"Uh-oh . . ."

"When the match ended—and, by the way, I couldn't make any sense of it or of the scoring—the chaps" (I could just see her eye-roll attach quotation marks to the word) "fell all over themselves and shouted till they were hoarse. And then this chap, Gareth, he waves to me from the field and tells me to follow the team to the pub. And that's when it happened."

"What happened?" I did not know what to expect; but from the tone of her voice, I thought she might have had a major accident. "Are you all right?"

"Only just. So, like, I try to catch up with them—with Gareth and the team—and the field is mucky with all the rain we've had and as I hurry behind them, the heel of my shoe sticks in the mud and I can't move. I'm, like, paralyzed there and I'm yelling frantically for him, like, Gareth, Gareth, but he's three miles away by then and my leg is out of my bootie and straight in the muck. Next thing I know, I'm almost sprawling on my face."

I remembered vaguely seeing a show on TV that involved a shoe getting stuck on a rugby field. I looked at Sam with suspicion. "Are you sure you're not mixing this up with some comic episode on the telly?" I asked as I tried to keep the laughter out of my voice.

It was as if I had never spoken. "Then we get to this, like, pub and this team has suddenly turned into an army of, like, jerks. They're downing gallons of ale like it's going to be banned tomorrow, and singing these godawful songs—like, rugby songs, apparently."

"Wasn't fun?"

"Like No-oh! I was such a misfit there, I couldn't wait to get the hell out. I thought they said these rugby blokes had class."

"Not seeing him again then, are we?"

"No way, Jose. Gareth is history."

"Well, there's always cricket," I said. "All you need to do is find someone to bowl a maiden over."

"Huh?" replied Sam.

As March brought come-hither temperatures, another one of my earliest fantasies involving metamorphosis into an airline stewardess became a reality. Benign weather and cornflower blue skies brought me renewed opportunities to snatch cheap flights.

Did I say cheap flights? What I meant were free ones. Yes, free, as in no fare, no taxes and no charges. Nothing. Nada. Zilch. My free flight to Cornwall, for example, became possible because Ryanair launched a brand-new route to Newquay. There were clearly no takers in March—which was why they offered online seats for free. The flight left Stanstead at an unearthly hour of the morning—meaning at 6:00 a.m.. I grabbed it although it meant leaving Holborn in the middle of the night—literally setting my alarm for 2:00 a.m.. I intended to spend three days on my own in Cornwall before my students joined me on a coach trip.

Dawn had broken above Southwestern England as our aircraft hovered over Newquay airport. Though skies were overcast, Cornish clouds parted to reveal leftover patches of snow above Bodmin Moor. Tarred roads crisscrossed like narrow black ribbons on a green counterpane. As icy winds whipped around me, my expectations of mild Cornish weather were shattered. Settling in the heated mini-bus that rolled towards Newquay, thundering Atlantic waves reached my ears.

My six-bed female dorm room at a hostel called *St. Christopher's Inn* could simply not be beaten for location. Perched high on a cliff, my room offered drop-dead gorgeous views. It would remain empty for the four nights I awoke in it to catch my breath at the startlingly beautiful expanse of pale jade ocean fading to foamy frills on surfer-lovers' Towan Beach. Cornwall is so packed during the summer that one wonders how the southwest of England doesn't bend down under the weight of all those ardent sun-worshippers. But in the off-season, its haunting emptiness and stark barrenness were simply too lovely for words.

I had come in search of Daphne du Maurier, the early twentieth century novelist, who set her renowned works in this striking peninsula. Menabilly is the town in which stands the mansion that the du Mauriers had rented for a while in Cornwall. It would become the infamous *Manderley* of her best-known novel *Rebecca* whose heartrending first sentence, "Last night I dreamed I was at Manderley again" rang in my ears.

I made inquiries at the Daphne du Maurier Literary Center in the seaside village of Fowey (say "Foy") for public transport to take me to the house.

Alas, the assistant said, *Manderley* is a private residence, closed to the public. No, I could not even catch a surreptitious glimpse of its façade as it lay at the end of a long private driveway.

Disappointed, I abandoned "Project du Maurier," focused on Fowey instead and, at the sight of boats bobbing on sparkling waters, was left deeply homesick for my beloved sailing village of Southport in Connecticut.

Insider information about Cornwall came to me from a rather unexpected source when I settled down, upon my departure from Fowey, at a bus-stop that overlooked a square stone tower. A lady who waited with her dog, a lively Jack Russel terrier, for the bus to arrive, informed me that the tower was part of a private residence belonging to one of Cornwall's oldest and most eminent families, the Trefoys. "They've lived there for centuries, maybe even for a millennium," she said.

In her flared skirt, colorful embroidered blouse, hand-knitted shawl and orange curls that flared around her head like a flaming halo, she appeared more like a Romany gypsy than a middle-aged Cornish granny.

"Oh yes," she responded. "My God, things have changed beyond recognition since I was a little girl growing up here. When I was a teenager, if I got into any kind of trouble, you could be sure Mother already knew about it before I got home. Everywhere I went, a hundred eyes watched my every move. Everyone knew everyone else in those days, here in Fowey. And by name. I could not possibly expect that today. The place is full of strangers now. It's just awful."

I had come to Cornwall hoping to walk in the footprints of Rebecca and Maxim de Winter and there I was obtaining a lesson on the evolving face of Cornish real estate from someone who resembled the disgruntled Mrs. Danvers. What were the odds?

When I alighted from the bus, I feasted on incredibly good Cornish pasties (say "pas"—to rhyme with "lass"—"tees") made to Grandma's recipes in a family-run bakery in Penzance. My Cornwall memories include padding around Padstow while following the aroma of fried fish and chips to the heart of TV chef, Rick Stein's empire to eat the flakiest cod clad in the crispiest batter. I gazed in the distance at the hazy outlines of the village of Trebeterick where, in the churchyard of St. Enodoc Church, one-time Poet Laureate Sir John Betjeman lies buried. Alas, I missed the last ferry that could have towed me across to his grave. When the tide receded, I strolled across the foot pathway that runs from the village of Marazion across the bay to the island of St. Michael's Mount. And my heart sank at St. Ives where, in the Barbara Hepworth Museum, I made the shocking discovery that this great twentieth century English sculptor had died in her bed as her house burned, bringing to a horrible end an intensely creative life.

But what I selfishly loved best about Cornwall was that I had it all to myself. Combing its length and breadth in public buses that kept me snug while mobile, I traversed snaking country roads observing the elderly who scrambled on with shopping carts. As it threaded through peaceful hamlets along daffodil-strewn trails (who planted all those bulbs?), my bus offered glimpses of aquamarine waters, fallow fields and chestnut horses in paddock as seen in Ben Nicholson's paintings at the Tate St. Ives from where I spied Virginia Woolf's Godrevy lighthouse, setting of her seminal novel *To The Lighthouse*.

I returned to London with an abundance of mental images that jostled for room. Though I wasn't able to follow du Maurier to Rebecca's secret hideout, when I joined my students who'd arrived later, the opportunity to climb the rock faces of Tintagel, legendary birthplace of Thomas Malory's King Arthur, more than made up for it. Scratchy crags were slapped by fierce Atlantic waters as spray flew sky-high to glaze my face. At the Eden Project's biodomes, I was transported instantly to the wilds of the Amazon recreated realistically by British scientist Tim Smith. He made a science project blossom into an ecological experiment funded by a UK Millennium Grant that attracts millions. As I strode upon its humid tiers and gazed at a cacao pod from which chocolate is made, I completely forgot that I was in the chilly British Isles. And at Boscastle, in a village almost wiped off the map by a flash flood a few years previously, I accomplished one more item on my to-do list by walking along the Cornish Coastal Path to meet breakers where land ended.

When Samantha called to say that she happened to be in London mid-week for a meeting and wanted to hook up with me for a walk, I ignored the warnings of every doctor and strolled off with her. My feet were coping admirably despite my accelerated explorations for warmer, brighter mornings called my name and urged me outdoors. I had stopped the Alternate Soaking but continued stretching feeling somewhat discouraged that early morning aches underfoot still persisted.

"Let's meet at the entrance to UCL," I told Sam. "There's something about which I'm 'dying' to talk to you. I could hear the quotation marks in her use of the word."

"Well, I have something I want to show you," I countered. "I'm 'dying' for you to see it."

An hour later, as we were heading into the grand campus of the University of London, she said, "So, like, you gotta hear about Arnold. I met him yesterday."

"Remind me," I said, "who is Arnold again?"

"My colleague's cousin, remember? She, like, set me up with him when you were in Cornwall."

"Oh yes," I recalled. "So how did it go?"

"Well, he was, like, very nice looking. I mean stunning. But she was right. I just can't get past his job."

"Which is?"

"Well, take a guess. He spent the evening talking about really weird things."

"Like what?"

"Er, he said he worked with, like, dead bodies. Throughout our meal, he talked about embalming fluids and morgue temperatures and that sort of thing. I was so, like, uncomfortable."

"Is he a forensic scientist?"

"He's, like, . . . get this . . . he's . . . an undertaker."

When I stopped in my tracks, laughed, and said, "Oh, that's why you were 'dying' to talk about him," she said, "That's it. I'm not telling you anything anymore."

Was it a good idea to continue our little excursion? I was taking Sam to see London's weirdest artifact—the "auto-icon" of Jeremy Bentham, one of the founders of the University of London and a renowned economist. As requested in his will, Bentham's body is preserved and stored in a wooden cabinet and is still occasionally brought to the meetings of the College Council, where it is listed as "present but not voting." In fact, naughty students once broke the case open, vandalized its contents, reportedly using poor Bentham's embalmed head as a football! A wax effigy replaced the original mangled head which is now, reportedly, secreted somewhere under lock and key in the university's vaults.

Samantha gawked at the glass case. "Is this your idea of a, like, joke?" she asked.

"I had no idea your last date was with Doctor Death."

"Doctor Death, who, by the way, told me his favorite movie was Dracula."

When I had seen the auto-icon for the first time, I'd been on my own and before you could say "Greatest Happiness", I had torn out of the deserted college corridor feeling way too creeped out. But after Samantha's encounter, the setting and the story behind the icon appeared inexplicably comedic. It was another indication that my fears were being slowly conquered.

"So I guess we won't be seeing Arnold anytime soon?" I said.

"Not on your life," she said, and then realizing what she had said, she roared too.

Nursing my sore calves at home, it occurred to me that despite the passage of several weeks, I hadn't been contacted by the NHS-appointed podiatrist. Absolute ages seemed to have passed since I'd been placed on the Waiting List by Physiotherapist Number Two Paul. It was time to contact UCL hospital for an update. But, numerous attempts to reach them by phone yielded only frustration. No one at UCL seemed to have heard of me. I simply wasn't, it seemed, in their computer records.

On impulse, I went in person, in search of Physiotherapist Number Three Coreen Curran, who, I hoped, would provide answers. Coreen had clocked off for the day but a West Indian female administrator invited me into her office and broke the bad news. I'd had at least five physiotherapy sessions with two different practitioners and never had my name entered into the system because the computers were perpetually down. It was time to get away from London.

Suffolk is a patchwork quilt of green fields closely knit together by a river that flows through its story book villages and medieval towns. Some of England's best-known artists, such as Gainsborough and Turner, had been inspired by these natural backdrops and had preserved them in their canvasses. Spring was decidedly in the air, although it was still a tad chilly when I set off with my students to walk in the footsteps—literally!—of Great Britain's most beloved painter, John Constable. Our study of his sketch pads had begun at the Victoria and Albert Museum and our examination of his canvasses had continued at the National Gallery where we'd analyzed *The Haywain* (an old-fashioned term for a hay-wagon), his most iconic painting. Our field trip to the banks of the River Stour (say "stoo-er") was to examine the exact spots where Constable had drawn inspiration from natural river-bank life. About two miles later, we would arrive at Flatford Mill which features in his famous painting.

Our coach dropped us off in the postcard-perfect village of Dedham, a one-horse hamlet so pretty that architect and art historian Sir Nikolaus Pevsner had written, "There is nothing to hurt the eye in Dedham." There was also nothing to attract the eye of a pack of post-teenagers whose idea of fun is being let loose at an amusement park or in gaming arcades. Still, they pushed on desultorily over rustic wooden stiles and bridges, seeing the same flocks of birds that Constable would have encountered and sketched, two centuries previously.

After trekking for a mile and a half, we caught our first glimpses of the rooftops of Flatford Mill that Constable has immortalized in his work. I planted myself in the scene where the haywain of the picture's title would have stood, just besides Willy Lott's Cottage, one of the world's most photographed houses. It remained the chief artistic high-light of my Nearly Perfect Year. But I felt tormented when I seemed to be the only one getting such a kick out of the visit. My students were still in search of roller coasters, electronic pinball machines and one-armed bandits.

Later that afternoon, in Lavenham, a guide named James Dickson led us on a walk through an exceedingly picturesque medieval guild town crammed with 'listed' buildings—those protected by strict conser-vation laws. The town stands frozen in time, a silent custodian of the past, when homes were constructed with thick timber beams filled with stucco plastered brick and painted pink by the addition of pig's blood in lowly whitewash.

Sam had also left me a message that morning. She sounded ecstatic. Keith Darling—yes, I kid you not—whom she'd met the previous night was "The One", she said, excitedly. "Call me back. This is, like, urgent."

I did. Mr. Darling from Canberra ticked all her boxes. He was a financial advisor on a posting in London from his firm based in Oz. He was single, heterosexual, employed and loved travel. "He's, like, really really handsome," Sam said. "He's very well spoken and he made me laugh. A lot." Those were the bonuses thrown in *gratis*.

"Hmm. Hmm. How'd you meet him?"

"On the net. He posted a, like, promising advert on NoStrings Dot Com. So I called him. And, get this . . . he lives like five blocks from my apartment. Now what are the odds?"

Sam sounded ecstatic but yours truly remained dubious.

Other than the message from Samantha which had led to our fraught telephonic exchange, I found another message on my voice mail. Would I call the podiatry place on Abbey Road to set up an appointment? I couldn't wait for the miracle cure promised by Physiotherapist Number Two Paul. The podiatrist would provide the answer to all my PF-related prayers, he'd sworn. My persistence had paid.

Hallelujah!

14

TALES OF SEVERAL CITIES

In the next couple of days, I was afflicted with yet another kind of PF—Phone Frustration! Over a hundred attempted calls to the Podiatry place on Abbey Road during varying times of day from my mobile achieved zilch. For a second time, I showed up at UCL Hospital to complain to Physiotherapist Number Three, Coreen. How could I possibly make an appointment with a Podiatrist if no one ever picked up the phone?

"Just send them a fax," she said, breezily (as if a fax machine was a standard fixture in every London home).

Through the assistance of my Gal Friday at NYU (Jeeves to my Bertie Wooster, remember?), a fax was sent to the clinic on my behalf. Two days passed in perfect silence. On the third day, a message blinked on my voice mail. My appointment had been scheduled three weeks thence at 9:00 a.m.. It was to be the day after Hubs and I would return from our travels in the ancient worlds of Rome and Istanbul. We'd be horribly jetlagged, no doubt, but I would haul my butt there on the dot if it was the last thing I did on this planet. Call, they said, if I wished to reschedule! But hadn't it been the calling that had failed in the first place? How could one reschedule if no one ever picked up a phone? The NHS had begun to stink like rotten fish.

I devoted a good portion of March to drafting the lecture I was to deliver at the University of Padua in Italy where I'd be travelling at the invitation of my friend Ludovica Fiorella, professor of English. The opportunity to lecture to graduate students in Italy's second oldest university—the same institution in which Galileo Galilei had once been a professor—was not to be sneezed at and I was wound up tighter than a coiled spring. The trip threw in a promised discovery of the Dolomites in Italy's gorgeous Veneto where in Vicenza, I was to be a guest in Ludovica's home. I was psyched.

At Stanstead airport before my flight out, I entered into conversation with a former academic from Cambridge, Peter Young, a Kiwi transplant in England who, in the course of our conversation said, "I'll be passing right through Vicenza en route to Lake Garda. Would you like a lift? I pick up my rented car right outside the airport."

"Oh would you?" I exclaimed, delighted at the unexpected offer. "That's very kind of you indeed." It occurred to me that my speech had begun to sound decidedly British and that I was deliberately ignoring a niggling voice that offered caution. Was it wise to accept a lift from a total stranger—albeit an intellectual? On the other hand, the ride would save me a train journey into Vicenza.

So, casting fears aside, into Peter's car I hopped as he swung it around in the direction of the Dolomites. He'd been stimulating company on the flight, and although my association with him was brief and uneventful, it was by no means, insignificant. Peter's ride gave me pause to wonder: Who was this person into whom I was evolving? Time was, when picking up the phone to schedule interviews with potential Anglo-Indian 'subjects' had seemed daunting. Yet, six months later, not only was I initiating dialogue with unknown fellow-passengers but taking rides from them while ignoring flutters of anxiety. My Nearly Perfect Year was making me free-spirited. And, it wasn't just my thirst for companionship that initiated these exchanges. It was also my quest for adventure, a desire to see where the road less traveled would ultimately take me alongside those who walked with me.

Dusk was falling softly over Andrea Palladio's classical city when Ludovica arrived in her smart black Mercedes at our appointed spot to whisk me off to her commodious three-bedroom flat. I spent the next five days with her affectionate family—architect husband Dario whose non-existent English made communication impossible and teenaged sons—her lean, lanky sixteen year old Franco and her ginger-haired twelve -year old Matteo.

For the next few days, Ludovica plied me with home-cooked Italian meals for which she shared recipes. I lent my shoulder to the wheel as *sous-chef*, thinking all the time: "This can't be happening to me. Here I am in a real authentic Italian kitchen with a real authentic Italian friend, cooking real authentic Italian dishes with real authentic Italian ingredients!" Who'dda thunk it? Before I left Vicenza, I learned to make savory pork tenderloin studded with rosemary and garlic and roasted Treviso radicchio; sautéed zucchini seasoned only subtly with olive oil, salt and pepper; *sofrito*-based chicken braised with olives in tomato sauce served over creamy polenta; spaghetti Bolognese made to an ancient family recipe passed down by her mother-in-law. How cool was that? And when we weren't cooking or eating or talking about cooking or eating, Ludovica drove me around the Veneto showing me little-known treasures of the region.

In the mornings, I breakfasted on Ludovica's homemade clove-studded pear and walnut jam with *Grancereale* biscuits, tangy blood orange juice and Lavazza coffee as I reviewed my lecture at a kitchen table that offered a view of the white-tipped Dolomites. As I worked, I became feverish with excitement because Ulrike and Giovanni were going to bounce back into my life in Padua. One short train ride from Venice where they were based would bring them zooming back on to my travel radar.

I toured Palazzo Bo, the oldest building in Italy's second oldest university after Bologna. Because my Italian is confined to words like 'cappuccino' and 'biscotti', Francesca, Ludovica's grad student, translated for me and played city guide. My favorite part of the tour was the visit to the Anatomy Theater used to demonstrate the dissection of cadavers. The tiny room, built like a Roman arena in concentric circles, allowed medieval students to stand in tiers and look down upon the body being deconstructed. Another highlight of my year was our visit to the lecture hall in which Galileo addressed his students at a podium that deserves pride of place in a room covered with the crests of Italy's most illustrious dynasties. A carved marble bust of the renowned astronomer has been placed on the podium out of respect for his prodigious contribution to Modern Science.

At the end of the conducted tour, Francesca and I hooked up at the famed *Café Pedrocchi* with Ulrike who arrived, breathless, bright-eyed and bushy-haired. We had a boisterous reunion. Three meetings in three different cities of the world—Athens, Berlin and Padua—that was the sum total of the ties upon which our friendship rested. And yet, we felt as close as two peas in a pod.

Francesca joined us on a brisk walk to the Basilica of St. Anthony of Padua where I prayed fervently for a cure from plantar fasciitis as I examined the tattered brown cassock of the miracle-monk displayed in a glass case. Faith could move mountains and I was going to put mine to the test in this celebrated Catholic venue. Everywhere I turned, testimonies to the cures wrought by St. Anthony reinforced my trust in the perfect cure and as I walked on my afflicted feet to his relics, my prayers continued.

As for my lecture to Ludovica's graduate students, I was seriously buzzed. What a dream! To be in a classroom in an ancient European university where the country's future leaders of commerce, politics and industry hung on to my every word! How blessed was I?

Over *tiramisu* and *panna cotta*, the same thought that had occurred earlier to me, also struck Ulrike—that our fledgling friendship was based on three meetings in three cities. As we sipped espressos, I couldn't help marveling at the combination of circumstances that had brought these young liberal European academics—Ulrike, Giovanni and Ludovica—to an *osteria* in Italy to share their views with me. This was not the sort of scenario I'd visualized at the commencement of my Nearly Perfect Year: frequent opportunities for intellectual discourse with fellow scholars. How well new and unexpected components of my dreams were coming together to flesh them out and make them real!

The rest of my travels in the Veneto comprised a mosaic of striking visuals that return periodically to nudge me: post-card views of Verona from the heights of the *Theatro Romano*. I see myself taking a mobile phone call from Hubs while seated on the pink tinged stone of the spectator stands in the Roman arena. Throughout the week, Ludovica had driven me around her region to show me its highlights. Palladio's vision and its execution in the palazzos he designed, especially the Rotunda, his most famous work in the Veneto after the Bridge at Bassano; sipping grappa in the town of Grappa where the fiery *apero* was created and is still produced prodigiously in gleaming copper vats; playing virtual chess on the gigantic ground board in Marostica's medieval square. Finally, on my last day in Italy, Ludovica played tour guide for the last time and drove me to Castelfranco to see Giorgione's *Madonna* in the Duomo and to Cittadella, another walled medieval city. I bid her goodbye and marveled at the fact that despite my skinny weight allowance on Ryanair, I'd managed to squeeze great wedges of Parmesan and Gorgonzola cheeses, vacuum-packed prosciutto and spec, packs of Lavazza coffee, Perugina hot chocolate mix and bags of Baci chocolates. My Inner Foodie was profoundly pacified in Italy. In fact, I had by then stockpiled so much European chocolate at home in Holborn that I gazed upon it lasciviously each time I opened my kitchen cupboards.

Later that week, my colleague Karina and I were neck deep in conversation at a major literary event at NYU where the semester's last week before Spring Break had brought Black British writer Andrea Levy (who passed away in February 2019) to our Bedford Square campus. Levy's novel *Small Island* had won some of Britain's most prestigious awards including the Orange Prize. Her work on black Britons excited me deeply as the immigrant experience so superbly articulated by her characters echoes those shared with me by first-generation Anglo-Indians in the UK.

Dressed ethnically in a grey tunic with matching head dress and a chunky beaded necklace, she read four portions of her novel while imitating the individual voices and accents of her characters. Herself of mixed race, (Levy had a white Scottish maternal great grandfather), she was the daughter of Jamaican immigrants who arrived in the UK on the notorious *Empire Windrush* steamer in 1948 and knew first-hand the strange dichotomy of rejection and acceptance with which the UK's people of color have been confronted for over half a century.

When her reading ended, we chatted together over a glass of white wine. When I told her the subject of my research, she said, "Keep at it. I am well aware of India's Anglo-Indian diaspora in London. And I do agree with you that not enough work has been done to document their struggle to attain a distinct sense of ethnic identity in Great Britain."

Pinch me hard! My research had received the blessings of a very special mentor. It motivated me to continue to identify, locate and interview as many Anglo-Indians as I could before my return to America.

But, more importantly, my conversation with Levy was an epiphany in that it alerted me to the intersection of academic research and personal introspection that had engulfed my year. With each interview I'd conducted among the UK's Anglo-Indians, I'd learned a little more about the complicated trajectory of India's smallest ethnic minority with whom I shared a common heritage. What had led me, I wondered afresh, to abandon my beloved childhood home in Bombay, a devoted immediate and extended family and the warming friendships of a happy young adulthood for the insecurity of an immigrant future? Where had I found the courage to arrive alone in the US with just two suitcases and only $500 in my pocket—the limit allowed by India's then strict foreign currency exchange regulations? Knowing almost no one in America, I'd undertaken graduate studies at St. John's University, earned a second doctorate and forged a successful university teaching career for myself in a country I'd grown to love dearly despite all my conflicts with it. Where had I found the resources to overcome severe initial emotional upheavals, a devastatingly destructive personal relationship that best remains undocumented, loneliness, homesickness for India and my family members, jobs I'd hated while completing post-doc studies, sporadic bouts with depression and recurrent financial hardship in those early years? It came from an innate determination to succeed. To not brook failure. To leave setbacks behind and stumble on. To hold no grudges, to bear no malice, to judge not lest I be judged. Quiet time in London and the completion of my fiftieth year provided the backdrop upon which I could assess the peaks and valleys of my life and fathom the reasons I'd made the choices that had impacted me and the loved ones who had made the journey with me.

Throughout the year, I had posed questions for self-introspection and private reflection. Was my incessant search for newer pastures, undertaken through several years of intrepid travel as well as during my Nearly Perfect Year yet another impulse of my cultural restlessness? Was this why my earliest thoughts, as soon as I became aware of my posting to London, had drifted towards a penetration of those dribs and drabs of Continental Europe that I'd never traversed?

For indeed, April of 2009 and my meeting with Andrea Levy marked two full decades, almost to the day, since I'd left the shores of Bombay, city of my birth, to become an American transplant. As I recalled my uncertain entry into Kennedy airport in April of 1989, my eyes swam. How much water had flowed under the bridge since I'd arrived, gawky, fresh off the boat, in my Indian garb, clutching nothing more firmly than a fistful of dreams! I had weathered the turbulence of those early years, had found Hubs who'd entered my life like a raft in a gale, had guided Dot's initiation into her own new rocky beginnings in America and could sit back, finally, and enjoy the sweet fruit of all that sweat equity. I had every reason to celebrate, albeit alone, two decades as an immigrant in the West.

A week later, Hubs arrived in London again for the start of what would be my two-week Spring Break. Determined to make his stay as much fun as possible, I appointed Samantha to drive us to Rye. She and Hubs simply couldn't wait to meet. I was also holding my breath about Sam's fine romance. Yes, her suddenly scintillating love life still involved Mr. Darling and I needed an urgent update on its progress.

We took the Tube to Richmond to meet Samantha. Fans togged out in varied shades of blue crowded the train, headed hours in advance to bag prime seats along Thames' river banks at Putney and Barnes for the famed annual Oxford Versus Cambridge boat race. Most of the chirruping lot melted by the time we hooked up with Sam. She had metamorphosed into a Woman in Love: cheeks tinged softly by natural blushes. Hair freshly shampooed and blown dry. Nails impeccably manicured. The soft whiff of lily-of-the-valley accompanied her every move.

In Rye, I paused to pay tribute to author E.F. Benson, once mayor of the town and creator of the Mapp and Lucia novels that he had set in the picturesque place that he'd once governed. Rye was all about strolling laughingly through cobbled streets past half-timbered houses that stood in higgledy-piggledy fashion looking as if they would collapse on themselves at any given moment. The town boasts a clock-towered church—scene of many a wedding in British movies—antiques shops crammed with yesteryear's possessions and quaint tea rooms stuffed with sandwiches, scones, tarts and English bone china. In other words, it was my kind of heaven. I was in a Tearoom-studded Paradise.

We lunched together in one such Mom and Pop-run tearoom where we eventually found out more about Sam's latest *beau*. Her Darling had expensive tastes—almost as glam as her own. Read Prada shades and Gucci loafers. He rode a Kawasaki motorbike and, come summer, she would discover the world on pillion with him. That put paid to our jaunts together. I suppressed a twinge of jealousy.

Hubs listened to our chatter and asked just one question: "So, Samantha, can you see yourself with him, say, five years from now?"

"Definitely," she responded. He's the guy for me. I know it in my gut."

"Well, well, well," I said. "So Operation Husband Hunt has been a resounding success, then?"

"On my part, yes," she said.

"And his?"

"Not sure about his yet. He seems, like, non-committal. Like he needs more time."

"Fair enough. Better not to rush it," I said. "Gives you more time to get to know him better too," but she did not seem quite convinced for she saw her year's deadline in the US looming urgently.

When the wind picked up and played games with our scarves, we headed homewards with one brief stop at Winchelsea. The pretty little village with houses sporting white wooden sidings was reminiscent of New England's seaside colonial village abodes just like in our very own Southport.

Hubs and I left London for the Continent, the next day. At the start of my Spring Break we shoved off together to Italy, once again—and then on to Turkey. Rome and Istanbul would keep us engaged for the next couple of weeks.

The Eternal City was bursting at its seams with tourists from every curve of the globe when Hubs and I arrived at Leonardo da Vinci airport. For the next few days, we were jostled and shoved and elbowed and nudged by every possible specimen of humanity. My feet were rather too delicate to undertake long spurts spent standing and surging human traffic hardly helped my fragile condition.

At the top of our Roman highlights was a "private' Papal audience, arranged most kindly by Hubs' cousin, a nun who'd spent several years at the Mother House of her order in Rome. Assuming we'd be cloistered with the Holy Father in an intimate room where we'd kiss his ring and pose for pictures, as is conventional, I was stunned when we arrived at St. Peter's Square, wagging tickets in the face of officious ushers, to find a sea—no, a whole ocean—of people filling its last crevice. Only then did the light bulb flash in my brain: overwhelming masses of people had converged upon the city to hail the fourth death anniversary of late Pope John Paul II. The 'private' audience with Pope Benedict that we'd visualized would include tens of thousands of Catholic faithful who turned St. Peter's Square into an arena resembling boisterous ancient Romans in the Circus Maximus. Go figure!

Pope Benedict XVI, we soon realized, shared the popular street cred of his erstwhile predecessor. The frenzy in the piazza reached rock star proportions when his Popemobile inched inside. The nifty glass vehicle passed just two feet in front of our seats (miraculously procured by ingenious twin elbowing of our way to the middle of the square). The Pontiff smiled, hands held out in communal benediction. Thoughtlessly abandoning every modicum of consideration for those behind us, we climbed our own chairs for prime shots. We would always cherish those few magical seconds when it seemed as if we had received our own personal Papal blessing. When the priest-emcee on the stage acknowledged the presence of a youth delegation from St. John's University in Queens, New York, my *alma mater*, I amazed myself by cheering lustily. It was at St. John's that I'd earned a doctorate in English, many moons previously.

Later, at St. Peter's Basilica, we went past metal detectors and manual frisking by security personnel who swarmed thicker than flies around treacle in the environs of Michelangelo's masterpiece. At its entrance, his *Pieta* gleamed in all its Carrara marble glory although far away from visitors. Despite viewing it from a distance, Mary seemed to us to breathe life into her dead son. Inside, Bernini shares the spotlight with Michelangelo for he strode across the Renaissance like a colossus leaving his imprint at the Basilica's altar and on the city's fountains that play in grand squares crammed with pizza, pasta and gelato joints.

All roads led to the Vatican Museum, the next day, where I saw Michelangelo's Sistine Chapel for the second time in my life, having last seen it, a quarter century previously, coated by centuries' worth of soot from smoky candles. I admired my own foresight in having procured tickets online eliminating an agonizing wait in a queue that wound around the block. While the ceiling remains the *piece de resistance* of any visit to Rome, marauding crowds can put any visitor off and I felt faintly disgruntled. Attempting to erase them from my consciousness was no mean feat, but Hubs and I bided our time patiently until we found seats upon which we trained our sights towards the superbly restored ceiling frescoes of which the Delphic Sibyl has remained my favorite through the decades. With all the time in the world at our disposal, we stretched out our personal encounter with Signor Buonarotti even managing to capture a couple of decent pictures of his ceiling *sans* flash.

But trudging through the overwhelming galleries of the Vatican Museum can exhaust the fittest among us and a plantar fasciitis-affected patient stands little chance of remaining upbeat. I was exhausted and prepared to give up hearing the Papal Mass later that afternoon. That was when the head of St. John's University's delegation materialized from nowhere and offered to permit us to join him at the front of the queue since I was an alumna. We were dumbstruck. And very grateful. Security checks to get inside the basilica were scheduled to begin in just ten minutes.

From then on, things moved like lightning. We were cleared quickly, although the crush of human bodies jostling to get past metal detectors was overwhelming. Racing with our over-enthusiastic American compatriots to the main portals of the basilica, we found ring side seats just about eight rows from the main altar. Hubs and I stared at each other in utter disbelief. How close we had come to abandoning the possibility of reaching anywhere near the doorstep of this monument! How much we'd have missed, had I chickened out! How grateful we felt for the kindness of strangers!

Through this opportunity of a lifetime, we beheld all the regalia of ecclesiastical Rome—impressive rows of magenta-clad cardinals, whole regiments of smartly striped Swiss Guards, a panoply of cassocked clergy and swarms of colorful youth bearing banners and flags in our faces and yelling, "Viva Il Papa"—anything to attract the attention of the Holy Father as he made his ponderous way down the main aisle, staff in hand, to Bernini's bronze altar.

My mind raced back to Bombay and the Eucharistic Congress of 1964, when, at the age of six, I'd joined my parents to glimpse another Pope from another era—Paul VI—now a canonized saint. I recalled the enthusiasm with which my Dad, an usher, had instructed me to yell, "Viva Il Papa" in exactly the same way the faithful around me were doing, this time in Rome. I recalled seeing Pope John Paul II in Bombay, twenty years later, when he'd visited Shivaji Park. Then, too, I'd joined throngs of Indian Catholics assembled to give the Pontiff a right royal Indian welcome. And now here I was, in my fiftieth year, in the midst of Catholics from every curl of the globe, having seen every Pope that had served in my lifetime—but for John Paul I who was Pontiff for a mere thirty-three days. This time I was accompanied by my husband whose faith matched mine and my parents'. It was the kind of coalescing of time and circumstance that repeatedly struck me as miraculous and providential as my Nearly Perfect Year marched on.

I supposed, after experiencing such stupendous Papal highlights, the rest of our Roman holiday would be humdrum. How mistaken I was! A long literary pause at the foot of the Spanish Steps took us into the room in which my favorite poet John Keats had drawn his last breath. Joining generations of loyal fans who'd trooped up the marble stairs on a solemn literary pilgrimage, Hubs and I arrived at Keats-Shelley Memorial House to retrace his last agonizing months—yet another highlight of my year. Wordlessly, I wandered through two large rooms while inspecting handwritten letters, locks of hair, manuscript fragments and heaps of sepia photographs. All the while, I tried to walk in young Keats' shoes—John as literary Romantic, John as lover of Rome, John as brother to George, John as friend of poet Shelley, John as fiancé of Fanny Brawne. . . . Imagine, I thought, being twenty-six, deeply in love and at death's door. Having strolled reverentially, a few years previously, through the London home in Hampstead in which he'd courted Fanny and where Keats had penned my favorite poem of all time, "Ode to a Nightingale," I came away from his Roman abode with a subliminal sense of having personally known a man whom I had grown to love only through his verse.

I didn't want to leave Rome without seeing one more grand *objet d'art* and I dragged Hubs off to accomplish this mission: Bernini's exquisite sculpture *The Ecstasy of Saint Teresa* in the Church of Santa Maria della Vittoria, off the beaten tourist track. Had Teresa lived in our times, she might have been the highest paid supermodel. She is simply ethereal and made far more lovely by the translucence of the marble in which she is carved.

Our next trail led us in the footsteps of yet another poet—W.B. Yeats, as we sailed—no, flew—to Byzantium.

On our descent into Istanbul, known originally as Byzantium and then as Constantinople, I was grateful for my window seat and the glimpses it offered of domes and minarets bathed in strong sunshine. As we skirted the mouths of the Bosphorus, nothing had prepared us, upon landing at Sabiha Gokcen airport, for the long wait in a restless queue to purchase visas at $20 apiece. About two hours later, following another complex journey (private *Havas* bus to Taksim Square, public bus to labyrinthine Sultanahmet Terminus, long colorful ramble on foot) we made it to our hotel, the *Sultan's Inn*. First impressions? It felt like roaming in Bombay's Null Bazaar. Maddening chaos and confusion made up the kaleidoscopic spectacle of Istanbul street life. The long-forgotten bustle of our Eastern childhoods came back to tickle us.

Somehow, our online bookings had been messed up. "Don't worry, Sir," the impeccably polite hotel receptionist reassured us. "We will find something very good for you. Very soon." We placed ourselves in his juggling hands, never for a second doubting his sincerity, and spent one night at *The Sultan's Inn*, one night in *Tashkonak* and the following two in *Deniz Konark* hotels. Wooden *yalis* that crowd Istanbul's ancient quarters are unlike any hotels we'd seen. In rooms reminiscent of my illustrated volume of *The Arabian Nights*, with brass lamps, kilim rugs and bathrooms paved in Iznik blue tiles, we slept in the hospitable arms of Ottoman culture, charmed each dawn by a differing view as we awoke to the haunting tones of the muezzin's call at daily *azan*. One day, we breakfasted on a geranium-filled terrace overlooking the Sea of Marmara, another day the Blue Mosque stared back at us only a stone's throw away as we sipped green apple and rose hip tea.

On the streets, incongruity abounded: fair-skinned beauties in Hermes *hijabs*, both in and outside the Blue Mosque, held hands with their *beaus*; signs led to a "spa" that turned out to be a traditional Turkish public bath (*"hamam"*). And in the Basilica Cistern, we walked along the archaeological remnants of an ancient water source created by the Emperor Justinian that continues to breed fish. In his book *Istanbul: Memories and the City*, Nobel Prize winning novelist Orhan Pamuk writes: "it was so thrilling to sit at a modern window gazing at the oddities, foreignness, and sudden humanity of the Ottoman ancestors we were meant to have left behind." Not only did we gaze upon the offspring of his Ottoman ancestors everywhere, we spoke, joked, ate and traveled with them as we beavered into Istanbul.

In the afternoon, we trotted off to the world's largest mall of sorts, the Grand Bazaar, when Trouble barged into our honeymoon paradise. More than four thousand stalls have shared space for centuries under one tremendous canopy in an ancient Eastern ritual of trading. I was eager to become part and parcel of its protocol.

"Beware of touts," instructed Hubs, well-schooled by guide books, "and ignore them firmly when they approach us."

For years before I'd arrived in Turkey, I'd intended to buy a brass coffee grinder from Istanbul, such as I'd seen the *Frugal Gourmet* use for pepper grinding on his TV food shows. With that in mind, I suggested we set out for the 'Antiques' part of the Bazaar. But, within seconds of entering the fray, we were accosted by a burly old codger who crawled, as if out of the woodwork.

"Good afternoon Sir. Good afternoon Madam." He dripped courtesy and old-world charm as well as impeccable English. Swathed in flowing robes and a stiff turban, he seemed like a soul that had drifted out of the Middle Ages.

I smiled in friendly fashion. Hubs ignored him and scowled at me.

"Would you like to see some carpets? Good quality ones."

"Well, it wouldn't kill us to just take a look," I hissed at Hubs.

"Come on, Madam. Nice showroom I have. Have a look. Just one look."

I entered the conversation. "Okay, one look. Only a look at your shop. We're not here to buy anything, okay?"

Hubs looked ready to burst a blood vessel. "We're not going to take a look at any shop," he said. "You've no idea how easily he'll suck us into buying a rug. Every book has warned us about this."

"Just one look," I said, determined to experience Turkish sales techniques first-hand and, much to the tout's triumph, turned to follow him through the dimly-lit interior of the bazaar. As we trailed him blindly through a labyrinth of narrow streets, we lost track of where we were heading. After what seemed like miles, we arrived at his emporium where another man—seemingly as old as Methuselah and just as wizened—emerged, clad in similar robes, reminiscent of fabled Constantinople.

"Welcome, Honored Guests," he said, ignoring Hubs' thunderous visage as he dropped a minor curtsy. "Take a seat, please."

"We're not here to sit down," said a surly Hubs.

"Some tea, if you please?"

"No tea, thank-you," said Hubs.

"A Coca-Cola then?"

"No Coca-Cola, thank-you very much. We're leaving . . . Now."

The confused owner looked to his slightly younger tout for help. Had this peculiar Indian couple only come into his shop to say they were leaving?

Suddenly, as if sensing my willingness to bend, the older man spun around with the agility of a teenager. He pulled a carpet down, opened it up and said, "See, Tree of Life design. Perfect souvenir of the city of Sultans."

Unable to stop myself, I gazed, not at the hypnotizing design but deep into his dark eyes. After a few moments, I felt weightless, as if floating away on a magic carpet towards marshmallow clouds. When I next became conscious of my surroundings, the smell of incense wafted around me.

"Would you prefer a smaller prayer rug with a Mihrab design?" he asked. "Muslims point it towards Mecca when kneeling on it in prayer. Would you like to feel it?"

I was still groggy and unable to respond. The salesman said, "May I?" and reached out to take my fingers in his to lead them towards the rug so I could feel the wool's softness. When his gnarled fingers touched my manicured ones, an electric current shot up from my middle finger to my elbow. I clutched at the crook of my arm in shock and continued staring fixedly into his eyes, feeling both weak and mesmerized.

Sensing something, Hubs asked me, "You okay?"

"You want? You buy? You buy now," Ali Baba said, sounding miles away.

"Yes, yes, I want. I buy. I buy now . . . " I responded, sleepily.

Then, much to the astonishment of both salesmen, my furious husband grabbed my elbow and hustled me out right out of the shop. I could barely glance apologetically at them and whisper a few fleeting Thank-yous.

"What are you doing? Where are we going?" I hissed. But Hubs was too bewildered to respond. I had never known him to be so actively animated.

Outside the stuffy shop, the bustle of the bazaar continued unabated as we breathed fresh air again. Pushing through a door, we found ourselves in a dark alley with nothing but stark brick walls staring at us. In front was the faint glimmer of daylight. The faintness I had felt in the shop rapidly dissipated. Had I imagined it?

"Home," Hubs replied. "We're going straight home!"

"But why? Haggling is supposed to be part of the market tradition. I wanted the full Turkish cultural experience." I did not mention how woozy I'd felt.

I could understand that Hubs felt a bit astonished by my obstinacy. But then, he hadn't been around to witness the ease with which I'd engaged with strangers all over Europe. He was unaware that I'd grown hungry for travel adventure.

"Do you realize what a close shave we had with a nightmare?" he asked, as we emerged out of the tunnel and into daylight.

What were we doing? Having a spat after being apart for months! Seriously! What was the matter with me? Why was I being so belligerent? All my husband had wanted to do was prevent what could have developed into an ugly scene. And I had to concede that there was more than an undertone of menace among the touts' velvet-tongued utterances. Ready to haggle with the best of them when he really wanted to make a deal, I understood that my husband did not wish to provoke shady characters in a Middle Eastern bazaar if he could help it. And I had not said a word about my near brush with the supernatural. Nor would I. My surreal experience was best kept private. Especially since I felt perfectly fine again, no trace of grogginess remaining.

When we emerged from out the spooky tunnel, we found our way to one of the entrances of the Grand Bazaar again. I clearly hadn't had enough of local color and managed to persuade Hubs to accompany me to the Antiques section again for I was determined to launch a search for a coffee grinder. I spied it finally in a crammed bric-a-brac shop run by an elegant old man who haggled in perfect English with style and class, just as the carpet sellers had done, obviously masters of their trade. I finally had the chance to try my hand at haggling. Ignoring Hubs' obvious discomfort, I got down and dirty with the salesman and pitched way too low. From there, it was uphill all the way until both the salesman and I felt satisfied at the deal we'd struck. There. I had the sensation I'd coveted. I had bargained a seasoned salesman down from two hundred to sixty Turkish lira and there hadn't been the slightest show of blood.

After money changed hands, the salesman beckoned to a passing tea boy who thrust a tiny hour-glass shaped beaker of strong black tea into my hand. It reposed on a white ceramic saucer upon which sat a sugar cube. I was enchanted by the uniqueness of our transaction's conclusion. Such charming civility!

Despite my disagreement with Hubs and faintly eerie carpet-buying episode, I warmed to Istanbul and to its people who basked in the peculiar light of tradition and modernity, of custom and commerce, of a need to please with a need to make a profit.

The next morning, we stepped out of our hotel towards the Aya Sofya only to discover that dozens of policemen, strung with machine guns, had swarmed the premises while we'd slept. Road blocks prevented not just auto traffic but pedestrians from gaining access to Sultanahmet's rabbit warren of alleys. Inquiring about the sudden new exhilaration that filled the streets, we made the discovery that our new President had chosen the very week of our arrival to make his first diplomatic visit overseas by currying favor with Turkey's political heavyweights. The fabled city intended to roll out a scarlet carpet but at the expense of annoying tourists, such as us, with only limited time to explore its attractions. It was my turn to be livid.

"How dare they close down national monuments?" I grumbled. "If it's sight-seeing he wants to do, Obama ought to come as a civilian—just like you and me."

Now don't get me wrong. I was as pleased about Obama's meteoric rise to stardom as the gal next door. No one was more pleased than I when his victory wiped out the last of Washington's neo-cons. But this didn't mean that, in the interest of improving East-West relations, I was willing to forego the pleasure of visiting the world's ancient wonders.

With Aya Sofya out of bounds, we were left with little choice but to consider another convoluted journey to Dolmabache Palace whose location on the other side of the Golden Horn probably still left it open to tourists. It was with much linguistic difficulty that we caught a local train whose tracks ran alongside the waterfront, past the romantic old stone walls of a Byzantine city, to its last stop at Sirkeci. We trawled through busy streets lined with retailers to the Eminonu waterfront. Roads less traveled lead to the most fascinating destinations and in delving unexpectedly into Istanbul's nooks and crannies, we found ourselves within bowing distance of Rustam Pasa Mosque. Approached by a zigzagging street that penetrates the Spice Bazaar, we were overwhelmed by the heady fragrance of burlap sacks overflowing with whole and ground spices—plump cardamom pods and mountains of smoky cumin, shards of cinnamon and fat whole pink peppercorns--as we hurried past Istanbullus going about their daily routine—counting worry beads, selecting oranges and apricots from vendors' carts, sipping tea in bazaars, gossiping.

Back in Sultanahmet, after visiting the jaw-droppingly opulent Palace which contains a whole complicated Baccarat crystal staircase, we found, to our relief, that President Obama had left the area, opening it up, once again, to lesser mortals such as ourselves. We entered the Church of the Holy Wisdom (Hagia Sofia in Greek, Sancta Sofiya in Latin, Aya Sofya in Turkish) that has stood on its site for over a millennium since Roman Emperor Justinian had built it. I'd never have been able to forgive Obama, had we missed it.

We would not carry home a rare carpet rolled under our arms, but we'd have an antique brass coffee grinder, boxes of *baklava* and Turkish Delight in an exotic variety of flavors from pomegranate to pistachios and honey by which to recall our colorful travels in Euro-Asia.

15

EASTERTIDE ADVENTURES IN BELGIUM AND WITH THE BARD

Orthotics!

I repeat—Orthotics!

Wonder Doc Rory Nottingdale, so-called Miracle Podiatrist, hyped by Physiotherapist Number Two Paul as the professional who'd make my PF misery history, presented me with Orthotics.

Returning jetlagged with Hubs from the cusp of two continents, my first priority was a visit to the clinic at Abbey Road to keep my 9:00 a.m. appointment, the very next day, with the NHS-appointed physician. I'd waited months for a consultation and the cure promised by his expertise. So there was no blaming me for being highly strung as we sat in his waiting room.

He was about my age, grey-haired and soft-spoken. In fact, he barely spoke at all. My "history" was reaffirmed. Plantar Fasciitis, I told him, still continued to plague me especially first thing in the morning. When I placed my feet on the floor, I still felt as if a thousand knives were piercing them.

"What line of treatment," I asked, hopefully, "would you recommend?"

"Have you been continuing the prescribed exercises?" he inquired.

"Religiously," I replied. "Like clockwork." I did not breathe a word about Alternate Soaking or homeopathy. Or the miles I continued to walk in defiance of all medical advice.

"In that case," he responded, "the only things I can recommend are . . ."

He turned his back on me, fiddled with something on a counter cluttered with rubber doodads and plastic thingamajigs, pulled out a drawer with theatrical aplomb and extracted something. Then he turned to face me and said in triumph, "These!"

Honestly! Like a conjuror who just pulled a rabbit out of a hat, he held them up for my perusal. Ta-Da!

The said Orthotics! Arched rubber inserts I could have picked up at *Boots* for a few quid.

"Get Outta Here!" I said, staring at him in disbelief.

He flapped them around and presented them to me, a puzzled look on his face. He wondered, no doubt, why I wasn't turning cartwheels in excitement.

Had I waited a miniature eternity for a fifteen minute long session with a podiatrist who handed me rubber insoles? I was hardly going to rejoice about the very things my American colleague Karina had recommended, months previously, was I? If this was meant to be a joke, I sure as heck wasn't laughing!

Thank goodness for Abbey Road's zebra crossing, near at hand at the intersection with Grove Street, made famous by a Beatles' album cover featuring the Fab Four striding across it. Of course, as die-hard Beatles' fans, I cheered up some when Hubs and I had our own picture taken *in situ*. It offered much-needed consolation.

The end of Lent found public parks blooming with parrot tulips and grape hyacinths, frilled daffodils and jeweled primroses. As Holy Week drew to a close, Hubs and I bought hot cross buns from what we had termed "our pantry" across the street—*M&S Simply Food*—and attended Good Friday services at St. Paul's Cathedral as guests of the Carringtons where we participated in interesting Anglican rituals associated with the Veneration of the Cross.

When Easter Sunday dawned, we sought out one of London's most opulent Catholic churches, the Brompton Oratory at Kensington, where we managed to squeeze ourselves into the grand Baroque nave that spilled over with ladies from nearby Mayfair in cultured pearls and Asprey silk scarves who wafted around in clouds of Chanel No. 5 that mingled with the pungency of incense. High mass in sung Latin was a trip down Memory Lane for both of us as we listened to young and old belt out the *Kyrie* from palm-sized missals such as we remembered from our own Indian school days.

And then, when mass ended and we trooped outside, we did it again. We had yet another royal sighting! On making our way to the parish hall for coffee at the invitation of the cheerful prelate who'd celebrated mass, we were awarded an unexpected brush with celebrity.

Two priests standing on the sidelines snapped suddenly to attention on spotting a gleaming black Bentley with a royal crest on its license plate that had arrived to pick up a smart threesome emerging from the interior of the church.

Going by all the fawning that went on, they were bound to be VIPs. I indulged in some shameless rubber-necking before I recognized the leader of the trio: Prince Michael of Kent. His beard makes him distinctive and I'd seen it in royal photographs, over the years, growing greyer at each public "do" that he was required to grace as a minor member of Britain's royal family.

I nudged Hubs hard and whispered, "That's Prince Michael of Kent. He's the first cousin of the Queen *and* of her husband, Prince Philip, Duke of Edinburgh, too. He and the Queen are grandchildren of King George V."

Hubs looked at me in astonishment. "How do you know all this stuff off-hand?" he asked. "And how the heck do you make all these royal connections?"

I had little interest in replying. I was too busy taking in the developing scene.

Standing beside Prince Michael, as their spiffy car drew near, was his very glamorous wife, Marie Christine, an aristocrat from a Catholic family of German-Hungarian descent. Known for being the epitome of glamor at all times, she was very elegantly turned out indeed in a sand-colored suit with a splendid hat that sprouted twin pheasant feathers. Near the woman who is known in Britain as Princess Michael of Kent, was yet another attractive lady, much younger and obviously embarrassed by all the fuss—undoubtedly their daughter, Lady Gabriella, a graduate of Brown. There was so much curtsying and bowing and scraping by the Catholic clergy—obviously unaccustomed to being graced by Britain's Protestant royalty—in front of the threesome that I had little doubt the courtyard would need repaving after their departure.

Then, just as I turned to pull my camera out of my pocket, Prince Michael turned directly towards us. Not even ten feet away from where we stood, he nodded smilingly at us before he followed his wife and daughter to enter the Bentley that swished almost soundlessly away.

Not just another royal sighting. Not just eye-contact with a true blue-blood. This time round, we'd received a smile and a nod as well! Like the Jeffersons in the 1980s TV sitcom, we were certainly "movin' on up"!

No, I was much too enamored by British royalty to ever be a Republican!

Easter Sunday would remain memorable not just because Hubs and I had another close encounter of the royal kind, but because we visited what is probably London's most unusual museum and one of its best-kept secrets. Bursting with *savoir faire*, I lead my husband to the East End to Dennis Severs' House at 18 Folgate Street in Spitalfields. The visit promised much more than a glimpse into yet another one of London's fascinating museums—this would be a dramatic journey into a previous century for entry to the museum required us to imagine we were honored guests of the home's erstwhile owner.

On the threshold, we received strict instructions, from an attendant dressed in a top hat and tail coat, to remain perfectly silent throughout our visit. No talking was allowed—not even whispering. We were not to touch anything and could take no pictures. We were entering, we were informed, the domain of a certain Mr. Issac Jervis, a wealthy Huguenot silk weaver, around the year 1724. How intriguing!

Talk about atmospherics. It was not just our senses but our imaginations that were fully stirred by the charade. It wasn't long before we realized that we were props in an elaborate tableau in which members of the Jervis family were collaborators. We were meant to make believe that they had departed each room silently upon hearing us enter it. In their wake, they had left behind subtle signs of their recent occupancy—a half-eaten apple on a tripod table, a just-lit pipe near a still-glowing fireplace. History buffs looking for an out-of-body experience could do well to follow their senses to this Huguenot home.

We were deeply enchanted. As we climbed higher, we drew ever closer to the present even as the extravagance of the interiors diminished until the attic that had once housed the family's servants proclaimed poorer nineteenth century residents. Behind the shaded blinds that hid the contemporary bustle of the capital, bells from Christ Church, Spitalfields, Sir Nicholas Hawksmoor's architectural master-piece, could be heard tolling sonorously. Their mournful tones were meant to suggest the grief into which the empire was plunged upon receiving news of the death of their beloved Queen Victoria.

This was real-life theater, all right. This was an exciting stimulation of all our senses. This was exactly what had been promised us. Indeed, it was much more than just another visit to a London museum. It was a willing regression into the eighteenth and nineteenth centuries.

As newbies in London, we had not received invitations to dine with any of our recent English friends that Easter Sunday. Left to our own de-vices, we ended Easter Sunday sampling victuals at *Rules*, a celebrated temple to British gastronomy at Covent Garden. It was apropos that we conclude our day in the eighteenth century having heard mass at a Baroque church and slipping into a Huguenot home in the East End, for *Rules* which holds the esteemed title of London's oldest restaurant, was established in 1798. As if its distinctive pedigree were inadequate, *Rules* is renowned as the stomping ground of Edwardian dignitaries and the literary likes of Sir John Betjeman and Graham Greene.

At a romantic table for two, we spoiled ourselves rotten on farm duck served with garlic spinach, crispy bacon and a sauce of chestnuts and red wine and succulent rabbit with a wild mushroom casserole. In a restaurant that serves such English classics as jugged hare, roe deer, snipe, teal, pheasant and grey leg partridge, proudly procured from the Lartington Estate in the High Pennines, "England's last wilderness," the menu reads like a manual on the game-based diet of England's landed gentry. As we awaited the arrival of our meal, we gazed upon walls covered with antlers of varying shape and size—a nod to the hunting and gaming traditions of the establishment.

Right after Easter, Hubs' departed Stateside and I left for Belgium, a country I had never previously visited. On my itinerary were the capital, Brussels, and the medieval town of Bruges.

Had it been Hubs' departure that filled me so suddenly with the deepest sense of malaise in Belgium? Earlier that morning at London's St. Pancras Station, I'd been full of beans. Three hours later, quite suddenly, I felt soporific—as if I'd swallowed a strong sedative. Was it a sightseeing hangover after two strenuous weeks in Rome and Istanbul that washed over me as I stood in Brussels' Grand Place taking in the wealth of medieval guildhall buildings that encircled it? I simply had to sit down somewhere, urgently.

Initial enthusiasm I'd experienced at dawn in London where I'd boarded the Eurostar train for my first ever Chunnel crossing dissipated quickly as the train sped startlingly through Kent. In the twenty-five minutes it took to cross the tunnel beneath the English Channel, I devoured my guide book as I had no idea what awaited me for the next four days in Belgium. From Brussels' Midi Station, I trundled my pull-along case along cobbled streets to find the Youth Hostel in a quiet square. Whilst still possessing a thimbleful of energy, I set out to meet the city on foot, and came face to face with the Belgian Dutch-named Mannekin Pis. He stood naked as the day he was cast in bronze, grinning cheekily—and pissing!

I'd hoped my rusty French would receive a thorough workout in Belgium, but, sadly, each time I opened my mouth to speak, I received a response in English. I became envious of the linguistic fluidity of modern-day Belgians whose polyglottal education allows them to slide facilely between English, French and Flemish. I made this discovery flitting in and out of one expensive *chocolatier* after the other, stuffing my face while sampling every conceivable *bonbon de chocolat* while saying "*Merci beaucoup*" only to hear "You're welcome" in return.

After a night of blessed silence in a lone hostel dorm room in Brussels, I left for Bruges, a town I'd long dreamed of visiting. Once there, I checked into *St. Christopher's Inn*, another youth hostel near the Bauhaus, where I settled into a 6-bedded female dorm room which appeared empty.

Bruges is pure eye candy. I was captivated fiercely by its Old Town and felt determined to comb every cobblestone, PF be damned! The previous day's *malaise* disappeared and my spirits soared like the towers that punctuate the city. Sauntering around, my camera worked overtime determined to record everything: gabled houses, red brick walls, curving bridges over mirrored canals and swan-filled lakes, cobbled market squares ringed by shops and churches and guild halls on pedestrian plazas paved completely with stone blocks. I finally understood why the white-grey stone, so popular among landscapers in the States, is called Belgian block!

Though something of a glutton for museums, I decided that my two days in Bruges were too precious to be squandered indoors. I elected instead to linger in every bewitching corner. Before the day ended, I'd picked out my favorite part of the city—the ancient brick Bridge of St. Boniface that spanned a narrow canal filled with shaded timber-faced buildings, a flowering cherry tree and a sculpted bust of Erasmus. I made the rare exception to wander indoors only to see the Church of Our Lady that contains the only one of Michelangelo's major works to be found outside Italy—an exquisite Carrara marble sculpture of the *Madonna and Child.* I also made a visit to the Basilica of the Holy Blood also known as St. Basil's Chapel. Built in the twelfth century, it wears its age upon its sleeve. Upstairs, a spectacular Baroque painted altar holds an extraordinary relic—in a silver receptacle is a rock crystal phial containing a minuscule scrap of cloth stained with the blood of Christ obtained after the Crucifixion by Joseph of Arimathea. I climbed the stairs leading to the altar to kiss the relic which is brought out occasionally and held in the hands of a church official. Apart from beholding the ragged brown mantle worn by St. Anthony in the Basilica at Padua in Italy, this was the holiest relic I saw in the course of my travels.

At the end of my first day in Bruges, finding a few more occupants in my dorm room, I befriended Tanaz, a grad student from Seattle, traveling on her own through Europe. Travel writers gravitate, as if by instinct, towards each other. So I wasn't surprised to discover, over a muesli breakfast, that my suitemate whose chest was as flat as a washboard and hips as narrow as test tubes was also a blogger.

"My Dad's Iranian," she laughed, explaining the origin of her name, "while my Mom's a white American from San Francisco. My parents were from the hippie generation and my Mom really did wear flowers in her hair. Like in the song." And no, Tanaz had never visited Iran but that was her next goal. "Someday," said the young adventurer, wistfully.

The next day, after strenuous walking, my thoughts turned to lunch and passing by the cutest restaurant overlooking a canal, decided to tackle my discomfort about dining solo. Samantha's American bravado had rubbed off on me. If she could venture into British pubs alone, I could pop into a family-style bistro to sample a few Flemish specialties before I left the Low Country.

Softly, squirming with awkwardness, wishing I were invisible, I walked towards the snooty *maître d'* and said, "Table for One, Please."

Well-heeled patrons eyed me curiously as I was seated alongside an elderly Flemish couple from Ghent who took pity on my singleness and smiled.

As I eyed the menu of unrecognizable offerings, I turned to them and said, "What would you recommend? I'd like to try something typical of this region, please."

"*Waterzooi,* "said the lady, kindly.

"Water, yes. But I'd like something to eat too.

"Jah. Izz to eat."

"Excuse me?"

"It's vary . . . how you say it . . . famooz."

"Oh I see," I said, "thanks, but, er, what is it?"

"Chicken Stee-you," said her husband. "Ist vary gut."

The waiter appeared. "The Waterzooi," I said, as he scribbled on his notepad.

"And ze drink?" he asked.

"Oh . . . and just some tap water, please."

"Hmmpph," he grunted with disdain. "Madam, vee do nat serve ze tap vater in zis restaurant."

Oh pardon me. I felt mortified and turned towards my kindly interpreters.

"Jah, that's normaal in Belgium. In zee restaurants, you must arder only the mineral vater," said the lady again.

Mineral water, for which, I noticed, at the end of my meal, I was charged 10 euros. Give me a break, I thought. The white Flemish stew with tiny fingerling potatoes was "vary gut," as promised, but I could have passed on the $15 rip-off with which I washed down my meal. I'd probably have paid less for a glass of wine. So much for peeling back my inhibitions and eating alone in restaurants. I'd never realized how fortunate we were in the US—tap water came free and haughty waiters wouldn't last an afternoon in restaurants where their lives depended on generous tips.

I had done it! Although being slightly humiliated by an uppity waiter, I had consumed a whole meal by myself in a restaurant. It was a small step for solo-gastronomy, a giant leap in phobia-slaying. Before reluctance paralyzed me again, I resolved to repeat the experience.

Patting myself on the back, I hastened canal-side, elated to discover that, with the first hints of sunshine, canal cruises had resumed. Spending less than seven euros, I had myself a memorable half hour under the bridges of Bruges. Incredibly, a canal cruise cost less than a glass of mineral water in the antiquated city. Seeing the city from another perspective—the hull of a boat—I felt slightly at odds with the passing sights in my jeans and hoodie. A flowing black cape with handmade lace at my collar in the manner of women in seventeenth century Flemish portraits might have been more appropriate. The only disappointing part of the cruise was our rower-guide who, in the interest of brevity, omitted key historical facts from his rather sketchy commentary.

Tanaz and I reunited later that evening in our dorm room where we passed a quiet few hours until the arrival of an occupant from Malaysia who shattered the peace. She made our night far less restful as she curled up and snored like a drunken sailor. Neither Tanaz nor I slept a wink.

At the shower stalls down the hall, in the morning, a bleary-eyed Tanaz said, "There really ought to be a law against admitting snorers in hostels unless they reserve private rooms! It should be written into the regulations."

"I hear you, girlfriend" I said, fervently. I'd have given anything for my ear-plugs which I'd unwittingly left behind in London. I could also have done with a roomier shower! The cubicles were no larger than aircraft loos and while they might have worked for slender Tanaz, I had to suck in my stomach to fit inside. No wonder the middle-aged do not touch these places with a barge-pole.

Biding Tanaz goodbye after breakfast, I left Bruges behind and arrived in Brussels on the train by lunch-time. Having set the ball rolling the previous day, I headed straight for the riotously colorful street called *Rue de Bouchers* lined on both sides with culinary delights. My tentative beginning at dining alone persuaded me to make a beeline for *Leon's* where, with no snarky waiter to cause embarrassment, I demolished an enormous tureen of *moules-frites traditionelle*, (mussels in cream sauce with fries) and a glass of foamy blonde beer. After my travels in Belgium, I conquered my timidity enough to start seeking solitary seats in restaurants without feeling conspicuous. It turned out to be far less intimidating than I'd expected. Never did I imagine on beginning my Nearly Perfect Year that I'd graduate to such independent pleasures without a single qualm.

Having skipped museums in Bruges, I returned to the Musee des Beaux-Arts in Brussels with a vengeance primarily to see Jacques-Louis David's *The Death of Marat*. Marina Vaizey numbers it among her 100 Masterpieces of Art . Over a quarter of a century, I had stalked her selections around the world's greatest museums and by the time my wide travels in Europe would end, later in the year, I'd have seen almost all of them.. My sense of accomplishment climbed one notch higher.

On my last night in Belgium, I went ballistic. The place was invaded by a hyperactive French school group of at least a hundred cretins who created a relentless din.

Where's the fire? I wondered as they ran, wild as horses in the Camargue, screeching through the hallways at the top of their pre-teen lungs. Their pathetic teachers had given up all hopes of ever regaining control.

It was time for me to take over.

"Fermez vos bouches!" I screamed. The most impolite French phrase I know rushed handily to my rescue as I left my bunk and strode into the corridor.

Sixty pairs of juvenile eyes turned in consternation towards the crazy lady in the blue silk PJs.

"Allez! Aux chambers!" I ordered.

They remained immobile, as if carved in stone.

"Maintenant!" I yelled again. *"Toute de suite."*

Shock caused them to simmer down for exactly six seconds. Then they turned away and fled, their voices swelling towards the next crescendo.

Arrggh! I remained awake half the night pining for my ear-plugs and my own bed. Don't get me wrong. I wasn't ready yet to relinquish the excitement of my nomadic life, but on nights like these, I so wished I was tucked up in the stillness of my own domain in Holborn.

Meanwhile, on the weekend when all of Stratford-on-Avon throws a party to celebrate the birthday of its most famous son, Samantha steered her Lexus into the town so we could revel in Shakespearean festivities. She was still upbeat about her Darling and had invested in a new wardrobe—off-white pea coat and sharp new leather boots ensured a spring in her step.

When I inquired if he'd ever join us on one of our jaunts, she said, "He's traveling. Again."

"Well, he's certainly being more elusive than the Scarlet Pimpernel," I replied and she said, "Scarlet who?"

Later, in Stratford's Visitor Center, she said, in wonder, reading from one of the publicity brochures, "Shakespeare was born and died on the same day. April 23. How weird is that?" Sam, who considered me an authority on British history and literary minutiae, turned to me almost defiantly and demanded, "Now did you know *that*?"

I didn't. But then how could I disappoint her or puncture her faith in my prodigious knowledge? So I crossed my fingers behind my back, lied smoothly and said airily, "But of course! *Everyone* knows that!"

After we'd visited Shakespeare's birthplace and Trinity Church where he was baptized and buried, I suggested we drive to the nearby village of Shottery.

"Shottery? Where's that? What's to be seen there?"

"Shottery is the birthplace of Anne Hathaway."

"Anne Hathaway?" she repeated. "Was she really born there? I didn't know you were a fan."

"A fan? Well, I'm not. Not in particular."

"Then why would you want to see her home? I can't really stand her."

"Er . . . you know her?" I asked, sarcastically.

"Not her personally, no. But I've, like, seen her movies. Wasn't she in *The Devil Wears Prada*?"

Only then did it occur to me that Sam meant Anne Hathaway, the American film actress. She had little idea that the Hollywood star shared a name with Shakespeare's wife. When I did explain that Shottery was significant for its association with the wife of England's most acclaimed dramatist, she said, "Fergeddaboudid. I've had enough of, like, Shakespeare for one day. Let's just get the heck out of here."

We headed straight to thirteenth century Warwick Castle, one of England's best preserved examples of medieval architecture. On the way out of the castle precincts, we learned from an attendant that if we walked about a quarter mile into town, we'd come upon a bridge that would provide a stirring view of the castle across the river.

When I returned to my campus office, later that week, I ran into my colleague Karina who asked excitedly if I'd seen the newly-unveiled Shakespeare portrait in Stratford. I stared at her in bewilderment. Whatever did she mean?

"You did not see the new portrait?" she asked, almost scandalized.

"Er . . . what new portrait?"

"Everyone's talking about it. It's a recently unearthed portrait of Shakespeare—probably the only one for which he actually posed. Mike and I saw it last week. It was one of the highlights of my year!" she said, fervently.

Whhhhat? Had I just been to Stratford and missed a newly-mined artistic gem? Well, if it was one of the highlights of Karina's year, then I realized (a) I had to find out more about it and (b) I had to make another trip to the city of Shakespeare's birth—with or without Samantha Prescott.

For that moment, however, I was rearing up for Dot's visit and my trip to France for a long-awaited reunion.

16

GRAND REUNIONS ON BOTH SIDES OF THE ENGLISH CHANNEL

Not squaddies on horseback or royalty in Cinderella carriages. Instead, it was bridesmaids' dresses in amethyst, jade and coral in the shop windows at *Monsoon* on the high street and tiered wedding cakes upon which gossamer butterflies had alighted in the Food Halls at *Harrods* that Dot photographed.

She had arrived in London in the merry month of May, giddy with pre-wedding jitters, to spend a Mother-Daughter Week with me. When I met her plane at Heathrow Airport, she had never looked more beautiful or more radiant. Shining hair, glowing skin, sparkling eyes. Being engaged agreed with her, no doubts about that.

I was determined to show Dot my London—the little nooks and crannies that few guide books had discovered or touted. Like *Persephone Books* on Lamb's Conduit Street, my favorite city book shop, where I felt like a flapper-girl as I bought beautifully bound silver-gray jacketed books whose end papers featured 1930s wall-paper designs with matching bookmarks. Or the Kyoto Gardens in Holland Park where peacocks strutted in proud disregard of my piles of term papers that I'd graded in their august company. Or the satellite map of London in the basement of architect Norman Forster's City Hall where I placed my finger on the exact corner of Grey's Inn Road and High Holborn where my flat was located. I felt compelled to show Dot everything I personally fancied.

"OK, "she said, after we'd kissed and hugged and finished exclaiming over each other's appearance. (Me:"You look fab, darling!" and She: "Mum, you look at least ten years younger!") On the Tube from Heathrow to Holborn, she said, "I'm all yours except for the evenings when I will need to get some work done on my computer. But during the day, I want to see it all. Bring it on."

The week provided an opportunity to check out something I'd wanted to investigate for a long while to see if it really made good financial sense: the loudly touted London Pass. Valid for three days for bargain-priced sightseeing, it opened doors at scores of popular tourist venues. Provided one did a bit of pre-planning, had oodles of energy and was willing to hoof it off as if on horseback from one venue to the next in attempts to beat the clock, the price made it a steal. Knowing her penchant for the edgy, I was afraid she'd reject the thoughtfully-created but challenging itinerary of my choosing. But, on the contrary, Dot was a trooper as we traipsed everywhere, even in an icy drizzle at the break of day through The Queen's Gallery representing the private art collection of Her Maj at Buck House. But by the time we reached Kensington Palace that evening after covering a quarter dozen venues in-between, all signs of dampness had disappeared. We sipped choice afternoon teas in the elegant Orangery in the same property that was once home to Princess Diana.

On Day Two and Day Three, we kept up our frenetic efforts at beating the clock as wild sightseers. In our London Pass book, we wanted to tick 'Been There, Done That' on all the venues we'd encircled at the beginning, some more esoteric than others. In-between swallowing huge doses of history, Dot and I feasted on a banquet of superb theater from Shakespeare's Globe to shows of her choice at the West End (*Duet for One* with Juliet Stevenson and Henry Goodman, *The Entertainer* with Kenneth Branagh), the stage being her own first love as a classically trained actor. She warmed the cockles of my heart with her enthusiastic reception to the city.

"I can't believe how differently I'm responding to London this time round," she often said in wonder. "In past years, I guess I was just too young to appreciate it. I always took it for granted . . . you know . . . it was just another European city."

"Ah, I'm so glad I've awakened your inner Anglophile," I replied, ecstatic. You have no idea how long I've waited to hear you say this."

"It's just . . . everything about this place," she said, nose glued to the windows of red double decker buses as her eyes roved over fat cherubs and flowery skeins plastered upon passing buildings that we perused at close quarters. "The architecture . . . it's just so different . . . so amazing. I now understand what you mean, Mum. Every time you turn a corner in this city, there is one more thing you feel compelled to explore. I now get it. I totally get it."

The next day, our sightseeing continued when Bishop Andrew Carrington treated us to a spectacular Insider's Supertour of St. Paul's Cathedral. Led into the winding spiral staircases of the steeples in which parts of some Harry Potter films had been shot, and up to the dome, we enjoyed 360 degree views of the city, albeit on a cloudy day. It was in Dot's scintillating company that I became a kid again as we tried out the efficacy of the Whispering Gallery.

I made certain she did not return to America without riding one of the old-fashioned Routemaster buses to the Tower of London where together we grew bug-eyed over the Crown Jewels. She adored the Albert Memorial and clutch of distinctive Victorian buildings that make up Kensington's 'Albertopolis.' It was a parcel of London that I discovered for the first time in Dot's company and it remains my most cherished time with her.

And how could I possibly resist giving her my own Highlights Tours of the main museums which, by then, I knew as well as the back of my hand? Before returning Stateside, she simply had to see my favorite pieces: Pieter de Hooch's *Courtyard of a House in Delft* in the National Gallery, Cornelia Parker's *Thirty Pieces of Silver* at the Tate Modern, the sterling silver Jeringham Wine Cooler in the V&A . While we split a scone over afternoon tea in the lavish Gamble Dining Room, she turned to me and said with the deepest affection, "I'm so glad I came. To see this city and its marvels through your eyes is extraordinary. I can't thank you enough for sharing it with me." Such lines uttered with spontaneous sincerity were as precious to me as priceless pearls. Despite the fact that Dot viewed London with Bridal Eyes, every aspect of it speaking to her in the language of love, while I was viewing it in professorial guise, every aspect of it speaking to me in the language of the academic, we loved our week together.

And just as she did each evening, Dot turned to her computer, worked diligently at sending reports to her office in New York before she donned her glad rags and set off with her friends to paint London scarlet. Getting to know these lovely young folk allowed me to grab a drink in a tavern I would not otherwise have entered or taste a meal in a pub I would otherwise have ignored. It was with Rohit that I connected especially firmly. Well-mannered, well-spoken and clearly fond of Dot whom he'd known since childhood, he had such a gentle manner about him. And in the tradition of young men who have been raised in India, he addressed me as "Auntie", until I told him to call me by my first name. By the time Dot left and returned to the Big Apple, Rohit and I had become BFFs, as the expression goes.

But for Dot, perhaps the most amusing part of her visit with me was the late-night stop we made at my 'local', The Mitre Pub in Hatton Garden, a block away from my flat. Dating from 1538, Shakespeare, no doubt, often came in for a swift half with his cronies. We'd spent an exhausting day sight-seeing and longed for a quiet table on the sidelines to nurse our ale and laugh. Instead of which we became the cynosure of all eyes as two blokes asked if they could join us, then proceeded to dominate our table before we'd quite gathered our wits about us. For the rest of the evening, Dot had a severe attack of the giggles as she watched the younger man assiduously hit on me, ask for my phone number and offer to walk us home—this after he'd made my day with profuse compliments.

"Pull the other one," Charlie said. "You're positively not sisters or friends then?"

He plied us with drinks. "Get us another round here, old chap," he said to the bartender, who hugely entertained by the unfolding drama at our table, beckoned Dot and me to join him behind the bar to draw our own draft pints—a first time thrill for both of us. The entire evening was a hoot. Much back-slapping and hail-fellow-well-met tavern cama-raderie followed. And Charlie even offered gallantly to walk us home. We thanked him, but refused. Before the grog loosened our tongues enough to indulge in reckless badinage, we beat a hasty retreat home-wards—without him. The last thing I needed was a walk with some drunken Charlie I'd picked up in a bar!

Yes, there were possibilities for casual flirtations all over Europe. But I ensured that any possibility for casual romance was nipped right in the bud during my Nearly Perfect Year as my gold wedding band and engagement solitaire had remained welded to the fourth finger of my left hand. There could be no mistaking the fact that I was well and truly hitched. Besides, I loved Hubs too much and could see no other man with romantic eyes.

Dot soaked the city in until her very last hour before we hopped on the Tube to Heathrow. She had proven herself to be a super trooper, pushing past jetlag and club-induced lethargy to trawl the city with a fine comb. It was only when we brushed past hordes of excited kids surrounding Ginger, an Egyptian mummy at the British Museum, that she said to me, "Okay, Mum, that's it. I really ought to get home to pack now. Can't believe it's been a week already."

As I hugged and kissed her goodbye, she said to me, "What a nice life you've created for yourself here in London, Mum." And when she said, "I loved it so much that I really do intend to come back again," I knew that she was leaving a part of her heart in my beloved city, just as I'd done so many moons ago. She would return to her New York life with Colin leaving me with a week of lovely memories to cherish.

I didn't have enough time to mourn over the loss of her departure or to wallow in sentimentality. Even as her flight jetted over the Atlantic, I turned thoughts to my departure the next day—to Lyon in France to reunite after twenty years with my pen pal of thirty-seven years, Salonge Chevalier, and to meet her family for the very first time.

A placard announced my name in block capitals outside the airport, held in the hands of a tall and very handsome Frenchman in khaki shorts and Roman sandals. I approached Salonge's husband smilingly and said, *"Bonjour Etienne!"*

"Ah! Bonjour," he responded, smiled widely and swiveling his head from side to side, planted not one, not two, but three smackeroos on my alternating cheeks. *"Bienvenue en France!"*

As we left the airport, Etienne proudly pointed out the new terminal building that resembles an exotic bird making a graceful landing. It was the handiwork of his wife, my friend Salonge, a civil engineer by profession and my pen pal since our thirteenth year. We'd been corresponding for thirty-seven years and had met thrice in that time: for the first time, when we were twenty-six and Salonge had made a trip to India; the second time when I was a grad student at Oxford and had traveled to her parental home in the Haute Savoie; and then two years later for the third and last time, when I had stopped off in Paris en route to

America. During those intervening years, Salonge had married the eloquent Etienne and had two sons: rakishly handsome thirteen-year old
Michel and timid, affectionate eleven-year old Benoit.

Etienne drove me from Lyon airport to their grand chateau -like
home in the *tres* upscale neighborhood whose name was a whole
mouthful—St. Didier sur Mont d'Or. For the next few days, members
of the Chevalier family were fabulous hosts. A well-established anti-
quaire in Lyon, Etienne welcomed me into their antiques-crammed
chateau. No slumming it in a youth hostel, thankfully, for me. On this
visit, I would enjoy the warmth and chaos of family life. I unpacked in
my spacious room with private bath and balcony that offered distant
views of Lyon's rooftops napping in the warm afternoon sun.

"*Mais* you have not changed," said Salonge when she returned from
work that evening and stepped back to size me up. "Not even a little
bit."

"But then neither have you," I laughed, after we'd hugged and kissed
and hugged again. "Fancy that. Meeting after twenty years like this."
Salonge was still as warm and bubbly as I remembered. She smiled
widely and, steeped in maternal pride and professional fulfillment,
introduced the three guys in her life. I'd last seen her on the banks of
the Seine; for it was in Paris, two decades previously, that I'd broken
journey en route to my new life as an immigrant in America. Funny how
vividly I could recall the details of my apprehensive crossing from one
stage of life to the next. That brief stop in Paris had been part of a red-
letter year and remained etched with crystal clarity in my memory.

That Saturday spelled the beginning of the long Ascension Holiday
in Catholic France and Salonge's extended weekend off from work.
After bidding her family goodbye, she drove me to Rumilly, a village in
which she'd been raised at the foot of the French Alps. It was here that
I'd spent several weeks with her Savoyarde family, twenty-two years
previously, and had made intimate acquaintance with her parents and
siblings.

I gathered with them, an hour later, over frog's legs and raspberry
tarts at *Le Pot Au Feu* in the village of St. Felix. During a luncheon treat
proffered by her mother, Mme. Juliette, I bonded again with the gracious elderly Frenchwoman who had written letters to me for decades
in faltering English when her own daughter had been too busy chasing
a career and kids. How different her siblings looked from the old

washed-out colored pictures in my album. How much they'd aged! Looking upon the faces that smiled back at me, I saw just how much my own fifty year old face had caught up with Time. No, you can't continue to live in the past, but you can cherish friendships that grow out of it.

My French was put through a thorough drilling and even garnered a few good compliments. *"Mais tu parle francais tres bien."* This was seconded with vigorous communal head-nodding, hand-gesturing, eye-brow-lifting, lip-curling and mouth-twisting in ways associated strictly with the French alone.

Before we returned to Lyon that evening, Salonge provided the icing on my gateau —a drive to Annecy, a lake-side resort town with a distinctly Swiss ambience, just across the border from Geneva. As one of the first European towns I'd ever visited in Mme. Juliette's company, while still in my early twenties, Annecy had a soft spot in my heart.

"I grew up in this bracing mountain air," sighed Salonge, walking down Memory Lane in my company, "and I often wish I could regress to those days when all I worried about was what ski outfit I'd be wearing for the coming winter. My life has become so much more complicated since you were last here!"

"Isn't that true for us all?" I remarked as I recalled my own wifely and maternal concerns, not to mention my worries as a daughter who lived so far away from her ageing parents.

Much as she adored her sons, I could see the extent to which juggling professional and maternal duties had stressed Salonge out. As in Ludovica's case in Italy, so too in Salonge's in France, being successful professionals and committed mothers meant a constant guilt-ridden balancing act. Whether in India, Europe or America, maternal ties bind with a ferocity that is breathtaking even as the lure of career fulfillment cannot be ignored. My generation of women had taken over the world but we had sacrificed time with our children as a consequence.

It was Michel whose unwitting remark tickled me pink. "Have you really been living alone for a year in London?" the wily teenager asked. "Hasn't anyone tried hitting on you?"

"Well, no . . . but I'll take that as a compliment," I said, blushing and laughing. "I happen to be married, you know." I pointed to my wedding ring, but he simply stared at it blankly.

I turned to Salonge and said, "Didn't he understand what I just said?"

"*Mais, bien sur,*" she laughed. "but remember, he is French. The fact of being married makes no difference at all to the possibility of indulging in a fling." Michel's teenaged libido was stirred by the French fondness for *l'affaire*—the *cinq á sept* extra-marital liaisons for which many of his countrymen are notorious. He thought it inconceivable that I had lived alone for most of a year in the UK and not indulged in the thrills of a torrid illicit liaison.

My fluency in French enabled deep and interesting conversations with Salonge's sons that I was never able to accomplish with Ludovica's. But my American tendency to pay for those younger than myself clashed with Michel's French sense of gallantry for he refused to permit me to put my hand anywhere near my pocket. With the aid of my guide book, I played tour guide as we traversed the famous *traboules* of the city—hidden passages through ancient apartment buildings once used by Lyon's famed silk-weavers and merchants to transport finished products from their modest homes to rivercraft on the Rhone and Saone, twin rivers that straddle the city. It was a subterranean adventure for the two of us as we often begged entry from occupants of today's privately-owned homes to let us into the wrought-iron gates that provided access to the underground passage ways.

I did not wish to leave Lyon without a long-coveted buy—a silk scarf designed by Antonio Canova, an Italian who made his home and *atelier* in Lyon so that the likes of European fashion houses like Hermes, Cartier and Ferragamo could use his top-notch services. Crossing bridges over two rivers, Michel and I walked and then continued our mission into the outskirts of the city to the beautiful courtyard mansion that Canova converted into an *atelier* and showroom, run immaculately by his daughter Claudette. She served me with the utmost patience and elegance and although I had inadvertently arrived on a day when the shop was closed, went the extra mile to open it for me and allow me to try on her father's wares.

Michel eyed my choices and expressed his opinion with the suavity of a Frenchman picking a scarf for his newest *femme fatale.*

"*C'est jolie,*" he said, fingering the fine silk then taking a scarf to the window to see it in the best possible light. Then again, with all the Gaelic charm he could muster, he said, "*C'est Vous! Certainement.*" It is you, for sure.

With such irresistible assistance, was it any wonder that I left Canova's *atelier* with not one but two silk scarves most exquisitely packaged by Claudette?

That Sunday, the Chevalier family planned a trip into Beaujolais country with me. Packing ourselves tightly into their car, off we left under brilliant lapiz skies to the peculiarly-named village of Oingt to taste *"le nouveau Beaujolais,"* swirling, sniffing, squishing and spitting before the selling began! Not a sound broke the intense silence of the neatly-planted vineyard slopes of which every architectural vignette looked like it belonged on a pricey wine label.

Next stop: Perouges, a medieval village of flint-sided structures and large, sugary crepes called *galettes*, and then a proud detour to Moinnay to acquaint me with Etienne's roots and distinguished family history. Served by a tiny toy railway station, this remote bit of rural France was truly a treat to discover. Had it not been for my lifetime of friendships and my year of escape, I could never have made such stirring rustic discoveries or ventured into such untrodden paths.

When Michel volunteered again, the next day, to escort me to Lyon's Botanical Gardens, I took him up on his offer on condition that I would pay for all our expenses. He agreed with a raffish grin, then invited along his best friend, Pierre—yet another pubescent Frenchman, tall, dark, handsome and eager to exhibit his chivalry. Much to my amusement, for the second time, I was taken under their wing by virile, handsome young Europeans. And what's more, this time they were not transvestites.

All went well until we arrived at the lake in the zoo where paddle boats bobbed invitingly on the water. I looked at them and sighed. "It would be so lovely to go out on a boat," I said. "Any takers?"

Both Michel and Pierre were enthusiastic. But when they discovered that boating did not begin until noon, they turned rogue. Moving purposefully towards the shed occupied by an attendant, they entered into rapid-fire French with him, militantly demanding to know why he would not rent them boats right away. Much fuming and fretting later, after the hands on my wrist watch had crept to noon, the reluctant attendant stubbed out his cigarette and walked in lackadaisical fashion to the pier to release moss-green boats available for the taking.

At that point, yet another issue presented itself. Each boat seated just two paddlers. When they realized that we'd need two boats between the three of us, my escorts became all seductive as each one attempted to woo me into his boat.

"Mine had a wider awning," said Michel. "You will be well shaded against the sun."

"But my boat is newer," said Pierre. "Yours looks a bit beat up."

"She is my responsibility," said Michel, his voice rising several decibels in annoyance. "Because she is my guest."

"But I am your guest too," countered Pierre, also becoming heated under the collar. "You invited me to join you so that I could improve my English, you said."

"But she knows me better than she knows you," said Michel. "She should go with me."

"Well, she'd get to know me a bit better if you weren't around butting in every time I try to chat with her," said Pierre. "Nothing doing. She should go with me."

"I'm a better sailor," said Michel. "My father owns a sail boat."

"This is a friggin' paddle boat," Pierre shouted. "Do you really need sailing expertise to get this tub out there?"

It was unreal. Two young teenaged Frenchmen fighting over Moi! This was a scene from Theater of the Absurd.

Just when it seemed as if I had ruined their friendship forever, they turned towards me. Then the savvy Michel said, "Okay, why don't we let her choose?"

"*D'accord,*" I agreed. "That would be fair. Let's see . . ." Turning to Pierre, I said, "You're so handsome, I can't resist you . . ." As Pierre broke out into a grin wider than the Cheshire Cat's, I turned to Michel and said, "But you're definitely the stronger of the two." It was Michel's turn to glance at Pierre and gloat.

"It's an impossible choice," I said. "Plus, I've caused sparks to fly between you. How about . . .?"

Suspense hung in the air as the two of them waited not daring to breathe. "How about . . . I put the two of you guys in one boat together so you can kiss and make up, and I'll go alone in the other one?'

For the next half hour, we shouted back and forth from one boat to the next as they pointed out pieces of sculpture I should not miss, an island that materialized in the midst of the lake and a luncheon kiosk. I sat in solitary splendor while all was forgiven between the two of them. Phew! Crisis averted.

The boys certainly hadn't made it easy for me to leave France. But across the English Channel, another treat was in store. I was left floored by one more unexpected brush with celebrity—a literal one this time!

London's Chelsea Flower Show is a big deal—and I mean humongous! Tickets are snapped up months in advance because England is a nation not so much of shopkeepers, as Napoleon had remarked, but of gardeners. Three hundred odd acres of the Ranelagh Gardens at Chelsea including the Royal Hospital are transformed for a week each May into a vast garden to showcase horticultural talents of the brightest and the best gardeners in the Kingdom.

On a survey tour of a series of show gardens, I had my next brush with celebrity. Literally. There I was, surveying some unusual garden sculptures when I found myself nudging elbows with the person on my right. I turned around, said "I'm so sorry," and found myself looking straight into the face of funny guy Ricky Gervais! Of course, for a few moments, I thought I was seeing things. But no, there he was, as large as life, wearing a prominent pair of shades ("glares"). No, I do not think he was trying to pass incognito because every second person at the show was wearing enormous sunglasses.

"That's OK," he said to me, softly, "It's a bit too crowded in here, isn't it?" Then he smiled—his crazy jack-assed smile—and moved quietly away without any fanfare or fuss.

Had I just seen things, I wondered. Was that a mirage? Rubbing shoulders with celebrity had not been a part of the afternoon's plans. Yet, there I'd stood, exchanging words, with one of my favorite comic actors of all time. I'd enjoyed countless guffaws over his shows, *The Office* and *Extras* while still in the States where the paparazzi would have stalked him. At the very least, a few star struck fans would have requested autographs. Yet, here he was on his own home turf, not causing the slightest stir. Browsing through the stalls in black hoodie, Bermuda shorts and goofball trainers in the company of a blonde, black-clad female whom I got to know years later was his live-in girlfriend, novelist Jane Fallon, he was ever so casual and ever so anonymous, making not the slightest attempt to stop traffic. He paused to pet a few black Labradors at one end of the show as the couple are devoted to animals. Then, he moved on, slowly, quietly, normally. Not that I expected him to turn cartwheels or sprout a clown's red nose or any-thing. Still.

Then, just when I thought I could not possibly have more fun, along hobbled a Chelsea Pensioner. War veterans who served their country well in military combat are provided retirement housing in the pre-cincts of the Royal Hospital. In their impressive red eighteenth century garb, they strut around the show, chests tinkling with medals accumu-lated in battle zones. Now while I had exercised enough restraint not to have requested a picture with Ricky Gervais, I wasn't going to stop myself from enjoying the rare privilege of being seen in the company of one of these revered old battleaxes, especially when he seemed just as eager to pose with me. He grinned widely in the photo we took togeth-er. A few years later, I saw the exact same model wearing the exact same grin, on huge posters, blown up larger than life size, at Heathrow Airport, welcoming visitors to London.

By May, with teaching done, grades submitted and my students safely back home in America, I was free to embrace London with no strain of responsibilities. My resolution to defeat PF was paying off handsomely. Discomfort, when I first placed my feet on the ground each morning, persisted; but PF cramped neither my professional nor leisure activity.

In fact, somewhat perversely, I launched on a new series of dares: I dared myself, for instance, to walk all fourteen miles of the Jubilee Walkway inaugurated in 1977, the year of the Queen's Silver Jubilee . I then dared myself to visit every single one of the churches Christopher Wren designed in the city after the Great Fire of 1666. Each Sunday, I received an unfailingly warm welcome from the pastor and sundry An-glican parishioners who invited me to stay for coffee and conversation, then led me down into darkened crypts to show me their display of antiquated treasures. I realized, as I covered Wren's creations, that church attendance was the quickest way to make new friends in Lon-don.

Why had I become so frantic, even obsessive, about setting new goals, accomplishing them, then setting newer ones? It had to do with getting PF in the first place. It made me conscious of the ravages of time and the dreadful limitations that age would set upon my most cherished ambitions. If, at fifty, I was plagued by a foot condition so trenchant and incurable, then where would I be, say ten years hence?

And then, at Hampstead Heath, I finally stumbled upon the perfect something I'd been hoping to buy all year! You might imagine a diamond-studded tennis bracelet for my right wrist. A divine Cartier Solo tank watch for my left? Or a vintage Vivienne Westwood cocktail creation from her Kings' Road dress shop.

You'd have imagined wrong.

Sound the trumpets and shout it from the roof tops! After almost a year of searching, my eyes had finally alighted upon a desk. And not just any desk. This was the sort of desk you'd see in an antiques-lover's fantasy. Lo and behold, there it was—a darling oak bureau-desk complete with the Tudor-style linen fold paneling I'd seen at Hampton Court Palace and the East End's Elizabethan Sutton House. With acorn pull handles, a warren of cubby holes concealed behind the drop-down front and three narrow drawers for stationary supplies. It left me hopping so insistently with enchantment that I was loath to inquire about its price tag. Should I? Shouldn't I?

I really shouldn't . . .

But then the desk called my name insistently and I did not want prolonged indecisiveness to rob me of the joys of spontaneity. I made a lightning decision, then and there, that if it suited my pocket, the desk was going home with me. Not just to London but to Southport. And never mind how.

"Gimme thirty quid, luv," said the bejeaned dealer Jackie, smoking like a chimney in the East End.

"Pardon me?" I said, certain I'd misheard her. That wasn't thirty she'd just said, was it?

"That's thirty quid and I have the key somewhere." She tossed her head up to blow smoke rings towards clouds in a vivid sky.

Thirty pounds! Get Out Of Hampstead!

There was the question of transporting it, of course, not just to Holborn, which was challenging enough but onward to Connecticut. But I knew, even as I gazed wondrously at the sort of desk I'd long coveted, that if I wanted it badly enough, I'd find the way. Meanwhile, because it was the very end of the day, Jackie was making her own attempts to close the sale.

"Oi," she yelled to a nearby co-worker. "Nigel, run this young lady 'ere 'ome, there's a dear." And turning towards me, she inquired, "Where'd ya live, luv?"

A few minutes later, Nigel was hauling my newest antique into the large trunk of his Landrover. Off we went, home to Holborn, where he saw it safely into my flat for the payment of another twenty quid. Mission Accomplished. The warmth of pure unexpected delight filled my being. This was the sort of desk I had always coveted—the kind I saw in the pages of Victoria magazine. Not just some glass and chrome contraption purchased from Rymans , but a piece that bespoke age and dignity, style and character in every vein of its solid wooden framework. It was one bit of England I'd carry proudly home with me.

I spent my last month in my Holborn flat culling through clutter in preparation for my move into my new loft at *Sweden House* in Farringdon. Much as I rejoiced at the gift handed me so generously by Providence—a loft to myself in the center of London—I must admit slight flutters of trepidation at the thought of becoming its sole occupant. Hopefully, my recently-conquered fears of solitude, especially in unfamiliar venues, would not return to plague me.

17

WITH COUNTRY SQUIRES IN FARRINGDON AND SUFFOLK

After an unexpectedly restful night, I awoke on June 1 to the stillness of a newborn week in my new Farringdon bedroom. As my eyes roamed over unfamiliar surroundings, it dawned on me that my fear of living alone had disappeared completely for I had spent a night, entirely on my own, in a vast, unfamiliar loft with no neighbors—indeed no one I knew within miles of my presence.

At dawn the previous morning, I had surveyed cartons and suitcases strewn all about my dinky Holborn flat and suppressed a shudder. It would be another couple of hours before my Moving Crew arrived. Between my English friend Raynah and Dot's friend Rohit who lent wheels and brawn respectively, we hauled and heaved, pushed and shoved, fetched and carried, grunted and groaned. Although I was only moving about ten blocks away as the Manhattan crow flies, one-way restrictions and street blockages in Farringdon around Smithfield's narrow lanes meant three trips back and forth from High Holborn. It took a total of three hours to move—lock, stock and barrel—into my new digs at *Sweden House*.

Even my precious desk made it safely while swaddled in pillows and sheets, shifted from the elevator in *Bishop's House*, into the little trunk of Raynah's car, into the elevator of *Sweden House* and thence into my brand new bedroom. There! All done and dusted! My prize find reposed in my new London pad where, amidst the plentiful antiques of the Carson's *pied-a-terre*, it looked decidedly at home.

Before I'd fallen asleep that first night, I'd carefully examined a Maggie Hambling self-portrait hanging just above my bed and wondered how little old me had landed where I was. Where would I be without friends who'd come so readily to my assistance? For I was being looked after in the most protective of ways in a foreign country by folks I'd met only a few months previously. As the lyrics of a song by ABBA had put it, "I believe in angels / Something good in everything I see." Right down on earth, on London soil to be precise, a host of angels were rooting for me, big time.

Still bleary-eyed with sleep, I drew back heavy linen curtains at my new picture window and gazed at the cobbles of Britton Street snaking below, lined by such iconic watering holes as *The Jerusalem Tavern*. In the clear light of day, the pointed white steeple of St. James' Church at Clerkenwell, stared directly back at me. Maybe I'd even hear the sacred tolling of bells. I sighed with satisfaction, "Ah! This is England." It would only be a few days before my loft started to feel like Home.

Very occasionally during the next two months, Charles and Lorraine made a foray into Farringdon from their country estate in Suffolk, creeping considerably in the dead of night into their master bedroom, to provide welcome company over breakfasts of *croissants* and coffee. I welcomed the company of my new landlord and lady and warmed to their varied interests. But, for the most part, I had *Sweden House* to myself.

June's glorious days egged me out of doors far beyond the confines of London. When, on one of her rare visits to Farringdon, Lorraine invited me to spend a day with her on her country estate in Suffolk, I jumped at the offer. I would witness the lifestyle of country squires in Suffolk.

"You can't miss the races," Samantha had wailed on the phone from Richmond when I told her about my proposed days in East Anglia. "Everyone who is, like, Anyone, goes."

"I'm so sorry," I'd replied. "You have no idea how much I wish I could join you at Ascot."

"I even have a hat for you!" she'd said, dangling her last carrot before my hungry eyes.

I declined. "No can do," I responded firmly. I am spending the day with the Carsons on their Suffolk estate. Lorraine's calendar is chocobloc. She cannot reschedule."

And so it was that I'd missed the most dazzling day on the British fashion calendar: Royal Ascot. Britain's upper crust leave their lairs on Page Three and turn out in regiments, the guys in tail coats, the gals in outlandish hats. Both genders sip champagne, nibble strawberries and ache to be seen. Sam couldn't bear to miss it and was there, on Ladies Day, strutting her stuff and reveling in the experience. Her Darling, aka the Scarlet Pimpernel, she told me later, had used my ticket and was all togged out in tails. "In Manhattan," she laughed, "he'd have been mistaken for a doorman at the Waldorf-Astoria." At Ascot, he fit right in. Meanwhile, I had yet to make his acquaintance.

Summertime brings a sporting social calendar to Britain—horse-racing at Royal Ascot, cricket at Lord's, tennis matches at Wimbledon, rowing at Henley-on-Thames. And the Trooping of the Color Ceremony on the Mall in London. Samantha and I had decided to do the rounds—which explains why both of us were disappointed when I nixed the first item at the onset of the season for I kept my date with the Carsons in Suffolk.

"I'll meet you at Wickham Market train station," Lorraine had said. "Let's pray for good weather because there's so much I want to show you in Suffolk."

A two-hour train ride from London's Liverpool Street Station bore me towards Iken to a vast land holding near the Alde river where on 800 acres of prime farm land, the Carson estate is devoted to farming. They live like England's landed gentry—squires who, in medieval tradition, still lease their land to tenant farmers while also running productive cottage gardens for their own tables. The astute Charles also became a property developer and used his Midas touch to turn wasted former factories and warehouse parcels into productive residential spaces in the capital. My loft at *Sweden House* was the end result of one such metamorphosis.

Lorraine's prayers had been enthusiastically answered as cushiony clouds billowed around the bluest skies from which the sun shone full and golden upon passing fields. In her snazzy grey Mercedes sport car, she awaited my arrival when I alighted from the train in a one-horse town, seemingly in the midst of nowhere. By the end of the day, I saw vast bits of East Anglia in the company of folks whose family had made it home for generations.

It wasn't long before we entered the gates of impressive *Sunnie Holme Farm* whose focal feature is a handsome yellow house on the banks of the Alde. Lorraine did the wise thing and gave me the Grand Tour in stages—starting with her own gardens.

"Oh, you even grow arugula!" I exclaimed, recognizing one of my favorite salad greens.

"Yes, except that here we call it rocket," she reminded me. "Would you like some in our salad?" And into the trug went a flavorful handful with tomatoes, lettuce and parsley. It promised to be a delicious salad indeed and I could not wait for lunch to try out her homegrown "veg".

It was, by then, nearly mid-day and her husband, Lord of the Manor Charles, left his office (all of twenty steps away) to join us in the lovely conservatory where he pecked me on the cheek in welcome as we sat down to eat a homegrown *Salade Nicoise* filled with her greens, olives, hard-boiled eggs and tuna fish. Their dog Zipper gratefully received tidbits that Charles passed her. In the elegant conservatory, surrounded by Lorraine's tropical potted plants, we enjoyed a remarkably simple meal. Encircled by the very essence of English country life, I had strayed into a feature story in the British edition of Home and Garden magazine as a guest at a charming table in the company of unpretentious English country squires. How had that even happened to me?

And then while Lorraine gave me a tour of the house, rather self-deprecatingly saying, "It's really not all that much," it caught my eye in the main hallway: a striking portrait of a British colonial officer on horseback was eyed by three red-clad infantrymen. A real sword swung just below the portrait's frame.

As I gazed at it, fascinated, Lorraine said, "There's a story behind that painting, you know. But you'd best hear it from Charles."

Charles looked up at it fondly and said in his clipped Cambridge-educated accent, "Ah yes. Perhaps you might be able to tell me a little more about it. The main figure in the painting is my great-great-great grandfather, a Lieutenant General Littler, Deputy Governor-General of Bengal."

I could feel the hair on the nape of my neck rise as their story progressed. The painting, depicting an ancestor on Charles' maternal side, had been passed down through members of the Carson family for generations, until it disappeared and was, ultimately, taken for lost. In their family records, Charles and Lorraine had pictures of it and were aware that it existed somewhere in the world. For years they had hoped to find it.

Then, one day, purely by happenstance, they found themselves in Sotheby's in London. Browsing through items that would come up for auction the following day, Lorraine spotted the painting and recognized it instantly as the one that depicted Charles' ancestor. She pointed it out to Charles who decided to bid on it and bring the missing painting home. Thus ends Part One of this serendipitous story.

But, in the manner in which some separated objects are simply fated to reunite after centuries, Lorraine found herself gazing, one morning, at the painting as it hung near the main door at *Sunnie Holme.* Her eagle eye alighted eventually upon the sword in General Littler's hand.

"I noticed that it most uncannily resembled a sword that had been passed down to Charles by his family members. In fact, having had it for a long while in our attic, I had just cleaned and refurbished it and gifted it to our son Bertram on his sixteenth birthday! The more I looked at the sword in the portrait, the more convinced I became that the sword in the portrait was right here in our house. Somewhere, in fact, in Bertie's room upstairs!"

Needless to say, I was, by this point in her story, hopping with anticipation. Wasting no time at all, Lorraine had sprinted up the stairs, found the sword, brought it down in trembling fingers and held it against the one in General Littler's hand in the painting.

"As I said, the more I looked at it, the more certain I became that I was holding in my hand the very same sword Littler held in his portrait!" she finished.

"Of course," said Charles, "it then followed that we reframed the painting in such a way as to have the sword, sheathed well in its own scabbard, hanging from the bottom of the frame. And this is what you see before you today. We'll never really know for certain, I suppose, whether this is General Littler's sword or not, but we rather like to think it is the same one."

At the conclusion of Part Two of the story, my knees felt weak. What an extraordinarily unlikely coupling of a colonial British portrait and a sword!

What struck me, most of all, by the end of my day with the Carsons was the completely understated manner in which they recounted their distinguished family history. Their totally unassuming way was both disarming and moving. They were nothing if not casual about their heritage, their collections, their pursuits. This was genuinely old Englishness. They exuded a down-to-earth spirit that carried not the slightest iota of snobbery or boastfulness. It underscored for me the truth about the old saying: Old money whispers, new cash screams! The more time I spent with them, the more endeared I felt towards *Sunnie Holme Farm* and its inclusive inhabitants who made me feel as if I'd always been a part of their abode.

I did not leave that lovely curve of East Anglia's coast empty-handed. Lorraine dispatched me to London with a bagful of home-grown Bibb lettuce and arugula and a fragrant bunch of sweet peas that blended perfectly with the fuchsia highlights of their living room in *Sweden House*.

We might not have bet together on the horses at Ascot but Samantha and I did make it together to a different sort of *chichi* gathering—the Grosvenor House Art and Antiques Fair in Mayfair. Considered one of London's best, to see it I made use of passes given to me by the Carsons . It was not on my To-Do List, but was the kind of impromptu opportunity that presented itself to me in the most unexpected of ways.

After we'd sipped champagne and passed ourselves off as super-loaded antiques' hunters from Hollywood and Bollywood respectively, pausing to examine a Victorian terracotta bust here and a pair of ivory-handled Samurai swords there, I insisted Samantha visit my loft in Farringdon as I simply could not resist the impulse to show off my fancy new digs.

And like almost everyone else who'd entered my pad at *Sweden House* and either stopped in their tracks speechless or couldn't stop exclaiming, Samantha found herself startled by the abundance of valuable Modern Art on its walls.

"Of all the luck, man . . . to have snagged this place. And there you were, only a few weeks ago, envying my little, like, hole in Richmond!" she said.

A half hour later, we were seated at dinner in one of London's most talked-about eateries because Sam needed to unload. There was something she wanted to confide in me, she said. All was quiet on the Romance Front—too quiet—and she'd begun looking for more action. Her year in London, like mine, would soon run out. Her Darling was still on the scene but her involvement with him was much too On Again Off Again for her liking. She could handle it initially when he was non-committal but he had become non-committed—it was too bitter a pill for her to swallow.

St. John's Bar and Restaurant seemed the ideal place to grab a spontaneous bite only because it was literally on my block. Though we had no reservations, *the maître d'* was able to squeeze us in.

"I mean," said Samantha, as if there'd been no interruption at all in her narrative, "he's fun and all that. But, like, I don't want to just be his pass-time in London, you know."

We glanced at the menu, crushed. I mean Pig's Ear and Oxtail? Give me a break. The menu featured more outlandish items such as Dried Salted Pig's Liver and Pheasant and Trotter Pie. Trotters! Uggh! Certainly not for Non-Foodies.

I surveyed the menu and my surroundings. The restaurant wasn't grand by any means. It was plain. Contemporary but plain: white walls, white linen, white china, white subway tiles on a backsplash in the kitchen, a blackboard with the Day's Specials casually chalked on with ads for *Nose to Tail Eating* by the restaurant's chef, Fergus Henderson, considered one of the world's finest who prided himself on using every single part of the animal to leave nothing wasted.

Through the open kitchen, we had a fleeting glimpse of the celebrated chef: crew cut, Coke bottle glasses ("spectacles"), focused expression on his face.

A few minutes later, a waitress made her way to our table, having given us adequate time to study the menu.

"For starters," I said confidently, "we'll have the Roast Bone Marrow and Parsley Salad." I recalled my mother's excellent mutton curry in India and the marrow bones over which my brothers and I had fought.

"Oh, I'm so sorry, madam," the waitress replied, "but we've run out of it. It's our most popular item. Would you care for something else instead? How about our snails with courgettes?"

Sam looked stricken and shook her head firmly. The waitress gathered that we were a couple of wimps, not adventurous enough to try something so far out of whack. We settled for Brown Crab Meat on Toast.

As we awaited our appetizers, Samantha surveyed the tables around us. "I don't really feel comfortable eating organ meat," she said.

"Offal," I said.

"Agreed. It is awful!" Sam responded while I laughed. It was like deja-vu, as Yogi Beara would put it, all over again as I recalled our Abbot and Costello routine in Scotland with Hank the Yank. "Organ meat is called offal," I explained. "O-F-F-A-L?"

"Really?" said Sam. "Well, I'm just a pot roast gal. Do you think we could share that?" She pointed me in the direction of a couple intent on demolishing a platter of pot roast.

"Fine by me," I said. "You choose."

"Okay then," she said, scrutinizing the menu. "Let's have the Pot Roast Smoked Gloucester Old Spot." And when the waitress returned with our starters, Sam placed our order.

"Perfect," said the waitress who disappeared again.

When the platter arrived at our table, Samantha glanced at slices of neatly carved ham, turned to the waitress and said, "Excuse me. This isn't what we ordered. We asked for the pot roast."

"This is the pot roast," said the hapless waitress. Then, riddled with doubt, she excused herself saying, "Just one moment please. Let me check."

She returned to our table only a few seconds later, and said, "This is exactly what you ordered. This is the pot roast."

"But this doesn't look like a pot roast at all," said a disappointed Sam. "This looks like . . . well like . . . sliced ham."

"Well . . . Gloucester Old Spot is pork, you know," the waitress said. It is a pot-roasted loin of pork."

"Ah, okay . . ." said Sam, but a few seconds later, she insisted, "we wanted a proper pot roast . . . look . . . like that couple there. What are they eating?"

The waitress craned her neck and replied, "That's roast beef."

"Well, yes," said Samantha. "That was what we wanted. But it's okay. Don't worry about changing it. Since it was our mistake, not yours, we'll just go with this."

Needless to say, neither one of us enjoyed our meal. "Frankly," said Sam, "my mother made better ham than this. I cannot believe we've just forked out £20 for two slices of ham and stewed peas. I mean this plate has cost us $40."

When the waitress came around with dessert menus, I ordered the elderflower sorbet, the menu's most unique item. "I'll split that with you," Sam said having lost all interest in our meal.

The waitress returned a few minutes later and placed pink sorbet at our table. "I'm so sorry, but we've run out of the elderflower sorbet, madam," she said, unhappily. Samantha rolled her eyes while I sighed. "But," the waitress continued, "we'd like to offer you this strawberry sorbet instead—on the house. And anything else you might care to try."

"Sam," I asked, "would you like to try this one instead? It's on the house."

Sam shook her head. Negative for me too.

Our joy in the evening had been slaughtered with our Gloucester Old Spot. "Okay, time I got moving," said Samantha.

"But, you didn't get to tell me what's bothering you. Would you like to spend the night at mine?"

"I really don't know if I should tell you anything. After all, you had warned me to take it slow with Keith. Anyway, gotta dash. Later . . ."

And with that last volley, she left me to stew in suspense. I would only really know what was tormenting her after the arrival of our mutual friend, Amelia, who would join us in a couple of weeks from New York. So I returned alone to my spacious loft to brood over her words.

I wasn't left with much leisure to agonize over them, however, as I was off to Oxford, the next morning, to spend a week with dusty tomes for company in the university town's venerable libraries.

18

IN OXFORD—IT'S DEJA-VU
ALL OVER AGAIN

"**W**elcome, my dear." Elsa Lonsdale greeted me warmly at the front door of her North Oxford Victorian Gothic manor and said, "Cuppa Tea?"

I admired her elegance, her tall slimness that veered very slightly towards the pronounced stoop that would mark her later years. She still sported the giant round glasses ("spectacles") and chic blunt bob that might have made her quite a catch in the 1960s except that her hair had silvered completely.

Then, when convinced I'd warmed up enough, she said, "Now let me show you to your room."

In a few minutes she unlocked the door to a darling little feminine sun-room with which I fell immediately in love. I adored its doll's house proportions, its position right above the car port and windows that flooded it with sunlight. Not even the fact that my old-fashioned tiled bathroom with claw-footed bathtub was one floor below in the basement dampened my enthusiasm for a typically Oxonian domestic experience.

Returning to Oxford for a prolonged spurt of research was less nerve-wracking than I'd imagined. I recalled the chilly December day, a few months previously, when I'd missed my Exeter College friends so profoundly that I'd actually wondered whether coming back alone as a research scholar after twenty-odd years was really such a good idea. But within minutes of alighting from a double-decker coach on The High, doubts were laid to rest. I spied the honeyed Cotswold stone walls of medieval colleges bathed in auburn sunshine and my prodigious love for the university town returned to fill my being.

As I made my way towards my new digs, I realized that though much remained the same, much had changed. I, for one. No longer a twenty-something slip of a thing, I was a mature middle-aged woman. No longer a grad student, I was an advanced published scholar with an invitation to lecture at Exeter. I was no longer resident in the Margary Quad of Exeter College where J. R. R Tolkien had conjured up Narnia and my favorite Pre-Raphaelite artists William Morris and Edward Burne-Jones had launched the Pre-Raphaelite Movement. This time round, I had rented digs in one of North Oxford's Victorian Gothic mansions where most of the university's faculty members and famous novelists lived. Renowned writers such as Colin Dexter of *Inspector Morse* fame and Nirad Chaudhuri would be my neighbors. Yes Siree Bob. Much had changed. But I was eager also to discover how much had remained the same.

Over the next couple of days, I grew to love the ivy-cloaked façade of St. Antony's College that peeked above tall stone walls on Woodstock Road. Research in libraries would have to wait until my ID card arrived through the excruciatingly slow grinding of the university's bureaucratic wheels. This did not stop me from discovering parts of the city I hadn't previously explored. At the Oxford Information Center, I picked up tickets for walking tours: "Pottering in Harry's Footsteps" and "Inspector Morse's Oxford" as I meant to saunter at leisure with my favorite fictional mates.

The next morning, after twenty-two years since I'd last lived in the town, I luxuriated in the supreme joys of awaking in Oxford! Every morning, in the Lonsdale dining room with its abundance of family heirloom silver and family photographs, I met my academic fellow-lodgers. Global diversity reigned on those summer mornings as we devoured Continental breakfasts of *croissants* and jam, crisp toast triangles served on silver slotted racks, hard-boiled eggs and that other peculiar staple of the English nursery—prunes soaked in cold tea!

That last week of term, as afternoons wore on and early evenings brought cooler breezes wafting around ivy-draped quads, weather-waned domes and gargoyle-covered towers, the staid scholarly city grew restless about the end of another academic year. For most of the week,

I gathered images that sank deep into my psyche and made me painfully conscious of my own past youth. During the day, clusters of students, mortar-board caps set firmly on their heads, red carnations adorning their buttonholes, walked briskly to and from Examination Schools to "sit finals" in formal academic garb. Others used humble bicycles, black gowns flapping madly, as they sallied furiously to their rooms at day's end. After sundown, knots of undergrads dressed formally in tuxedoes and gossamer frocks attended end-of-term dances in their colleges, bringing, to the soft dusk of spring, the shimmer of a sequined bodice and the toc-toc-toc of strappy stilettoed sandals.

For most of the day, I sat in the venerable interior of the Radcliff Camera, most ornate of the set of buildings that comprise the Bodleian Library, distracted from my research by the glory of its Baroque sky-blue ceiling with gilded highlights and full-sized wiged sculptures. Reveling in the privilege that permitted me to sit at a desk and read from dusty documents besides a gum-chewing teenaged student (who might well become a future Prime Minister), I was often the first reader to enter the library when it opened its door at 9:00 a.m.. It was only hunger pangs that drove me out at 2:00 p.m. in search of a sandwich before I returned to my books and incessant note-taking. Then, as dusk gave way to iridescent twilight, I sank down on the banks of the Cherwell (say "Chawell") watching crew members invest sweat equity as their coxes roared. At 9:05 p.m., when in accordance with tradition, Old Tom, the mammoth bell that topped Tom Tower in Christ Church College Quad, tolled the hour one hundred and one times, I walked again in the footprints of my past along Banbury Road to my lovely little room. It only remained for me to make plans to see Shakespeare's portrait in Stratford that my NYU colleague Karina had extolled.

Since the only objective of my long and meandering bus ride through idyllic Cotswold villages to arrive at Stratford-on-Avon was to see the portrait for myself, I made a beeline for Henley Street. I found the portrait next door to the gabled Tudor house with exposed beams known as Shakespeare's Birthplace.

I tried to slip into the shoes of Irish country squire Alex Cobbe seated in the drawing room of his mansion outside Dublin. He'd spent his entire life, sipping his Bailey's and being gazed at by the oil-painted portraits of an unknown Elizabethan couple hanging on his drawing room walls. In 2006, purely by coincidence, he made a trip to London's National Portrait Gallery for a special exhibition entitled "Portraits of Shakespeare." As he stared at likenesses of the Bard, he saw a striking similarity between one of the canvasses at the exhibition and the anonymous bloke whose portrait hung in his mansion. He brought the uncanny resemblance to the attention of the powers-that-be . . . and next thing he knew, Badabing, Badaboom! He'd become an instant gazillionnaire for he was informed that the two nameless folks whose portraits he had inherited were William Shakespeare and . . . get this, not a woman at all (as he's always believed), but a man, albeit a rather androgynous man—the Bard's patron, Henry Wriothesley, Earl of Southampton, better known to the world as the "Mr. W. H." to whom Shakespeare had dedicated his sonnets. Thankfully, Cobbe did not collapse in shock but lived long enough to gift his portrait to the world.

Furthermore, reputed scholarly opinion confirmed that the portrait of Shakespeare in his possession was probably the only one for which the dramatist ever posed during his own lifetime. Cobb loaned the portraits to the Shakespeare Trust so that fans could examine the closest likeness to the Bard that might possibly exist. Only a chance conversation with Karina had allowed me to peruse this singular portrait with my own two eyes and to ponder the complex scholarly initiatives undertaken to prove its provenance. Truly, from unintended accidents of encounter are the finest discoveries made.

Ever the avid sight-seer, I hopped at Oxford into one of the Stagecoach network of buses to Woodstock, that most picturesque of chocolate-box villages at the entrance to the Cotswolds. On the threshold of this picture-perfect hamlet of golden stone cottages surrounded by poppy-scattered fields lies John Vanbrugh's other *magnum opus*, Blenheim (say "Blen-um") Palace. Having combed through Castle Howard in Yorkshire with Hubs the previous August where my year-long adventures had begun, it somehow seemed right that Vanbrugh's two masterpieces should act as book ends to my Nearly Perfect Year.

On another evening, I jumped into a local bus to Witney, a medieval market town, to meet a very old Oxford friend, Sidney Seymour, who'd served as Hall Steward during my summer term at Exeter College more than twenty years previously. Having stayed in touch over the years through the exchange of Christmas cards, I didn't wish to leave Oxford this time round without making sure I spent quality time with Sid. At 77, ill-health had dogged him for several years. Despite knowing how poorly he'd been keeping, I was startled by his appearance for he'd sprouted raccoon-like bags under his eyes and an inordinate amount of weight that had settled on his bent frame causing painful knees.

At the bus-stop in Witney, Sid grinned and said in his characteristic mumble, "Luv-lay ta see ya again." And at the end of our meal at a local pub, I took Sid's swollen arm and walked towards the bus stop so we could go our separate ways. While I was deep in the heart of my rumination, he turned to me and said, "So how old are you now?"

"An old, though not necessarily wise, half-century," I laughed. Only an aged Englishman could ask a lady so blunt a question without so much as a by-your-leave.

"Exactly like that singer who died today," he said. "He too was fifty."

"Which singer?" I asked, fairly certain I wouldn't know him.

"I can't remember his name," said Sid, "American bloke. Black. Haven't you heard? It's all over the telly."

"I haven't been watching anything for the past few days," I responded. "I have no telly in my room here in Oxford."

"Well, this is big news. Huge," he said. Then, not wishing to be harassed by his failing memory, he turned to a teenager seated on the bench at the bus-stop and inquired, "What's the name of that singer who died today, Miss?"

"Michael Jackson," she smiled.

Whoa! What was that she said? Michael Jackson? Surely I'd misheard her.

"That's it! Michael Jackson!" said Sid.

"Michael Jackson?" I repeated. "Are you sure?"

"I know . . . it's shocking . . . the world's stunned," the teenager said.

"Michael Jackson," I said again to myself, softly. Blimey! How was it possible?

"How?" I asked her. "An accident? A plane crash?"

"A heart attack, I think," said the girl, smiling, visibly amused by my reaction. "But no one's really sure."

"A heart attack? But he was so young. And so fit . . . I mean he wasn't fat and flabby like Elvis or anything . . ."

Issues of death were still on my mind as I kissed Sidney goodbye when he alighted at his village of Eynsham (say "En-shim"). I waved at

his departing figure, wondering if or when I would ever see my sincere
friend again. Witney Market Square would always be associated in my
memory with the loss of the King of Pop.

While my ID card remained snagged in inter-departmental mailbags, I
discovered Oxford's hidden cracks and crevices on an 'Inspector Morse'
tour. The series had made British actor John Thaw an international
household name. I'd seen every one of the thirty-five episodes of *Inspector Morse* mysteries on American PBS channels and was, apparently, one of the millions of women viewers world-wide (including the
Queen, no less) who swooned upon hearing the name of the fictional
ale-swigging, opera-loving, crossword-solving, Jaguar-driving detective
of the Thames Valley Police. Morse's acerbic personality had been
created by fiction writer Colin Dexter, a Cambridge alumnus who'd
made Oxford his home and set all his novels amidst its dreaming spires.
Against the backdrop of medieval architecture, Morse and his sidekick
Sergeant Lewis, played by Kevin Whately, solved murder mysteries
written with the sort of suavity that gave them the reputation of the
most sophisticated crime solvers on TV.

I joined a large group of fellow-devotees led by a rather dapper
gentleman clad in a beige linen suit. Adrian Taylor had a booming voice
and a twinkle in his eye. Well, I sure did luck out! His knowledge of
Dexter's books and the TV series was profound and his naked passion
for the subject highly infectious. By the end of the tour, I was convinced
that I hadn't spent a better ten quid in my entire time in the UK and, in
the additional nuggets with which he left us, Taylor motivated me, in
the days that followed, to go out and toss back a fine ale at Morse's
favorite watering holes. Sadly, the Harry Potter tour wasn't half as compelling, or maybe it ought to have been restricted to young readers
alone. There was nothing in it to engage me.

So steeped was I in Morse memorabilia, that I found my way by local
bus and on foot for over three miles, that evening, to the Trout Inn in
Wolvercote where I ordered a Pimm's, "Oxford's quintessential summer drink" according to a blackboard at the bar. I sat by the river as the
sun disappeared beyond the western horizon and the muffled roar of a
gushing weir reached my ears. Taking the Morse Tour had crossed one
more item off my To-Do List as did the five mile Walk along the
Thames Path that followed. I undertook the return journey on foot to

Oxford along the banks of the Isis past ruined Godstow nunnery that gave the nearby Lock its name. God was in his heaven, all was right with the world.

Or very nearly.

For just when I thought my seemingly unending tryst with plantar fasciitis was slowly becoming a concern of the past, I had another severe physical setback in the tiny Cotswold village of Chipping Norton. What's that they say about the spirit being willing but the flesh being weak? It became apparent to me as I attempted to jump into a bus that had just left the curb that although my mind was still agile, my body's reflexes, at fifty, could no longer keep pace with them. I clearly misjudged the size of the leap that would land me in the bus and, as it sailed away slowly, I heard the sickening thud of my left kneecap as it slammed the pavement and brought me to my other knee.

Dazed and deeply embarrassed, I sat motionless, clinging to the curb, massaging my knee. Occurring, as it did, right opposite *The King's Arms Hotel* where Hubs, Dot and I had once stayed on a driving tour of the Cotswolds, I longed for the care and concern of my family members.

Jennifer Ilman at St. Antony's College came splendidly to my aid that evening by fixing a doctor's appointment for me at the Summertown Health Center.

Oh boy, I thought, the NHS. Here we go again. The more I tried to avoid dealing with it, the more my mishaps pushed me towards the UK's socialized healthcare.

That evening, the local GP, a Doc Nottingdale with salt and pepper head of hair and gentle bedside manner, took a quick look at my knee, examined it closely and made a diagnosis.

"You've suffered obvious trauma to your kneecap," he said. "It will ache for a few days. Might even swell. No cause for alarm, though. There are no cracks, no tears. No bones broken, no ligaments stretched. No fluid in the knee. Nothing. Take a pain killer, if you need to. But you should be as right as rain in a few days."

No, he neither recommended X-rays nor CT scans. For the second time, I found myself deeply impressed by the speed and confidence of old-fashioned British diagnostics. I am convinced, after a year of dealing with the system, that the best thing about the NHS is its physicians. But it's very definitely all downhill from there!

Why was fate working so hard to thwart my plans of retracing my youthful footprints? Was this Nature's way of reminding me that I could no more stop Time's inexorably slow march than I could hold back the waves of an ocean? Was it a wake-up call, sent to recommend that I slow down, take life at an easier pace, be mindful of my physical limitations? Well, Fate and Nature, I decided, were going to be ignored. Though I was afraid to awake the following morning, expecting my knee to have swollen like a balloon, I was relieved to find that but for a residual ache, the sickening fall might never have happened. I resolved to pretend I had imagined it all and to meander at leisure, as I'd intended, through paths I'd once known and others I'd yet to uncover.

19

LAST HURRAHS

Spring sprang. And I stepped into London's theaters to enjoy a new 'season' on its Victorian stages. It was time for some more adventure-ridden 'dares' as I continued to put my endurance to the test. One afternoon, at a matinee show, I regressed to my teens, doing something I'd never considered before. I set myself a dare: I would see if I could pull off rushing to the 'stage doors' of the theater after the show to bag autographs of the play's stars.

At the end of *Three Days of Rain*, I raced off to have current heart throb James McAvoy, star of such films as *The Last King of Scotland* and *Atonement*, autograph my Playbill. Even as I stood there, in all my half century glory, with a bunch of giddy teenyboppers hopping impatiently first on one foot, then another, for a glimpse of their hero, I had to pinch myself hard. Was I really doing this? Waiting for a movie star at a London stage door to make an autograph appearance? Half an hour later, I was the proud owner of signatures from all three of the show's actors and the possessor of a Playbill that would probably fetch premium price on Ebay.

And how could I possibly stop there? I soon found out that my favorite actress of all time, Judi Dench, was soon to be on stage—yes on stage—meaning in the flesh and not just on celluloid. I had loved her ardently in my favorite British TV series of all time, *As Time Goes By*, of which I had watched repeated re-runs on PBS in America. And shortly she would appear at the West End in Yukio Mishima's *Madame de Sade*. I was willing to go through hell and high water to snag tickets. So imagine my shock, my utter consternation, my downright devastation, when I heard Dame Judi flub her lines on stage. For at least ten seconds, she blanked out, having several serious Senior Moments, until Frances Barber who matched her histrionic prowess, scene for scene, came to her rescue. Without batting an eyelid, the veteran actress floated effortlessly on with her lines and movements, as if the gaff had never occurred.

Did this dampen my enthusiasm for the talented thespian? Far from it. It somehow made Judi more human, more like any of us, really. More like the lovable Jean Pargeter she'd played so vulnerably in my favorite show. When the curtain came down on yet another dazzling night at the Donmar, I was at stage door—an old hand by then at obtaining autographs—and was within a hair's breadth of my idol.

A few days later, I was at it again for success had made me hawkish. I stood at Leicester Square outside the Odeon Theater at night to see stars glide in and out of the London premier of the newest James Bond film, *Quantum of Solace*. More celeb-stalking. More possible bragging rights to be garnered, such as: "I have to say . . . Daniel Craig is just as dishy in person as on the big screen . . ." I could dream, couldn't it?

Alas, I did not catch the slightest glimpse of 007 as the other agent that called the shots in my life—PF—issued marching orders that sent me straight home.

However, when Harry Potter and his friends came to town, I rushed out to meet them, fired once again with a fan's zeal. It was too good an opportunity to be missed—to see Harry, Hermione, Ron and their creator, J. K. Rowling herself—especially as I'd spent the better part of several months devouring their wizardly escapades.

Leicester Square was transformed into Hogwart's School of Witchcraft and Wizardry for the occasion. Banners and logos representing the houses of Godric Griffindor, Helga Hufflepuff, Rowena Ravenclaw and Salazar Slytherin blew in the breeze in a riot of colors. A huge wooden stage set way up high enabled onlookers to catch a glimpse of their idols. And yours truly, unbelievably, was a part of it all.

Theatrical productions aside, in June, I became a player in a real life drama for I very nearly saw the inside of a British clink. I was at the royal ceremony called the Trooping of the Color, when, if you recall, I had narrowly missed getting nicked for climbing a forbidden terrace on the Mall for a better view of the proceedings.

How was I to know that free tickets are distributed by lottery, several months ahead of the event? Lucky ticket holders find assigned seats on the Horse Guards Parade from where they watch a series of military maneuvers. Or something of the kind, anyway, for nobody seems very clear exactly what goes on there! Non-ticket holders are welcome to line The Mall. Yours truly had set out to bag a spot when the policewoman had put paid to my ambitions. To rot in a London clink was, by no means, my idea of fun. The road to hell is truly paved with good intentions. Spotting the Princess Royal, Anne, the Queen's daughter on horseback, had been my motivation. The sight of her remained the only silver lining in an ominously grey cloud.

I had just begun to leave the Mall filled with despondency after my near run-in with the Law when I overheard an Englishman in conversation with his family: "Later, the royal family will appear on the first floor balcony of the Palace and wave to the crowds below. We really ought to try to make our way towards Buckingham's gates. Shall we start moving, dear?"

His teenaged daughter, assertively chewing gum and glued to her I-Pod, was most unenthusiastic. "Is this all? Is this what we woke up so early this morning to see?" she scowled.

"Well no, there's more," continued her Daddy, trying his utmost to remain upbeat, "A few minutes after that, you will see a fleet of planes zooming overhead. They fly in formation above the Palace and all the way along the Mall leaving smoky streaks in the sky. Come on, buck up, darling. It'll be fun. You'll see. You can tell all your friends at school that you saw William."

I didn't wait to find out whether Miss Top of the Pops complied or not. Nor did I have the stomach to move towards the Palace gates myself. I'd had more than I could digest for one damp squib of a morning.

As each new spring day presented itself, I sought out flowery bowers in which to spend it. It was finally time to use the annual membership to the National Trust that I'd purchased when I'd first arrived in England in August. Since the older I grow, the more firmly convinced I become that in a previous life I was an Edwardian lady, I headed to the home and gardens of Vita Sackville-West in Sissinghurst, Kent, where, with her diplomat husband, Harold Nicholson, she created some of England's most breathtaking gardens in the ruined precincts of a Renaissance castle.

Sissinghurst is one of the few National Trust properties easily accessible by public transport. But by the time I got to Kent and had spent most of the morning on my feet, I was ready to sink down somewhere for a long sit-down amidst its famed giant white delphiniums. By a sheer stroke of luck, I found a shaded arbor planted with lately-bloomed wisteria vine. Then, conjured, as if by a magician's wand, they appeared—the sweetest pair of ladies you could ever imagine.

And so, to my enormous delight, I found company and had another close encounter of the Anglo kind, this time with two little *memsahibs*—a remnant pair of biddies from the British Raj. Their antecedents stretched all the way to Calcutta, where they were born, as their imperialist daddies had seen the sun set on the British Empire. Jeannine and Beatrice, octogenarians both, were polished and charming, the kind whose global exposure left them open to spontaneous exchanges with fellow travelers on the road of life. Jeannine's slim frame was coolly clothed in a white Indian-style linen *kurta* while Beatrice wore a straw hat. Both sported sunglasses and beautiful tortoise-shell handled walking sticks.

"We loved India so much," said Jeannine while Cousin Beatrice commented, "My daughter was actually born in Calcutta's Elgin Hospital. Where is she? She's here somewhere . . ."

Out on a day's excursion with their daughters who were both roughly my own age, the ladies, originally from Yorkshire, were on a gardening tour. "Vita Sackville-West was almost our contemporary," said Jeannine, "and visiting this garden is a bit like making a pilgrimage to a revered shrine, isn't it, Betty?"

"Neither one of us has been back to Calcutta in over fifty years," Beatrice added, "but my, don't we have the happiest memories of our days there?"

"We did fail you though, didn't we? The British, I mean," said Beatrice, as Jeannine nodded her head in agreement. "What did we ever do for the poor Indian? Nothing. Nothing at all. It was a crying shame, the Empire. Simply disgraceful."

"And then when we returned here to England, we were such misfits, weren't we? We longed for those days back in India, for our girls-only schools in Mussourie and Nainital and our diplomatic dos in Calcutta where we were the belles of the ball."

"No, old girl, we didn't fit into England at all. We hated it. The cold and the rain and the fog. All that fog. We don't have any of that anymore, really, do we?"

"Well, with central heating now, Jeannie, there are no more charcoal fires burning . . . you see."

"And we missed all those servants, instantly at our beck and call, didn't we?" Beatrice chuckled.

"No wonder we couldn't stand it here when we returned."

I gazed at them in disbelief. I had always been enamored by the Edwardians and now there I was, literary me, devotee of colonial novels and films seated right besides two of them—women who could have walked right off the pages of a novel set in an Indian hill-station. This pair of cousins, endowed with the compassion of Paul Scott and the sensitivity of E. M. Forster, brought me face-to-face with the Raj. How much of a coincidence was that? It seemed to me as if it was simply meant to be.

I could have sat there forever conversing at ease with these articulate grannies whose global vision had endowed them with open mindedness and curiosity. On the strength of their combined memories, they had whisked me back, not just to Vita and Harold's Edwardian roots, but indeed to the Calcutta of Lord Curzon, half a globe way. On a brilliant morning under Kentish skies, I had been permitted entry, if only vicariously through their memories, into the gracious world of imperial yesterdays.

Awash in the spirit of Vita Sackville-West whose journal entries in her own handwriting had charmed me no end in the special exhibition set up in a converted barn, I resolved to find a way by public transport to Knole House, abode of her birth, also run by the National Trust. I knew that the two venues would work like a jigsaw puzzle to fit together the missing pieces that comprised her privileged life.

Reaching Knole House, home of Vita Sackville-West in Kent, got, as the English would say, my knickers in a twist. Public transport—or the lack of it, really—to the bastions of medieval aristocracy—often plunked in the midst of a hundred acres of parkland—so fatigued and frustrated me that I felt severely drained. When I arrived at Sevenoaks, no signs of any kind existed to guide me towards Knole. I stood, bewildered, outside the railway station, hoping divine intervention would send me an angel to guide me on my way. It was a one mile walk to the top of a hill and a further two-mile walk from there to the Park's entrance.

Was I up to the challenge? In shoes stuffed with Orthotics? On feet only reluctantly recovering from inflamed ligaments? I didn't think so. Not when I discovered that the house sits in the middle of a vast property, a further mile from its main gate. By sheer Providence, I found a couple headed to the house and into their car I jumped in for a ride to the venue taking another huge chance with my safety. Clearly I continued to believe in angels.

Knole House had belonged to Thomas Cromwell, then King Henry VIII, then his daughter Queen Elizabeth I, then her favorite courtier Robert Dudley, Earl of Leicester and then her cousin Thomas Sackville, Earl of Dorset, who then passed it on to his descendants until it fell into the hands of Vita's father. Sadly, as his only child and being female, she could not inherit the manor that was passed on to her uncle in 1928. Shattered and then newly married to Nicholson, Vita purchased nearby Sissinghurst and poured her resentment into its gardens.

After the execution of King Charles II in 1685 and the national confusion that accompanied it, the owner of Knole House at the time, Charles, fourth Earl of Dorset, ransacked Whitehall and Hampton Court Palace so completely that he seized any item on which he could lay his avaricious hands. Considering that British newspapers were rocked, during my year in London, by the scandal of contemporary MPs whose snouts were stuck firmly in tax-payers' troughs, it was plain to see that the crooked ways of Ministers hadn't changed a great deal over the centuries. Knole House is simply cluttered and I mean cram-jammed with stuff.

While still unmarried and living in her parental home at Knole, Vita had a lesbian affair with the novelist Virginia Woolf who was her frequent guest. A facsimile copy of the original manuscript of Woolf's novel *Orlando* is on exhibition, having been gifted to Vita by Virginia. In fact, so familiar did Virginia become with Knole House that it is said to be the model for the house she describes in *Orlando* for in it, Woolf had written, "Indeed, the house was surrounded by a park fifteen miles in circumference and a wall ten feet high". Virginia was right on the money! I knew. I had traversed those fifteen miles—fortunately as a hitch-hiker in a car produced by angelic intervention. Woolf also wrote, "The great hall had never seemed so large, so splendid or so empty . . ." She had ended by penning this lovely passage that exactly describes the abundance of furniture: "there was no room in the galleries for another table; no room on the tables for another cabinet; no room in the cabinet for another rose-bowl; no room in the bowl for another handful of potpourri; there was no room for anything anywhere; in short, the house was furnished."

Was I glad I made it to Knole through such a convoluted route and such centuries' worth of clutter? You bet your last farthing!

Feverish! I was actually feverish with anticipation, a few days later, when Amelia Tolbrook, my American friend and favorite travel companion, arrived from Manhattan. It was she who had introduced me, through cyberspace, to the irrepressible Samantha. We passed by million plus-pound homesteads that punctuate the walk from the Tube station to the tennis courts at Wimbledon. We weren't privileged to cheer for tennis stars that afternoon as we did not have access to the corporate tickets that Sam had snagged. Undaunted by disappointment, Amelia and I anticipated larger rewards. For Sam had organized a post-match party and I was finally going to meet Mr. Darling, also known as The Scarlet Pimpernel, at a pub supper. Strawberries and cream and sporty star-gazing took a backseat to the thrills of meeting Hizoner at last.

After months of hearing so much about Keith Darling, to see him actually in the flesh in our midst was simply too much of a let-down. People and places grow in stature, the more you hear about them. Blame imagination for lending enchantment to the view. Believe you me, I tried hard not to stare. Call me dreadfully superficial for my age, but I was convinced my Sam could do better. Sam's Darling did not earn my approval right away. But I decided to withhold the formation of an opinion until I had the opportunity to know him better.

Amelia was fully in cahoots with me. Not only did she also withhold judgment on Sam's *beau* but when we met again, the following day, she said, "Okay. Let's get down to business. Time to tackle your To-Do List and knock those last lingering items right off it."

I laughed, delighted to have her with me in London for two whole days before she vamoosed to Croatia with Sam on a planned European cruise of the Adriatic.

"You asked for it!" I said. "Today, we shall conquer the Monument. Tomorrow, when we walk in Chiswick, I shall have completed every single one of those twenty-five self-guided walks I'd intended. How's that for focus during a terribly crippling year—pun intended?"

Amelia high-fived me and off we went to scale the three hundred and eleven steps from the Monument's pedestal, my battered knee-cap notwithstanding. Christopher Wren had designed the pillar to commemorate London's dreadful Fire of 1666 that had started in a bakery in the vicinity. Conquering its heights earned us a certificate each and the knowledge that it was exactly as tall as the distance from the fire's origin on nearby Pudding Lane to the site chosen to mark it.

Later that afternoon, Amelia disclosed that Sam hadn't squirreled her Darling away after all. It was he who had remained AWOL for most of their months together. Not sure how to end it with Hizoner, she had remained conflicted for weeks. She was not yet clear, apparently, where to take their relationship—whether to end it or to give it (and him) some more time. She hoped that a getaway with her girlfriends might sharpen the picture.

Two days later, Amelia left on a voyage with Sam and her gal pals to little-known hamlets along the Adriatic coast. For my part, I headed towards weeks of swotting in London libraries by day. And in preparation for my return home, I packed and taped boxes frantically after dark.

Little did I expect that at the fag end of my London sojourn, I'd meet another comrade-in-arms. Amelia was not the only one in cahoots with me in getting my To-Do List ticked right off. Fate stepped in quite handily at the eleventh hour at an Anglo-Indian barbecue party in Wembley at which I was (almost) the only odd-one-out. Before long, my visual radar zeroed in on Jaffar (Jaff) Alam, another Singleton. He appeared just as ill-at-ease amidst the geriatric conference of seventy-plus invitees who comprised the party. Understandably, we connected and after preliminary introductions, much to my amazement, my handsome, newly-divorced, fifty-something companion glanced at my infamous To-Do List (quite handily tucked into my handbag) and joined forces to cancel every last entry on it.

"We're only a stone's throw from two places you want to see," he said. "Come on. Let's get you off to Wembley Stadium first!"

Woo-Hoo! A sexy articulate South Asian about my age with an educated British accent, oodles of enthusiasm and a car to boot? Where the heck had he been hiding?

"Better late than never!" he said, reading my mind. And then, "And now I'd like you to meet someone. Say hello to Suzie."

Suzie was his little Mini Cooper, cute as a metallic button and just as shiny. As we skirted the precincts of one of the world's most famous stadiums, I took in the iconic arch that spans its skyline, stuck my head out the window, threw inhibition to the wind and screeched, "Wembley Stadium! Hulllllloh! I'm here! This is my Laaaast Hurraaaaah!"

"Second Laaaaast!" corrected Jaff as he joined in the yodeling. I had found a partner to accompany my gallivanting.

"We're heading off to Harrow School next," he said, firmly. "Do you need me to take your picture to immortalize these moments?"

He got it. He so got it. He became instantly attuned to my personal obsessions. When he said, "Madam, your carriage awaits. Just let me know where else Suzie can take you," I wondered anew why I hadn't run into him earlier in the year.

Jaff subsequently became one of the firmest friends Hubs and I had across the pond. Suzie joined the three of us to make up a formidable foursome that swallowed up almost every tourist mile on Britain's motorway network as the years went by and I remained smitten by Britain.

Meanwhile, I planned another trip that put me solo in Soho. I felt deeply compelled to follow my gastronomic taste buds to *The Gay Hussar*, a fine Hungarian dining place in Soho that had been serving a chilled Cherry Soup to faithful patrons since the turn of the last century. Eager to put my new solo dining skills to the test, I approached the hostess and whispered, "I'm only here to try your legendary cherry soup, please, as I've read so much about it. I thought I couldn't leave London without a sample."

As I took my first tentative taste, my eyes closed involuntarily to savor the sublimity of the sensation. Divine. It was simply divine. Sour stewed morello cherries had sunk to the bottom and as I fished them out with the greatest tenderness, I determined to combine cherries, cherry juice, milk, crème fraiche, sugar and a dash of salt to replicate the concoction at home. What a steal for a mere £4.75 a bowl!

I complimented the waitress and requested my bill. Then, to my amazement, the Manager himself popped out to say, "No charge, Madam. Soup is on the house!"

No way! "Why ever not?" I asked in both wonder and embarrassment.

"Your appreciation is payment enough," he said with the slightest Eastern European flourish that harked back to the days of the Austro-Hungarian empire.

Dissed by a waiter in Belgium for ordering tap water with my meal, then served a celebrated bowl of cherry soup with the compliments of the chef in a Soho establishment. My adventures in solo dining were a true study in contrasts.

A full three hundred and sixty-five days had passed since I had blown out fifty candles on my cake in my garden in Southport; but I placed thoughts of celebration on hold as I had far more urgent priorities. My prized desk, for instance, needed to be packed and shipped home to Connecticut with every ounce of TLC that I could bestow upon it.

On my fifty-first birthday, partridge-shooting Khan Saab came splendidly to the rescue when he sent his Merc and his Man Friday, Minaz, to transport it to a warehouse in Acton for its onward journey to the New World. The reputed forwarding and clearing agency known as Headleys Humper—a name that never fails to produce a snigger—was delegated the task of schlepping it across the pond for me. When next I saw it, it was three weeks later, swaddled professionally in packaging material and delivered to the doorstep of Holly Berry House in Southport.

I spent the afternoon of my birthday shopping for gourmet groceries at *Waitrose* with the intention of putting together a summer no-cook meal for my former Holborn neighbors, NextDoor Tom and Brenda. With Buck's Fizz cooling in the fridge, couscous with Moroccan preserves and a variety of salads and Prosciutto di Parma on the table, we had dinner that ended with a Black Forest Gateau. But for the cards that decorated my dining table, my former neighbors and current BFFs would never have known that it was my special day.

And finally, my last day of solitary exploration dawned. After wondering long and hard how I would spend it, I decided it would be with Samantha. She drove me to Salisbury for the last time in her ink-blue Lexus to give me the latest update on the goings-on with her Darling—who, much against her fondest aspirations, had faded into the annals of her colorful dating history.

"We're so done!" she said. "I'm going to chalk it down to British experience. It was good while it, like, lasted, but now it's time to move on. He was fun and we had some good times together. So, no regrets."

"Are you sure" I asked suspiciously, "that you're over him? You did seem to fancy him."

"Yes, I did . . ." she responded, "for, like, two minutes. But then nothing was ever straight with him, was it?"

"Never say Die," I said. "Tomorrow is another day, as Scarlett O'Hara said."

"Scarlett who?" she responded.

Because we had just reached Andover, I was prevented from replying.

So in conclusion, dear reader, sadly, Sam did not keep her tryst with marital destiny in England. But because my vivacious friend did not have a single foolish bone in her body, I knew that when the right time came, she would marry the right man and marry him for entirely the right reasons. Three cheers to her, as the Brits would say: Hip-Hip-Hurray!

Although Salisbury is acclaimed for the spire of its cathedral that is reputedly the tallest in the land as well as for holding one of the few original copies of the *Magna Carta*, the 1215 document that outlines agreements signed at nearby Runnymede by King John and his barons, it was for a quite different reason that the city gave me one of my year's highlights—my quest for the spot at which John Constable painted his famous *View of Salisbury Cathedral*, as, for the second time, I attempted to place myself inside a painting. Luck favored me when a 'Salisbury local' gave me the most precise directions to the exact spot.

"Right. You walk straight ahead past the Cathedral Close, go under the gateway, make a left at the pizza place, then over a bridge on the river. Follow the road as it bends past the Meadows which will be on your left. You will see a road leading to the railway station and on its left a foot path leading to another wooden bridge. Cross that bridge and you will see the Cathedral on your left from the exact angle in which Constable painted it."

Would you even believe it? Such precise directions, so confidently delivered? He simply had to be a fellow art-lover.

And there I found it. Exactly as he'd said I would. I could have hugged the man. Tall bulrushes almost obscured the sight, but the Cathedral spire still rose proudly, the landscape completed with the flowing Avon and grazing cattle that had become the proud focal point of a composition that Constable had immortalized. My last bit of solo searching had yielded admirable returns.

When I went to bed that night, my solitary year came to a close. I would awake alone for the very last time as Hubs was due to return to Blighty when morning dawned.

From the moment I opened the door of *Sweden House* to him, Hubs and I became honeymooners all over again. Absence does make the heart grow fonder—take it from me! We floated around together in a romantic fog, arm in arm, as we took our last looks of London. I'd missed my husband dreadfully, yet how healthy the year-long separation had been for our marriage. It had brought us together in the sweetest ways, providing excuses for trans-Atlantic crossings and Continental holidays during which we both realized how much we meant to each other.

Above all, my Year of Nearly Perfect Living had provided me with extended time to think about those things that ought to matter most in life—the emotional, psychological and physical well-being of those we most love. The Year had brought out the best in me as I'd coped with unforeseen tumbles and excruciating physical pain. But it made me want to return home to be the best daughter, sister, wife, mother, friend and colleague I could possibly be. In delving deep into my psyche in perceptive moments of solitude, I saw how much I'd gained by spending the year alone—not merely in terms of forging powerful and enriching new friendships but also in terms of acquiring priceless insights.

When Hubs and I decided to throw a farewell party, *Sweden House* provided the perfect backdrop for such a gathering. My newest friends trooped in from far and wide, bringing their British buoyancy with them. As *pakoras* and Cabernet circulated amidst the antiques in my art-crammed loft, so did introductions. Lorraine and Charles, mine hosts, were present to welcome our guests, some of whom, like Jaff, were meeting Hubs for the very first time. Even as I took memento pictures with sets of friends, I stared at them and hoped my swimming eyes would communicate what my tongue was too heavy to articulate: "A year ago, I did not know a single one of you. How can I thank you all enough for having enriched my time here in the smallest but most meaningful of ways?" Wherever life took Hubs and me, we would always have a special place in our hearts for those individuals who had found a place for us in theirs during my solitary life in London. I fought tears away until our last guests left; but then I clung to Lorraine and let them rip. They flowed copiously down my cheeks as I hugged, kissed and thanked her for her incredible generosity and her gift of lasting friendship.

Cindy Byron, Director of the summer program at Exeter College, Oxford, introduced me briefly and then I was off as I traced main movements in Literature in English from the Indian sub-continent inspired by Great Britain. As students took copious notes and chuckled on cue, my shot nerves relaxed. To a roar of applause, my lecture ended and when Cindy invited me right there and then to return to give another lecture, the following summer, she crowned my Nearly Perfect Year with its brightest highlight.

Hubs and I had made it, at dawn, on a coach that is known picturesquely as The Oxford Tube so that I could deliver my lecture on South Asian Immigrant Fiction from Great Britain. What a long way I'd come in twenty-two years! From Bombay to Oxford; from Oxford to New York; and then back to Oxford again; I'd traveled full circle. Where once I'd hung on to the words of wisdom of the university's dons, there I was delivering my own. For the nth time that year, I wondered how such a thing had happened. It would be the last crowning highlight of an incredible year.

For when we launched upon the final leg of my Year of More Perfect Living and conjured our last idyllic week of holiday bliss—our week in France—the calamity that awaited me across the Channel simply never entered the picture.

20

FINALLY IN FRANCE

In a hospital! Yet again! Seeing more doctors. Not NHS ones in the UK. Not a homeopath in Bombay. This time round, I was being seen by *medecins en France*. Just when I thought that our last week in Europe was going swimmingly and that I'd kissed my misadventures *au revoir*, I had one more collision with the ground—this time across the English Channel on a bicycle—that brought me in headlong contact with the French healthcare system.

We'd left London to board a train to stay with our friends Guillaume and Marie-Christine Leblanc in Normandy. Guillaume awaited us at the train station at Lison and drove us past the charming town of Saint Lo before we arrived in the tiny village of Quibou where our friends live on a sprawling eight acre homestead named Hotel Bonheur with their boys, Alain and Rene, baby daughter Sarah, a cat named Misti and two brown horses.

We'd had a most unusual day on Guillaume's brother Jean-Paul's farm and were returning to *Hotel Bonheur*, when it happened. There I was one minute pedaling my bicycle contentedly past fields of black and white cows when I encountered a slope. Downhill I went, at a higher speed, the wind threatening to send my baseball cap flying right off. I didn't want to lose my cap and I knew I could not apply my brakes too suddenly while going downhill. Instinctively I raised my hand to hold my cap down, losing both balance and control on a steep hill. In seconds, I hurtled towards the ground landing astride my front wheels in an untidy heap on manure-scented Normandy soil. Behind me, Hubs' voice ended in a tortured screaming of my name.

Half an hour later, I was entering the Emergency Room at Paul Nelson Hospital. Within minutes, the place sprang to life as nurses and paramedical staff obtained details of my fall.

It wasn't long before the gorgeous, young, Dr. Claude Beaumont came to my assistance. Despite my fears about a possibly fractured skull, I wondered whether, in another avatar, he'd ever played Dr. McDreamy from *Grey's Anatomy*.

"*J'ai tombé de mon velo*," I began hesitantly, as I told him that I had fallen from my bicycle. I then asked if he preferred to speak with my friend Guillaume in better French than mine.

"*Pas du tout*," said Dr. McBeaumont. "*J'ai tout a fait compris. Vas y. Vas y.*" Even in the midst of my worst fears that I was slowly bleeding to death inside my head, I was vain enough to feel tickled when he complimented me and, at the end of my account, said, "*Madame, vous parlez francais tres bien.*" His smile was warm and I discerned a distinct twinkle in his charcoal eyes. All those weeks spent boning up on my French in England hadn't been in vain. *Ouuiiiii!*

Preliminary examinations were carried out before the delectable *docteur* opined that everything looked good, prima facie . However, he prescribed X-rays to rule out internal damage.

About ten minutes later, I was in the Radiography Department, where another paramedic named Marc Thevenet directed me most politely to do his bidding. Eager to practice his less-than-perfect English, he said, "Leave your *epaule* 'ere, *madame*, if you please" and just as I tried to figure out how to leave my shoulder behind, he said, "Okay, okay, now turn your 'ead and sleep 'ere a little bit."

Less than a half hour after my pictures were studied, Dr. McBeaumont told me there was no cause for concern. Expect bad bruising upon awakening, he said. But awake, he assured me, I would.

I had escaped without serious head injury or a longish stint in the ER. Leaving my global medical insurance information behind, I had only to await a bill from the French hospital—a bill that would be delivered to my home in the States, they said.

Three days previously, our penultimate escapades had begun in France's capital, when our Eurostar train had swallowed miles to bridge the waters of the English Channel. We were in Paris before we could quite say *Bonjour*!

Just off the Champs Elysses, my heart leapt on surveying the grand *fin de siècle* building, complete with massive iron grilled gates, spacious internal quadrangle, gleaming floors and walls, that was to be our home for the next few days—an *appartement* that belonged to our friend Frederic and his teenaged daughter Chantal who had opened their domain to us for a most gracious visit. As we entered the minuscule old-world lift, we were hoisted into eighteenth century Paris, architectural showpiece of Baron Haussmann.

Massive wooden doors were opened to us by Chantal who kissed us three times. A slender Parisienne with silky blond hair to her waist, sparkling blue eyes and the most perfect smile, she welcomed us warmly into her *appartement* and ushered us into a room with a marble fireplace and French windows that led to our own private balcony. Overlooking a courtyard brushed by the abundant branches of sturdy oaks, we had an undulating view of the rooftops of Paris from our fifth floor perch. For the next few days, Frederic, a high-powered corporate lawyer in a multi-national firm, and his daughter Chantal, played perfect hosts. Tall, slim and sporting a well-trimmed beard, Frederic exuded Gaelic elegance. His week was made when we offered to grill him duck breasts marinated in a spicy yoghurt bath."

"*Maigret du canard a l'Indienne*! I love it," exclaimed Frederic.

Two days later, Paris unexpectedly presented a wonderful sporting spectacle when we became onlookers at the *Tour de France* bicycle race. For days before the event, I'd noticed signs all over the city announcing the end of the famous international cross-country race on the Champs Elysses. Of course, it did not escape me that we were staying in a building right in the thick of the racing action.

"Imagine that!" I said in awed excitement to Hubs. "We're going to be here the day the *Tour de France* arrives in Paris! We really ought to watch it!"

"Have you any idea what the crowds will be like?" said a surprisingly unenthusiastic Hubs. "It'll be crazy."

What was the matter with him? He was supposed to be the sports junkie. I thought he'd jump at the idea of watching the end of the race in person. I mean, what are the odds that we'd actually be in Paris, living right off the Champs Elysses, where the race ended? Well, I didn't know about him . . . .but I intended to be there, one way or another.

When we returned to the *appartement* , I asked Frederic if he thought we could possibly watch the conclusion of the race.

"*Mais, bien sur,*" Frederic said, "Very easily done. I used to go downstairs every year. Just take my ladder with you. Prop it up on the sidewalk and you'll get the best view."

"A ladder?" I stared, doubtfully, not sure I'd understood him correctly.

"*Oui, Oui* . . . it's not a big deal. We have a very light one. When Chantal was little, I used to take her down and place her on my lap to watch."

"A ladder?" I repeated, very unsure about the idea.

"Ok, I'll tell you what?" said Frederic. "Take my step stool instead. That's the best thing. It's smaller and lighter. You can stand on it and look above the heads in front of you."

Hubs and I stared at each other thinking the same thought. Improbable as it sounded, the step stool could just work.

And, two days later, crazy as it might seem, we did exactly that. At 4:00 p.m., amidst the *bleu, blanc, rouge* flags merrily lining the Champs Elysses and the frenzied spectators cheering on that great American legend, Lance Armstrong, we stood with Frederic, on our step stool and with an uninhibited view of the avenue, yelled madly.

"Mind your wallets," warned Frederic. "Pickpockets abound here."

"Did you hear that the French have renamed the race *Tour de Lance*? I shouted above the noise.

As Hubs and Frederic laughed, the first 'sprinters' entered the Avenue to the roar of the assembled crowds. To be there, in Paris . . . to be part of a race that we'd watched on TV for years in the States . . . to salute the sprinters who'd first made their way on to the Boulevard to complete the last nine rounds that would end the event . . . and then to see colorful clumps of cyclists, exhausted after days of cross-country pedaling, make their entry . . . to listen to the reverberations that rose and fell like waves each time Lance and his compatriots whizzed past us—*Quelle chance!* Carrying that stepstool and setting it on the Champs Elysses and climbing it to take pictures of the athletes was the most inspired move we'd made in a very long while.

Thus, as my Nearly Perfect Year came to an end, we had another celebrity sighting—Lance Armstrong who'd made cycling history, our compatriot, was only a few feet from us on his final spins into the record books. We carried extraordinary memories of France's capital city with us as we boarded a train to Normandy, the next morning, for the set of adventures that led me straight to a hospital at midnight.

When Guillaume had asked me if there was anything in particular I wished to see in Normandy, I had my answer pat.

"Two things, please. The Bayeux Tapestry and the D-Day beaches with the American War Cemetery."

"*Pas problem*," Guillaume had replied. "Quite easily done. We shall cover that tomorrow. And the day after, I shall take you to my brothers' farm to show you some interesting aspects of modern French dairy farming."

True to his word, Guillaume had driven us on a dripping morning to Bayeux to see the famous Tapestry woven to commemorate the conquest of the Anglo-Saxon King Harold of England by William of Normandy known as the Conqueror at the Battle of Hastings in 1066. Widely believed to have been embroidered by contemporary Normandy Queen Mathilde and her ladies-in-waiting around the year 1070, the tapestry is displayed in a room constructed specially to accommodate the 70 meter long work which comprises 58 small panels, each one telling part of the story that brought England under French rule and forever changed its culture, language and administrative systems. Having perused the battle-field in the town of Battle with Samantha when the blizzard had begun in the throes of winter, it was hardly a relief to be in Bayeux where the heavens opened again.

Later that day, our mood underwent a sea change following our drive to Coleville-sur-Mer whose beaches were selected as the landing point upon which to launch the Allied conquest of Europe on June 6, 1944. Scenes brilliantly depicted by Steven Speilberg in the opening shots of his film *Saving Private Ryan* were uppermost in my mind as I gazed out at the English Channel, deceptively placid on a day when rain clouds had finally parted to reveal an anemic sun.

"We should try to get to Point du Hoc also," said Guillaume. "So let's hurry."

The main objective of the Allied forces, he'd explained, was to destroy German guns positioned on the promontory where the two beaches, now named Utah and Omaha, meet. Infantry soldiers could then penetrate Europe to destroy Hitler.

As we drove away from the cemetery, it was hard to fathom the enormity of the figures that had been tossed out at us in the adjoining museum. Ten thousand men had died and fifteen hundred went missing during the infamous land attack. At Point du Hoc, as we walked with other silent visitors upon ground pockmarked by falling bombs and punctuated by the remains of German bunkers, we strode straight into history textbooks. Only a few weeks previously, we'd missed another close shave with our President—this time on French soil—as President Obama had laid wreaths in commemoration of the sixty-fifth anniversary of the Anglo-American landing.

It was after the sun had sunk low in the west and long before darkness had swept over the farms and fields of Normandy, that Guillaume had suggested a bicycle ride along the country roads to the dairy farm run by his brother Jean-Paul. Alain and Rene brought us our bicycles and off we pedaled, along narrow country roads past fiercely barking dogs that leapt at us from behind the gates of sleepy dairy farms until we arrived at Jean-Paul's farm.

"Here you will see how mechanized dairy farming has become in Normandy," Guillaume said as Jean-Paul led us to the barn.

We watched, astonished, as eighty giant black and white Normandy cows trooped into the barn, to be milked, one at a time, the electronic tags on their ears read by a computer as they passed its sensor. Once in, a gate slid shut automatically, holding them captive. As they turned their heads to munch on a trough of cow treats, a set of suction cups, led by a robotic arm, searched, found and firmly attached themselves to their udders as milking began. Even as the cow stood there, the chemical composition of her milk was analyzed automatically before it was deposited in a large vat, to be siphoned off later, also automatically. Should a cow not produce the requisite nutritional levels required by the bottling plants, her milk would be diverted to a secondary vat to be discarded at a later stage. When the milking session ended, the gate opened, the cow was discharged and the next one in line took its place. Incredibly, the entire operation occurred without any human intervention of any kind.

"This means," explained Guillaume, as we stared open-mouthed, "that since he installed this system, my brother can laze on the beach during the summer knowing that his cows are being milked regardless of his absence."

"Unbelievable," Hubs said. Jean-Paul grinned, then asked if we'd like to see his week-old calves.

"*Mais, bien sur.*" How cute, I thought, to see a few calves gamboling around in the hay. Another photo op waited in the wings. And, truly, that was all I expected.

We were ushered into the 'maternity barn' where we found a cow right in the throes of labor. There, before our disbelieving eyes, stood a huge pregnant animal with the hind legs of her calf just beginning to emerge from a region just below her upright tail.

"This is just about the most WTF moment I have had during my entire year," I whispered to Hubs, my voice filled with wonder. As I readied my camera to shoot this once-in-a-lifetime opportunity, Jean-Paul jumped into the stable to help with the delivery.

Suffice it to say that we spent the next half hour listening to the plaintive lowing of a cow in deep labor and the grunts of one, then two human males—Jean-Paul and Guillaume—as they tried to yank the calf out of its mother's belly. They used a thick rope and a metal contraption to steady their feet and keep them firmly rooted to the ground as they pulled.

Just when it seemed as if they were ready to collapse in exhaustion, Hubs jumped into the fray. He could not stand passively by and watch as our friends struggled through the tug-of-war.

"Where are you going?" I shrieked.

"Doing my bit in the maternity ward," he said.

"Well, then, I'm damned if I'm standing tamely by," I said, as I joined in the endeavor.

Helping to deliver a calf in Normandy! For the umpteenth time I wondered, Who'dda ever thunk it?

Under the direction of Jean-Paul, we pulled and we tugged—the four of us—and we pulled again in unison, and then we let go and then we tugged again, to the repetitive chorus of "*Un, Deux, Trois*".

To say it was not an easy birth would be a classic understatement. The wearied cow finally just plopped on the ground even as I became an active participant in the miracle of birth. Meanwhile, oblivious to all the trouble, pain and anxiety it had caused, her calf, covered in slime, reluctantly slid out and said *Bonjour* to the world.

Whoever expected that I would come to Normandy and participate, in person, in scenes that had left me spellbound on TV's *All Creatures Great and Small*? The privilege both moved, subdued and filled me with ironic wonder. Hubs and I had started my Nearly Perfect Year in James Heriot Country near Thirsk in Yorkshire, recalling the many accounts of animal calving that the prolific vet had described. Little did we dream that we would end my Year by becoming twin participants in the drama of veterinary surgery in France.

That evening, flushed with the knowledge that we had assisted in bringing life into the world, Hubs suddenly pulled me close to him and said, "It is just so good to be back with you again. I have missed you so very much."

Taken completely by surprise at his words, I said, "But . . . but . . . you never ever said so."

"You have no idea how much I missed you." I could hear the depth of emotion in his voice.

"Then why didn't you say so before? I always wondered."

"Because I never wanted you to feel guilty about being in London. I wanted you to be free to complete your research and have the year you'd always dreamed of."

I stared at him, speechless. "If I'd kept telling you how much I'd been missing you," he continued, "you might have felt guilty for accepting your work assignment. And I didn't want anything to spoil your enjoyment of your special opportunity."

Those precious few moments of intimacy between us filled me with a profound sense of understanding and a wealth of new insights. Our year apart had tested both of us severely, emotionally and psychologically, but it also played a role in drawing us closer together. Yes, it is true! Cliched though it might sound, absence does make the heart grow fonder.

A day later, we left *la patrie* together and returned to the UK. My biking mishap and midnight visit to the French ER ended my Nearly Perfect Year with a bang! Literally! How could anyone top that, right? I'd had my fair share of adventures, but causing my husband as much alarm as I'd done in Normandy upon hurtling to the ground, had definitely not been on the cards. For the hundredth time I assessed my many physical mishaps. I'd survived inflamed tendons in London, a flying fall that had traumatized my knee-cap in Oxford and a bicycle debacle in France—all within what was supposed to be a Dream Year! I'd return to Southport, battle-scarred and travel-weary, with a spectacular black eye to proclaim my misadventures.

Back across the English Channel, I tried to fall asleep in *Sweden House* on our last night in London. But the highlights of my year rewound mentally, like a slo-mo documentary, kept me awake as so many images assaulted my mind.

Through the flurry of crazed activity of that final morning, our day was saved by my forgetting to put my wrist watch one hour back after returning from Paris late the previous night. So while I thought it was 10:00 a.m., it was actually only 9:00—Omigawd! Changing Time Zones had gifted me an extra hour!

Then in a bizarre repetition of our arrival in London one year previously, the cab-driver who was supposed to drive us to Heathrow, failed to show. We were in the process of tearing fistfuls of hair off our heads when, magically, just as Mahen had done a year before at Heathrow, another mini-cab driver called John happened to be cruising down our street. He piled our baggage into his shiny grey BMW and took us to Heathrow. I fought back tears throughout the ride on Cromwell Road past the museums of Albertopolis that had been my second home for a year. I rebuked myself to behave for I wasn't even out of the city and I'd already begun to experience intense symptoms of withdrawal syndrome.

Darkness had fallen over New York by the time we landed across the Atlantic. On the Van Wyck Expressway headed into Connecticut, America looked familiar and yet so foreign. I made my first call in the USA to Dot who simply said, "Welcome Home, Mum!"

EPILOGUE

One month after I blew out candles on the Black Forest Gateau of my fifty-first birthday in my Farringdon loft in London, I awoke in my favorite village—Southport, Connecticut. I had savored every single second of my perfect mid-century birthday present. I bid a lingering goodbye to my year as a Singleton in London and embarked, once again, upon my normal roles as a dutiful wife, mother, university professor and museum docent in America.

I resumed my professorial career in The Big Apple where I still teach and advice students who plan to study abroad in T-Smoke. I picked up the threads of weekend traipsing through galleries filled with Old Masters' works at the Metropolitan Museum of Art where, after twenty-two years of weekend museum-guiding, I am now an Emeritus Docent.

Dot and Colin did not marry and Hubs changed international banking positions as the world's financial failings were gradually rectified.

I'd taught humanities and writing courses throughout an academic year at NYU-London. I'd carried out research at six libraries beginning with the Grand Daddy of them all—The British Library, the Senate House Library, the Library of the School of Oriental and African Studies, the National Archives at Kew, and at Oxford, the Library at St. Antony's College and the Bodleian.

I'd interviewed seventy-five Anglo-Indians ranging in age from sixteen to eighty-five all over London plus Essex, Barking, Maidenhead and Oxford. Their words are documented in the ethnographic book I wrote and published in 2017 under the title, *Britain's Anglo-Indians: The Invisibility of Assimilation*.

In a single year that marked half a century of my being, I'd traveled through three Continents (Europe, North America and Asia). I'd visited thirteen countries (England, Scotland, Spain, Greece, Northern Ireland, the USA, India, Germany, Belgium, Norway, Italy, Turkey and France). I'd spoken—or attempted to speak—twelve languages (English, Spanish, Greek, Gaelic, Hindi, Marathi, German, Flemish, Norwegian, Italian, Turkish and French). I still had coins from six sundry currencies rattling around in my purse (British pence, European cents, Norwegian kroner, Turkish lira, Indian paise and American cents).

At the beginning of my not-so-ordinary year, I'd expected unflagging tourist zeal to provide my fondest escapist memories. But, it was the people I met and befriended—those who took me to their hearts and under their wings—that greatly enriched mine. Those bonds made my year Nearly Perfect.

Samantha took a year-long break from husband-hunting as she globe-trotted during her own Gap Year that followed mine. After traveling around the world, just as I had predicted, she found the love of her life in her own backyard—at her firm in America!—and settled down to wedded bliss in Pennsylvania. She regularly cooks Mr. Right her mother's pot roast.

NextDoor Tom and Brenda remain close friends. When they visited us in Southport, Tom took over my kitchen to fix us chef-grade stuffed artichokes, Irish stew made with Guinness stout and cinnamon-scented pears poached in red wine for dessert. Although I had thought that my year of magical happenings was a one-off, I had stellar opportunities to return for long research stays in London and never fell out of love with the capital. My subsequent stays in T'Smoke were unfailingly punctuated by dinner parties at their Holborn home which allowed me to return to my former building to say hello to concierge Aren. Their offerings of medallions of veal, perfectly grilled steaks, sizzling, succulent pork chops and 'puddings' of breadcrumb ice-cream and prune parfait remain branded on my brain.

The Carringtons, now grand-parents, made trips across the pond and stayed with Hubs and me during idyllic Connecticut vacations. Because their 'boys'—now high-achieving solicitors in Chancery Lane— recognize me as Celia's 'sister', they continue to call me 'Auntie'. I spent many a subsequent summer as their guest in the glorious brick-clad manor that Christopher Wren had designed, awaking each morning to the tolling of cathedral bells from nearby St. Paul's and the sight of the Goddess of Justice atop the Old Bailey from my window at *Amen Court*.

Lorraine and Charles Carson, also grand-parents, sold their Farringdon loft and 'downsized' in Holland Park, only a couple of blocks from where *As Time Goes By,* my favorite British TV series was shot. I made memorable repeat visits to their Suffolk estate to say Hello to their oil-painted, sword-brandishing, Raj-defending ancestor and to comb soporific country lanes in their company.

Rohit never fails to break bread with me on my frequent London visits, and Raynah, who with him made up my small moving crew from Holborn to Farringdon, actually bakes me loaves of it when I stay in her Battersea home. We share a passion for foodie experimentation from Cyrus Todiwala's Parsee-influenced cuisine at *Café Spice Namaste* to Bombay's street delicacies at *Dishoom*. I still draw the line, however, at eating pig-ears and trotters—even if Fergus Henderson has concocted them. Everywhere I go, I hear Samantha cheering my judicious menu choices.

I returned to work regularly in Oxford and to see my landlady Ela Lonsdale who still rents rooms to international scholar-lodgers. Although I never did stay in my darling little sun-room again, I never leave the spired city without taking an affectionate turn through my temporary home at Norham Gardens which Penelope Lively immortalized in her own memoir.

I'd used 14 forms of transportation (planes, overground trains, underground trains, even an underwater Train—the Chunnel). I'd been a passenger on ferries, canal cruisers, boats, coaches, buses, trams, cars, taxis and bicycles. But my favorite form of transportation remained my severely Tried and Tested Feet! I had been treated by at least a dozen medical personnel—doctors, physiotherapists, radiologists, homeopaths--in three countries (England, India and France). Back in the US, I saw private orthopedists who put me on to Dansko clogs (from which I did not remove my feet for a whole year) and prescribed night splints to encase both my legs as I slumbered. It took a full five years, repeat five full years, before I bid PF farewell.

I shot, downloaded, edited and captioned 5,000 photographs, all of which reside in my laptop's hard drive. I wrote over 365 blog posts numbering several hundreds of thousands of words. The number of museums, art galleries, churches, cathedral, castles, country estates, rivers, bridges, tunnels and gardens I traversed is countless.

I'd survived the worst economic down turn in recent history that severely affected dollar-pound exchange rates for the worse. I'd mustered and discovered latent financial prowess that led to astute monetary juggling that allowed me to meet all my travel goals on the slenderest budget. I had attempted to regress to my youth through stints in dismal hostels with thoughtless young folk. Riding on a hormonal high, they had fascinated, amused and annoyed me all over Europe. While I had watched an international terrorist attack unfold on the telly in London, I came face-to-face with its impact in Bombay—and lived to tell the tale.

I had endured a litany of medical ailments, acute physical pain and discomfort and negotiated my way through three baffling foreign public health systems that left me deeply frustrated and oftentimes angry. I'd experienced roller-coasting emotional upheavals—guilt at having turned my back on my wifely and maternal callings, unbridled loneliness and longing for the presence of those I most loved, and near delirium when they joined me, no matter how briefly. Through it all, I often found myself wondering, Would I do it all over again?

So, let me put this plainly and in the lingo of my Yankee compatriots. You betcha! I would relive every moment of that crazy breathless ride all over again for the extraordinary chance that went hand-in-hand with it—the opportunity, during my fiftieth year, to unleash my Anglophilia in my beloved Blighty.

The End

ABOUT THE AUTHOR

Rochelle Almeida is professor of global cultures in liberal studies at New York University. Author of three books of literary criticism and three anthologies of scholarly essays, she specializes in Anglophone world literature, post-colonial cultural studies, migration theory and ethnographic research on diasporic Anglo-Indians. She has taught writing in India, the United States, the UK, and most recently, in Uzbekistan as a Fulbright-Nehru Fellow based in Bombay. Her travel writing has been published in international periodicals. She is emeritus docent at the Metropolitan Museum of Art in New York City. As an international freelance writer, she divides her time between Southport, Connecticut, where she has lived for three decades, and Bombay, India.